HorrorScope

Books by Gian J. Quasar

HorrorScope • Then Came The Dawn • The Bermuda Triangle II

Scarlet Autumn • A Passage to Oblivion

Distant Horizons • SOMA • Recasting Bigfoot

They Flew Into Oblivion • Into the Bermuda Triangle

Gian has a real talent for finding the facts in our folklore. If you're interested in the truth, his books are a must read.
— Matt Jolley
Edward R. Murrow Award for Journalism.

You have opened my eyes for the first really serious look at The Bermuda Triangle. I think that your book is, as you say the first of its kind in 25 years, and I think the best. — Whitley Strieber

Quasar's THEY FLEW INTO OBLIVION is not only the best book by far on the iconic Flight Nineteen, it serves as the gold standard, in my opinion, for readers and future writers who seek to explore the complex facts (which make a mystery no less wonderful) rather than soothe their biases with fairy tales.

— Randy Wayne White

We wondered about the author's name, Quasar, which in normal parlance means any of a class of celestial objects that resemble stars but whose large redshift and apparent brightness imply extreme distance and huge energy output, and if it might relate to the book (Bermuda Triangle) and we weren't disappointed.

— New Yachting Magazine.

HorrorScope
The Zodiac Killer Exposed

"The police shall never catch me because I have been too clever for them."

By

Gian J. Quasar

BRODWYN-MOOR & DOANE

2025

Cataloguing-in-Publication Data

Quasar, Gian Julius

HorrorScope: The Zodiac Killer Exposed

First Edition

Copyright © 2025 by Gian J. Quasar
All Rights Reserved

978-0-9888505-9-0

No part of this publication may be reproduced, broadcast, transmitted, distributed or displayed— except for brief quotations in reviews— without prior written permission.

Contents

Introduction	"This is the Zodiac Speaking"	7
Chapter 1	The Sign of the Crimes	11
Chapter 2	Sadistically Gunned	21
Chapter 3	Silence of the Peacocks	35
Chapter 4	Murder Said Easy	47
Chapter 5	Gamester of Death	59
Chapter 6	Good Times in Vallejo	65
Chapter 7	Ceremonial Bum	71
Chapter 8	Car Door Score	80
Chapter 9	Zodiac	97
Chapter 10	Ante	105
Chapter 11	Autumn of Angst	114
Chapter 12	Comic Strip Crusade	128
Chapter 13	Skillful Player	138
Chapter 14	Paper Tiger	145
Chapter 15	Southern Exposure	160
Chapter 16	Billowy Wave	182
Chapter 17	Titwillo	189
Chapter 18	Fiddle and Far . . . out	198
Chapter 19	"Clews"	207
Chapter 20	East By Northeast	215
Chapter 21	Steve H.	219
Chapter 22	Riverside Ruse or Proto Zodiac?	226
Chapter 23	The Omicron Suspect	235
Chapter 24	Signed, Yours Truley?	249
Chapter 25	Through the Triage Glass	257
Chapter 26	The Iota of Omicron	263
Chapter 27	Dead Ringer	269
Chapter 28	The Shadow	295
Chapter 29	Joker in the Deck	305
Chapter 30	The Spook	315
Chapter 31	The Zodiac Club	333
About the Author		342
Index		

Acknowledgments

The author wishes to thank all those who throughout his 13 years of investigation lent advice and help, in particular Dr. Jim Kern and Mike Turrini, Vallejo Historical Museum; Steve Doran, weapons expert; Jason Schreiner; William Fiesterman, artist; David Hardin, Katherine Terry, Cara Lebonick, and Jessica Battle, of the Military Personnel Records Center in St. Louis; Karen Paaske, Lompoc Historical Society; Lee Gnesa, Brian Donelson, Bobby Domingos' old friend and cousin who journeyed with me to the Gaviota crime scene; Ricardo Gomez, Zodiac investigator. Various county records offices of the Superior Court made it easier for me to obtain records, in particular Ventura County Superior Court Records and Contra Costa County Superior Court Records.

The 'Zodiac' Killer is referred to herein alternately as the ZODIAC or ZODIAC. "The Zodiac" was his own handle, but police frequently dubbed him just "Zodiac." For all intents and purposes they are interchangeable.

FOREWORD

THIS IS THE ZODIAC SPEAKING

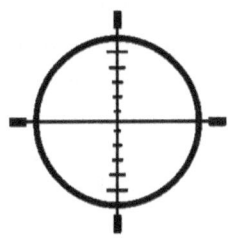

C IVILIZATION HAD NEVER SEEN SUCH A THING BEFORE. THE FABRIC of American society was viewed as coming apart. National curiosity was now dissolving into national disdain and even national jitters. A counterculture within the younger generation was spreading like a contagion. They cast off the conformity of the "establishment" to become dropouts, long-haired hippies, anti-war flower children, and radical student yippies. San Francisco was the center. An elegant, established society tiptoed around the psychedelic flamboyance of peace, love, and drugs, wondering when this unnerving fad was going to ebb. Yet a year and a half after the momentous Summer of Love there was no end in sight. The river of youth had become a torrent, entering the city's tenderloin and parks to reside in "Love-ins," to adorn themselves in peace symbols, tie-dye, Indian feathers, to smoke hashish, and to hear the preaching of the Age of Aquarius.

There could be nothing more at a contrast to this mixture of giddy colors and staid culture, diamond tiaras, minks, and daisies behind the ear, than a midnight, lonely rural road near Vallejo, a utilitarian city across the bay. Shots rang out. Gun powder flashed. Two teenagers lay dead, a boy and a girl.

The victims weren't licentious members of "Love-ins." They were John and Jane Q. Citizen. Now in December 1968 the mainstream youth still looked like their parents— clean-cut guys with thick-rimmed glasses, and gals with coiffured hairdos. These were the victims: kids at a petting spot. Here the terror began. Like a drop that starts a ripple, it began here in this drab, unlikely place and grew wider and wider with each victim until it sent San Francisco and the metropolitan Bay Area into a panic.

The perpetrator was the most unique murderer in history. He not only marketed his murders, he marketed them through a fabricated alter ego he created in print. It was the summer of 1969 when he introduced himself to the world. In the manner of a pompous comic strip villain, he proclaimed:

This is the Zodiac speaking.

The killer made it plain that his victims were merely pawns in a game of death, a game he intended to play randomly throughout the entire metropolis. To keep his readership intrigued he included cryptograms which the public was to decipher. When the first code was cracked, it began in gleeful but simple syntax: "I like killing people because it is so much fun." He forewarned more murders and rejoiced over the fact his victims would be his slaves in his afterlife, thereby invoking some primitive, arcane religion that seemed inspired by the esoteric mysticism of the disturbing hippie movement. He became so devoted to his game that he brought his alter ego into the real world. While wearing a sinister black hood with the celestial zodiac symbol sewn thereon he knifed two victims in one of the strangest crimes ever. Finally after his 7th victim he reached crescendo. He now threatened to become a sniper and wipe out a school bus.

Throughout the frightful autumn more letters followed. Each began with the above preamble: "This is the Zodiac speaking." Each letter was signed by the symbol of the celestial zodiac— a circle with a crosshair through it. It looked little different from a gunsight, and the double meaning was no doubt intended.

A bizarre villain was being born in print and published in the newspapers and talked about on radio and on TV. He was The ZODIAC. He is one of the few serial killers to give himself his own handle. It doesn't reflect police categorizing or witty press sensationalism. It reflects his own megalomania as the celestial controller, the master of the game of fate— in his case the game of death.

When all was said and done, 5 victims were dead and 2 went on to live with their viciously inflicted wounds. His murder spree lasted for only a short time, but his love for publicity kept him writing poison pen letters for years, each claiming more and more victims and each threatening to take more victims. Often with tasteless humor he demanded appeasement, either from the public or the police, to stave his hand of death. Each letter was sluiced with sarcasm, and with his dark humor each in its way was a sinister chuckle. Then he played the ultimate hand in his game. He vanished. To this day the San Francisco Bay Area has never forgotten, and the most bragged about murders in history remain unsolved.

This, in essence, is the crime spree of The 'Zodiac' Killer. He is inexorably linked with the summer and tumultuous autumn of 1969, but his legacy is decades of anxiety that he'd return, decades of frustration that a killer escaped justice; not just a killer, but the most boastful, haughty killer in the annals of crime. "The police shall never catch me," he crowed in one letter, "because I have been too clever for them." He won. He got away. The faded ink of his bragging rubs this fact into our face even today.

But his gloating words have done more than cause us to collectively bristle with indignation. The letters and their bragging ink have continued to rub into our faces the alter ego. The taunting ZODIAC we remember. The reality behind this facade has been forgotten. We pored over his words, but we forgot the context of his crimes.

From the very beginning opinion was divided as to what exactly were the ZODIAC's motives. His victims were teenyboppers at petting spots. Yet at a stark contrast his publicity game presented him as a grand comic book specter looming diabolically over Gotham. He used the syntax of a cheap pool hall punk in his letters, jeering a ridiculed establishment, but then at the same time he also brought discredit upon the counterculture by implying he was inspired by some of its occult fringe beliefs. Those who have laboriously contemplated the mesmerizing case cannot help but be frustrated by the utter lack of coherence. The one constant was his desire to inflict societal terror. If he was indeed mad, he still proved himself a disciplined manipulator.

Identifying the ZODIAC by his real world name does not really solve the case. As the reader will soon learn there is much more to it than merely putting a name and face on a man. One must explain not just one motive but multiple motives. This was a killer who limited himself to convenient victims but used the moniker of the Universe in print in order to intimidate all society. He was brutal in act, crazy in print, ridiculous in *claimed* motive, but cunningly successful at evasion. The 'Zodiac' Killer case smacks with the evolution of a thrill seeker, and he reeks of arrogance, the arrogance of a man who was certain he could never be outed.

The first half of this book is devoted solely to restoring the actual historical context of the crimes. During this period of my research I did not actively pursue anybody as a potential ZODIAC suspect. This means the first half of this book is not a text narrowly designed to support a suspect. It reflects objective investigation. Only by reliving the crimes and times of the ZODIAC, as the reader will soon do, can we get back to the truth and reveal that one kernel that leads to the identity of this cerebral braggart. Through the narrative the reader will relive the volatile and colorful era and be stunned by the actual execution of the brutal crimes.

The rest of this book, the finale of 13 years of investigation, is the result of a long and frustrating journey to solution, to a frustrating solution.

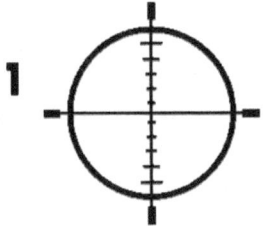

THE SIGN OF THE CRIMES

THERE ARE FEW MOMENTS IN ANY GENERATION WHEN AN EVENT IS so momentous it becomes a reference point for dividing a way of life and attitude "before" and "after." One of those in the 20th century is the counterculture movement. It smoldered through 1966 and then in June 1967 the events in San Francisco were broadcast from coast to coast. The Summer of Love inaugurated a movement and 1967 became the dividing line between the way the past would be viewed —traditional and idyllic— and the way things would become thereafter— immoral, dark, and drug strewn.

The elder generation's negative attitude about the 1960s grew more rancorous in the 1970s because they blamed the current dystopia on the counterculture. It was a pervasive attitude that the time before counterculture was "How Sweet It Was!" Children heard of a time when people didn't have to lock their houses or cars; when kids didn't have to check their Halloween candy for razors and pins. Men had looked like men—Cary Grant and Paul Newman; women were classy—Ava Gardner or Audrey Hepburn. We were united. We blew the "Krauts" and "Japs" away and currently we held the pinkos at bay. Now America was suddenly bad. Vietnam War protests, anti-Nuke protests, rent-a-protest, urban riots.

The slide to hell in a wheelbarrow began with the Boomers and their bizarre adaptation of rebellion— long hair, smoking hashish pipes, moving to ashrams and "Love-ins," free sex, VW van vagabond living, anti-materialism, and the beatitude that LSD would guide the user to a real universal consciousness of enlightenment that would empower peace. Despite the ennobling claim made by its chief protagonists that they were resisting the Cold War, there was nothing in the above that would address Soviet arms production. Frankly, it could not affect US arms production either. The Great Generation understood the motives for rebellion— world peace— but its expression in counterculture made no sense.

Ironically the Great Generation, parents of the Boomers, was antiestablishment in mentality. However, their attitude was not belligerence against their culture; they were skeptical of the powers-that-be. As children they had seen the corruption that dominated major cities of the Roaring '20s. In the 1930s the Great Depression was a reminder of incompetence at high levels. That generation then fought World War II and viewed its cause as another masterfully engineered bit of incompetence from the establishment.

The Great Generation never forgot the Munich Appeasement or the fact the United States sold Japan most of the scrap metal it then shot back at the US. They came to adulate Franklin Roosevelt for taking a strong hand and cleaning out corruption and leading the nation through the war. The most glorified guiding light of the Great Generation had been Ike Eisenhower. "Everybody liked Ike." In his farewell address from the Presidential office in 1960 he warned the nation of the growing power of the military industrial complex. For the Great Generation, "government bears watching." For the antiestablishment Boomers, it needed to be dismantled through acid dreams, guru inspiration, and cordite.

But the elder generation's attitude did not make the 1970s a darker decade. It was darker because the Boomers had lost their idealism. Ideals of a new world had motivated all 1960s protest, from lofty arguments over war and peace, to forsaking the materialism of the current culture. Ever since Berkeley 1964 the Baby Boomers had sought to cure the ills of a materialistic society they felt had brought us to the brink of nuclear holocaust, but by the 1970s too many events had robbed them of the tenets upon which their expression of rebellion had been justified.

The counterculture/antiestablishment movement had never really been one and the same. Counterculture indulged in Eastern mysticism and in the ideology of taking drugs, largely LSD, as the pathway to world peace. Antiestablishment was more aggressive and protest oriented, wanting to change the world politically and ideologically and not just through their own inner experience. Both coexisted, sometimes comingled, and then both coincidentally met their demise in 1970.

The radical protest element of the antiestablishment movement's "New Left" had set off one too many bombs, one at the University of Wisconsin which killed a lab student that year. Disenchanted, the sober element of 1960s' protest walked away.

The philosophic counterculture and its belief that world peace could be found not in objective truth but in LSD-induced inner peace fell apart after the disastrous Altamont in December 1969 and then the ugly ending of the festival on the Isle of Wight. Counterculture saw what people on drugs could do, and it obviously wasn't the cure-all it had been preached to be. As an ideology drug taking stopped. Drug taking increased, but it was recreational. The motive was now escapism— a trip for a trip's sake.

In diluted forms, both went on. Counterculture continued mostly as a mindset which 1970s' mainstream merchandising tailored (or watered down) to fit the inquiring mind. Books expounding every sort of esoteric topic were bestsellers. Yet without the counterculture's world purpose, it was only marketing a mindset without any real focus or philosophy other than to sample anything that was contrary to the establishment's tenets.

This made the occult deeply popular in novel ways. If the 1960s were viewed as "being shot to hell," then hell shot back in the 1970s when every form of hybrid occult religion filled the void, including "devil worship," the devil being promoted as the ultimate rebel. Where else but in San Francisco would such a thing as the Church of Satan take root? Clad in black robes and hoods, the Black Mass was declared by its adherents:

In nomine dei nostri Satanus luciferi excelsi
  In the name of Satan, the ruler of Earth, king of the world, open wide the gates of hell and come forth to greet me as your brother and friend. Grant me the indulgences of which I speak, for I live as the beasts of the field rejoicing in the fleshly life. I favor the just and I curse

the rotten. By all the gods of the pit, I command that these things of which I speak shall come to pass...

... Blessed are the strong, for they shall possess the Earth. Cursed are the weak, for they shall inherit the yoke. Blessed are the bold, for they shall be masters of the world. Cursed are the righteous and humble, for they shall be trodden under cloven hooves — Hail Satan!

As a footnote, an irony should be noted: what constituted evil was still being defined by Judeo-Christian values. Those reciting the Black Mass sounded like Sunday School kids gone bad. There was nothing original in their attitude; they were just inverting the pervading norms of their Christian upbringing.

As for antiestablishment, it too had filtered into mainstream. Although the universities had quieted down, society had not. Crime waves were rampant. Now there were chic urban guerillas like the Symbionese Liberation Army. Dressed in leather jackets and stylish tam-o'-shanters, they largely just liberated money from banks. The Zebra Murders were a bizarre spate of gang murder. Race riots plagued the early 1970s— Brown Power, Black Power. America: Love it or Leave it!

Protest finally trickled down to the frivolous. Carrying signs that read "Don't Bust My Bust," women protesting for equality held a topless parade down main street in Santa Cruz. Where else, again, but in Santa Cruz would drugs and the current fascination with the devil be combined? To celebrate Halloween, a local rock band performed in the public park. They were dressed up in black witches' costumes and tall conical hats while they passed around free joints to the audience. The banner behind them read: "Halloweed."

In sum, counterculture and antiestablishment had become two different commodities, but both basically failed at the same time. The former essentially disappeared because it was deprived of its ideological base; the latter became something of a mainstream contrarian attitude. Altogether the younger generation was disenchanted, and the darker, dystopian 1970s was upon us. An inquiring mind may have been one of the good side-effects of the era, but it is undeniable that the most toxic elements had also been emboldened to commit the most audacious crimes this country had seen during a time when anxiety ran high.

This little summation of the times and seasons does bear on the subject at hand. The first criminal to dovetail on the volatile sign of the times was not a militant who claimed greater political or social motives. He was the exotic 'Zodiac' Killer. He struck while counterculture was still lively and he struck at the cradle of the movement's inception. He mixed counterculture occult ideas with the terror methods the "New Left" would come to rely upon. His motive was more than terror merely to serve his tastes to inflict fear. His motive became societal domination through terror— it was the ultimate thrill, the ultimate "kick." And he had the intelligence or just the evil good luck to know that the high anxiety of the times made it possible for an individual to set upheaval in motion with a bullet and the stroke of a blue felt pen.

History has shown us that in 1969 network news would be at its apogee. The colorful antiestablishment movement was part of the reason TV news scored so high in American homes. Racial tensions in the nation, anti-war protests, and the latest news on the war in Vietnam were other factors. The moonshot had long been promised and in the summer of 1969 it would be fulfilled. Political assassinations had drawn Americans to the TV. It had only been 6 years since President Kennedy had been assassinated, 4 years since Malcolm X had been brutally gunned down, less than 2 years since Martin Luther King Jr. and then Bobby Kennedy's assassinations. News was really happening, and it was news that had mattered. It was news at hand.

Whether this phantom killer's publicity campaign of murder is a reflection of the era or inspired because of the massive stage news could give, preying upon the fears of the time became an integral part of his game. His threats of a "killing rampage" rode the crest of a popular wave of fear the likes of which was never to be seen again. Indeed he made such a success out of it that despite the fact he is only one of several killers who stalked lovers' lanes he is the second most famous serial killer in world history, ranking only behind London's Jack the Ripper.

No city had been set on edge to the extent San Francisco would be in 1969 since the socially tumultuous year 1888 saw London go into a panic over this faceless night stalker. His crimes began from some individual motive until he too sought to dovetail on the racial and social tensions of the time. He then tried to incite riots against Jews and protests against the government— an interesting evolution to a crime spree which had begun by killing prostitutes in the East End's Whitechapel district.

In many ways the pompous ZODIAC was identical, and it seems the convulsive times influenced his evolution as well. He had started late December 1968 on a dark rural road with the pointless and cowardly murder of two necking teens, but until the summer of 1969, seven months later, he had let it remain a mystery. Only after his next murder did he confess to the newspapers. Thus began his thrill to use his rural crimes to set the public stage for a game in which every citizen of the San Francisco Bay Area was a potential player if he decided to target them.

And it seems the time was indeed ripe for terror campaigns. Only a week after the ZODIAC had sent his first series of letters threatening a "kill rampage" if his enticing cryptogram (included therein) wasn't published in the newspapers, Los Angeles too went into a panic over a spate of audacious and savage murders known as the Tate/La Bianca Murders. Acting upon the racial tensions of the time, the killers had etched "War" in a victim's stomach. With the victims' blood, the killers had written "Pigs" and "Rise" on the walls of the victims' houses to impress upon the police that this was a guerilla movement of Black Panther militants out to kill whites.

Until December of that year Los Angeleans didn't know the murders had been committed by a hippie cult on LSD at the instigation of their mesmeric guru leader Charles Manson. Months of fear had gripped the city between that hot, bloody August and that cold, shocking December.

And we are back to the first pages of this chapter— the psychedelic and once fascinating 1960s came crashing to an end in 1970, with the total destruction of the counterculture leaving unfocused the residual contrarian mindset.

But of those audacious crime sprees that had inspired so much awe, the case of the 'Zodiac' Killer continues on. It was the one which was never solved. The Mansons were imprisoned, the SLA battled and broken up, and the Zebra killers caged. The ZODIAC, who only had the courage, if that word should even be used, to pounce upon unsuspecting teenagers at petting spots as the base to create his terror campaign lived on incognito never to be identified.

It is impossible to separate the ZODIAC's crime spree from the times and place of his crimes. But there are obviously different elements involved in his case that do not exist in the other terror and murder campaigns, one that allowed him to go unidentified. One, of course, is that he most likely acted entirely alone. All the others had accomplices, and identifying one led to others. But it is a fact that all the major crime sprees were committed by those who could be called members of the antiestablishment. The ZODIAC's crimes were not militant in nature, and the language in his letters was that of a pool hall thug, not those of an angry idealist. In fact, he went out of his way to make himself sound uneducated. Unlike the others he was most likely the establishment, a spectator of the new movement and morality from afar.

The San Francisco Bay Area was actually the perfect place to inspire a killer to become the first fruits of a bizarre combination of the establishment and the philosophic counterculture.

San Francisco was the center of an industrious, profiteering culture. Stately and cosmopolitan were surrounded by the Bay Area's unique rural ambiance— the sea, the fog, the farms, the bays and quays, the old towns. The city was affluent and yet adventurous. She was a great modern Venice. She was Queen of the Pacific, and through her passed the trade of the exotic Orient. In fact, when antiestablishment began at Berkeley in 1964 Jack London's San Francisco could still be felt in the pungent smell of the brine and tar of the docks wafting over the once-raucous Barbary Coast. The unique past of the city was heard in the cable car bells clanging up and down the famous hills.

There was, however, a huge difference between the San Francisco of the summers of 1964 and 1967. Antiestablishment had rated news in 1964, but its visuals were understandable: student mobs hurling smoking bottles and carrying protest signs. Phalanxes of police in riot gear marching behind shields. Angry orators commanded the steps at Sproul Plaza. Now in 1967 counterculture was in the spotlight. Its visuals were garlands of daisies crowning heads, stoned faces and lotus positions.

The Summer of Love was in full swing. Youth from all over the United States had been coming to the Haight-Ashbury district as if an invisible pied piper had summoned them. It had begun in the fall of 1966. At least 30,000 had come for the "Sit-In" in Golden Gate Park. It was such a success that the "Human Be-In" had been scheduled for January 1967. This too had been a great success. Many had remained, faithfully awaiting the greatest festival yet announced— the "Love-In."

Since March, Scott McKenzie had gone to the top of the charts with *San Francisco*, announcing as a herald the coming Concordia. Music videos (though a term not yet used) showed him walking about landmarks in an Eastern tunic— one patterned with daisies, of course. As January saw the Be-In, the gathering to understand and to "be," so the Summer of Love was to practice it. It would be a summer of drugs, love, music, peace, enlightenment— debauchery painted with a philosophic brush.

The Haight had begun to swell during the spring. Guru leaders were instilling the vibe, the third eye and every other hybrid Eastern concept into youth. Posters still kicked about the streets or hung in shop windows showing the "Be-In" swami, cross-legged, ratty hair, the triangle and third eye in his forehead. Some were pasted over with the new ad— psychedelic posters advertising Timothy Leary as a speaker. With palms pressed together—"follow the way"— he urged youth to "Turn On, Tune In, Drop Out." Philosophic TV jargon. "In" was the new word. To be "in." Not in the fad sense, but in the philosophic sense of "with it." With the vibes, man. "Tuned in." On the right Bat Channel. For Leary, this meant LSD and the drugology of the inner journey.

Geographically, the Haight was situated perfectly to become the unintended incubator for the Flower Children movement. There is one way into Golden Gate Park here on Fell Street and one way out on Oak Street. Only a few blocks down Oak Street from the park and turn right— this is Ashbury Street. The center of the Haight is the intersection of Haight & Ashbury streets. Renting was far more affordable here. After the Sit-In and Human Be-In, Flower Power naturally started to bloom here. The Haight was quickly becoming the navel of the hippie culture.

The response to the Summer of Love was enormous, beyond anything planned. What was intended to have been a brief flame, a brief Concordia of spiritual empowerment for the "hip generation," continued to be a fire stoked all summer. What was to be a folk festival with metaphysical preachers and a choir made of the greatest rock bands became a culture, and those here created a Constitution of life without using paper or print.

Like blood circulating in the body through the heart, the "hippies" coursed through Haight for rooms, for washing, sleeping, kitchens for bread, and then always back to the heart— Golden Gate Park.

Teens, little better than waifs, stood in the park mindless, with vacuous expressions, flowers behind their ears, and twirling fig leaves in their numb fingers; their faces painted with pastel daisies, their eyes dull and "far out." New converts to hippiedom still sported short hair, but they had been painted all over with bright colors by the unofficial welcoming committees. Hippies danced to the bands. Danced? They were more like drunken storks trying to fly, arms flailing under multicolored ponchos. Some gyrated to no rhythm at all in their drugged stupors.

Music was everything. It was the soul. Flower Children hung out in small groups around folksy amateurs or crowded around the professionals. Flowers were always in their hair— *always*. Bare feet, painted faces, smoldering joints passed along lips to puffing lips. They were reverting to their concept of innocence behind a drugged stupor. To a civilized world, it was galloping immorality.

Innocence to the hippies meant sexual freedom too. Marriage and anything organized was the oppression of the establishment, the establishment that gave them the Cold War and the angst of living in the shadows of potential nuclear holocaust. When San Francisco saw that these sedentary vagabonds weren't going to move on, a medical facility was set up to treat venereal disease. Hygiene was deplorable. There were communal baths or, more accurate, rotational tubs.

This was *not* the San Francisco that any San Franciscan had known only 5 years before. For any "outsider" looking in, it was a potent experience.

This was not just a contained carnival. The press loved the movement. It represented something exciting. The press themselves were made up of those who had fought in WWII and Korea, and despite them being the distrusted generation (those over 30) by the hippies, the audacious message of living a new lifestyle to bring in universal peace was something they indulged. Hollywood enjoyed the message too. Escapist movies weren't vogue anymore, and neither was all the artistry of Technicolor epics. Current events were the new vogue, and movies and TV shows began to integrate the antiestablishment themes, both seriously and in comedy. It was one of the most powerful and financially profitable formulas. In short, the whole concept could be commercialized to the mainstream.

Those closest to San Francisco, especially the youth, could naturally partake firsthand in the extreme examples of the counterculture as represented in Haight-Ashbury. . .well, dabble at least. Mainstream youth certainly weren't allowed to adjust their image to Flower Children— parents wouldn't allow it and PTAs were aghast at the thought. Schools, whether public or private, would still enforce dress codes. But this is only appearance and appearance is only a manifestation of communal reinforcement. Mentality was changing in the individual mainstream youth. Many were embracing some of the concepts of the counterculture even if they weren't morphing in appearance.

The rural areas of the Bay Area may still have moved to the tempo of rustic traditions and the work whistle of the great ship building yards, but flower power symbols were popping up along with marijuana and the new morality. Casual sex was becoming so, well, casual with the young everywhere so that movies, of all things, had to moralize. In the family trials of *Yours, Mine & Ours*, also set in San Francisco in 1968, the *pater noster* had to advise his stepdaughter that love is found not in going to bed with a man but when you wake up and have to endure the trials of everyday life with him.

Moralizing though it may have been, it reflected the elder generation's indulgence of the younger. Hellfire and brimstone for fornication was not something going to be found in TV and movie parental guidance. Of course, the fundamental chunk of society found this compromise to be immoral. To them, society was going to hell in a VW, pure and simple.

However you view it, things that had once been done behind closed doors were now being addressed in public. Society was changing, and it was changing openly. Some extremes were quite weird and unnerving— Flower Children and hedonistic hippies. But the mainstream liked some of the message. It too was beginning to change, if only subtly in attitude.

History moved on. Events came and went. The clock ticks slowly and we come forward. The Summer of Love was long over by the end of 1968.

Passing headlights break the suspended animation of the late night countryside. Trees, scraggly and bare, emerge from the inky anonymity. Subfreezing temperature makes the bloodless light sharp. The glare passes along, stinging each arthritic branch, each twisted trunk; fence posts as weathered as old grave markers.

The headlights sweep a parked car in a turnout. They coast up beside it and stop. A car door clicks open.

A flashlight beam streaks about, weak and round. There is shouting. Two gunshots. Shouting. A struggle. A head, an ear— close up. A gunshot! The beam is speckled with dot-like shadows. A shriek. Running footsteps. A teen girl dashes from the blurry fringe of the flashlight beam. The beam slices through the ink to find her. Her bright purple dress glows as the beam casts a halo on her back. Gunshots soil the bright cloth with red. One, two, three— the girl slows, staggers. Gunshots— four, five. The bright purple of the dress drops from the halo into the ink.

The beam coasts over the frozen road. A girl lies bloodied in her purple miniskirt. A boy moans. The beam darts over the gravel and finds him. He is on his back, blood trickling from his head, the slightest spirit of breath from his lips. The light has only weakly captured the station wagon by his feet. It glides over the profaned and bloody gravel and stops at a brown car. Shoes, heavy under the weight of the villain, turn on the gravel. The light snips out. Footsteps crunch on the gravel in the darkness. A car door opens. An engine starts.

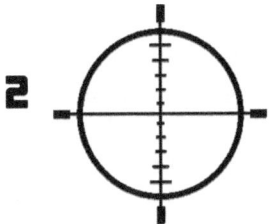

SADISTICALLY GUNNED

A WINTER NIGHT MAKES LAKE HERMAN ROAD A LONELY STRAND OF frozen ink trickling through the rolling countryside. These oak-studded hills are a beautiful sight for Vallejoans at sunset, especially in summer when the golden chaff is glowing pink and orange. But at 11 p.m. on a freezing December 20th they were only an undulating black silhouette set against an indigo, starry sky. There were few reasons to be on this backroad. Lake Herman cottage and campground were closed, so anybody going past the lake was simply going to or from Vallejo and Benicia.

There was only one other reason.

There was a gravel turnout just past the lake. It was wide like the spout of a funnel, narrowing to a locked cyclone gate. The turnout was at a rise in Lake Herman Road, at a point where you could look over rolling prairies to distant Carquinez Strait. Not only was the turnout at a rise, it was at a bend in the road. Coming from either direction, it was impossible not to see cars parked in the turnout.

Naturally, it became a petting spot for teens. Everybody local knew it, and anybody who often used the road could easily deduce it from the parked cars.

This night at 10 p.m. Bingo Wesner drove out the gate (after tending his sheep) and passed a white 1960 Impala parked in the turnout. He paid little attention. Darkness clutched the area again as his headlights swept onto the road and sailed along to Vallejo.

An hour or so passed. We have no account of the road in this time. It's only known companion was the weather— a below-freezing 22 degrees. So cold you could almost shatter the pockets of mist into bright, glassy confetti. Now and again twin cones of effervescent headlights coursed carefully along the black artery. A few nightshift workers were driving to the new Humble Oil refinery in Benicia. Otherwise there were a couple of ranches, but who would be driving to town at this time?

As it happens, Stella Medeiros was doing just that. She lived on the outskirts of Vallejo on a ranch about 2 miles from the turnout. She was headed to Benicia. It is about 11:24 p.m. according to her car clock. She is mounting up the rise approaching the turnout. Dim red lights ahead are the reflection of her headlights off the rear reflectors of a car parked in the turnout.

At the top she takes the bend. Her headlights sweep a parked Rambler station wagon, causing its windows to burst with bright sparkles. A young man lies on his back beside the car; a girl lies about 30 feet behind the rear bumper. She is on her right side, facing the road. Long rivers of blood trickle from both of them. She hits the gas and speeds off to Benicia. On the outskirts she locates a police car. She honks her horn and flashes her lights. She reports what she saw.

What greeted Benicia police, then eventually Solano County sheriff investigators (it was ultimately their jurisdiction), was a scene of pointless brutality against a couple of teenagers. David Faraday was only 17 years old. He lay there, his head and shoulders in a pool of his own blood. He had been shot pointblank in the head, through the top of his left ear. It was scorched black from the gunpowder. His feet were near the rear tire on the station wagon's passenger side, his arms over his head, one limp in the pool of blood.

Twenty eight feet from the rear bumper of his dad's Rambler lay his date, 16-year old Betty Lou Jensen. The killer had taken particular pleasure in shooting her. Her purple miniskirt, fringed in a ruffled white collar and cuffs, was riddled with holes; five in her upper right back, grouped in an ovoid pattern. She lay face down, streams of blood issuing from her nose, mouth, and abdomen.

Betty Lou was dead, but David was still breathing— shallowly, very shallowly. The ambulance rushed him to the hospital in Vallejo, but it was too late. He was pronounced dead on arrival.

Next morning the lead detective, Sgt. Leslie Lundblad, stood at the gravel turnout. He looked somberly at the putrid bloodstains and white chalk outlines. His features seemed tired, perhaps just resigned to the wave of pointless violence gripping the nation. Lundblad was the old school. His thin hair was salt and pepper. Wearing his dark trench coat and fedora, he was the image of a crime noir detective. But this wasn't some mob hit scene or sordid gin hall murder. These were two kids. Now the shadows of their presence were large, dark bloodstains, and the white chalk a hollow tracing of where kids died on their first date.

Russell Butterbach, Lundblad's partner, looked modern. The thin lapels and tight cut of his dark suit were entirely 1960s. The thin dark tie was perfectly drab and businesslike, a sliver over his white shirt. Hands in the pockets of his narrow pants, he looked about and pondered the morbid scene more logistically. Despite his gray temples, he was young. Close cut hair and dark-rimmed glasses, he represented the establishment that was, at least locally, growing more and more worried about Haight and the hippies.

What was left today was only the residue of last night's carnage. Cold winter sunlight vanquished the cloak of horror, but the black scars of blood trickling from the empty chalk frameworks strangely symbolized life drained away. The crisp breeze from Suisun Bay seemed careless as it gently blew away the chalk, slowly erasing the violation of the rustic innocence of pastoral winter.

Amidst the klieg lights last night the crime scene was revealed to be full of clues. The Rambler's doors were all locked except for the front passenger side door, which was found open when the police arrived. There were two bullet holes in the station wagon, both carefully placed in the rear of the vehicle. One had shattered the rear side window; the other was in the roof of the car just above the rim of the rear passenger side door. Ten shots had been fired in all. Eight shell casings peppered over a fairly tight area by the passenger side of the car. One was found on the passenger side floorboard of the front seat; another about 20 feet away from the car. The killer had used only a .22 caliber, a small game or target practice weapon.

Neither Dave Faraday nor Betty Lou were wearing jackets. Coupled with the location of the shell casings it was thus quite easy to put back the chain of events.

The petting couple's attacker had fired a shot through the Rambler's roof and then through the rear window to force them to come outside. He must have ordered them out the passenger side door. They opened it, letting the warm air rush out. Betty Lou was first out, then Dave slid over and got out. Facing them was their attacker, close up now and pointing the gun at them while they trembled by the open door.

A couple of clues indicate David challenged the attacker. His class ring was found between the tip of his ring and index finger, barely held into place by both fingers. He had a lump on his cheek, as if he had taken a punch. It seems likely that David, a lightweight wrestler at Vallejo High, had tried to wrestle the gun from his attacker. This is hardly surprising. With two bullet holes in his car, David Faraday must have known what awaited them. The position of his ring, just dangling there, indicates he had clutched and pulled around his assailant's waist.

Sadly, he hadn't succeeded in his struggle. The killer had pulled him to the ground. David lay there on his back, arms locked around the hulk on top of him. The killer fired the .22 into his head. Faraday's arms fell limp over his head.

Nothing indicates Betty Lou had tried or had time to help David wrestle the attacker, but she had stood close by. Patches of blood sprinkled the gravel between where she lay and the bumper of the car, so it was easy to follow her trail. Perhaps before he was shot, David yelled at her to run. Perhaps the killer, angrily standing up after shooting Faraday, ordered her to run in order to juice his fun. In any case, she took off.

The killer started pumping bullets into her right away. A single grain of gunpowder had been found embedded in Jensen's dress by one bullet hole, indicating it was the first bullet fired when she was close enough so a grain of powder could still reach her dress. She continued to dash away. With each step she took, the killer squeezed the trigger again and again. He did not chase after her. The shell casings grouped by the car prove he had remained by David Faraday's body.

Within the trail of blood from the bumper to where she lay there was found one of the spent bullets. It had gone through her and fallen down as she ran. This bullet was only one of three bullets that had passed through her. One exited the left breast and left a hole in the front of her dress. Another ricocheted through her body and came out at her panty elastic and lodged in her underwear. The other, the one mentioned first, had come out her stomach and fell down into the "blood splattered" path.

In her final moments, she could not have been running anymore. She was found face down, with her feet facing west, the direction to which she had been running. The physics of momentum cannot be violated. If she had been running she would have fallen forward with her feet facing east. Thus at the end she was only staggering, still trying to escape; the killer still shooting her. She had been shot once through the heart. This must have been the last. She fell to her knees and first slumped onto her side.

This is not indulging in the macabre for the sake of it. These are clues to the character of the attacker. The killer got the boy out of the way quickly. The girl was then shot several times until she fell. He watched, coldly enjoying shooting her as she had fought bitterly to escape, shooting repeatedly from the beginning to the very end.

In all, 8 bullets were retrieved from the victims and car. Ten shots had been fired, so it seems 2 went wild. Perhaps the attacker fired a warning shot in the air first, thus accounting for the shell casing found 20 feet from the others. Perhaps as he rapid fired at Jensen he missed once or when she collapsed the last shot went across the dark road and into the fields.

With both victims dead, this left Leslie Lundblad with no witnesses and, for 1968, with no real theory as to why someone would do this. Crazed killers were known, of course, but this seemed like revenge aimed at both of these teens.

Right now as Butterbach and Lundblad left the bay breeze to disperse the chalk, David Burd at Bureau of Criminal Investigation and Identification in Sacramento was going through their files trying to identify the killing weapon. It was a .22 caliber, of course. Ammo was Super X. Ballistics only revealed there were 6 lands and grooves, in a right turn; nothing too unique about that. In fact, they were so common that Burd could only match the bullet to a model, so he stressed that if he had the actual weapon in his hand he could not prove it with ballistics.

The weapon most likely was a mass-produced J.C. Higgins Model 80 automatic pistol. They were exclusive to Sear's. Over 200,000 had been made and sold between 1957 and 1961, when the model was discontinued. These were used for target practice and small game hunting. (A squirrel was even featured on the owner's manual.) The weapon was not something that could have been purchased recently, but it fit the circumstances. It would be owned by someone who liked small game hunting in the rural areas. Yet as dumb luck would have it, it was a weapon that could not be traced.

Press reports had already said that a rifle must have been used—scuttlebutt that had come from Leslie Lundblad's initial reaction. He had been surprised by the grouping of the bullets in Jensen's back, considering it to be a "remarkable close pattern." However, now that a pistol was definitely involved the mystery deepened. How in such darkness did the killer have enough light to not only shoot Jensen on the run but group his shots? The press speculated that since the turnout was at the high point of Lake Herman Road the moonlight from distant Carquinez Strait had peaked through the bosom of the rolling hills and illuminated Jenson enough.

It is practically impossible to place a stranger on a road at any given time when there are no witnesses. Lundblad knew this. In this case, the freezing temperature had even assisted the killer. The gravel turnout was too hard to show tire tracks or footprints. The killer might as well have been a ghost. There was only one chance of trailing this maniac. This was the possibility that these murders were motivated by revenge or jealously. If so, they therefore had a good chance of finding a classmate or acquaintance of either victim who was unaccounted for at the time of the murder, and go from there.

Word was coming back that David Faraday was going to turn in someone for "dealing grass." There was also a strange teen named Ricky Burton who was terribly infatuated with Betty Lou Jensen. A

J.C. Higgins Model 80 was the kind of weapon a 15 year old teenager might have. Jealousy seemed to fit best. After all, there was unique vengeance taken on Jensen.

Significant to the theory above, there had been no secret that the cooing couple was coming out here that night. In fact, more teens were planning on coming out to the turnout after a Christmas concert, it was said. Freezing weather probably turned the others off. In the end, only Dave and Betty Lou came. Only someone in their inner circle would have known the others opted not to come. Then he seized the opportunity and came to the turnout ready to kill. As a working hypothesis, this fit.

This was their first date, and hotly anticipated by the young 17 year old David Faraday. They did not attend the same High School. He was Vallejo High. She was Hogan High. The cocky lightweight wrestler had been attracted to the 16 year old Betty Lou from an event at Pythian Castle. He was an extrovert, a Boy Scout leader, and already a member of a few organizations. She swooned and accepted the offer. She primped her blond/brown hair into a lovely hairdo. She donned her purple miniskirt, with its ruffled collar and cuffs, and fastened a bright broche. David arrived in the tight corduroy slacks that were fashionable, a button-down collar, long sleeve dark blue shirt, a comb in his back pocket, and a big toothy smile on his face.

By Christmas both had been buried.

One thing the detectives were certain about. They had narrowed down the time in which the crime had been committed and thus the time that all potential suspects had to give account of their whereabouts. Lundblad and Butterbach had made an impressive recreation of who had been on that road between 10 and 11:30 p.m. that Friday night. Over the days following the murder, a chain of events fell into place.

Homer and Peggy Your had been in Sacramento for most of the day, and around 11 p.m. were back in Benicia. But before going home Homer wanted to check on the day's work along Lake Herman Road. Humble Oil refinery was still under construction and he was responsible for some of the piping. He took the isolated Lake Herman Road cutoff on Highway 680 and his car plunged into the natural morass the foothills create at this time of night. The headlights pushed aside the inky atmosphere as they continued on. Approaching the turnout, their headlights glittered off a parked station wagon in the turnout. Since the turnout is off to the left (from this direction) on the curve, it was easy to see two youths inside. The girl was snuggled close to the boy, her head on his shoulder. The boy was leaned back in the driver's seat. Taken by surprise, the boy quickly leaned forward and put his hands on the steering wheel.

Homer didn't turn around here but continued on to the bottom of the rise. Here he turned right into the entrance to the Marshall Ranch. It's a deep, wide entrance with corral fencing around it and a gate protecting the dirt road to the ranch. Here they suddenly came across a parked red truck. Next to it stood two men by the wood gate. One had a rifle. Peggy told Homer to "get the hell out" of here. Homer turned around and drove past the turnout again en route back to Benicia. Peggy noted the station wagon was still there (only a minute or so had passed).

Those two men at the Marshall Ranch turned out to be old Frank Gasser and young Bob Connolly. They had been out hunting raccoons in the foothills of the ranch. They had arrived around 9 p.m. and were now preparing to leave. They estimated it was around 11:05 p.m. when they left.

Peggy Your was certain that it was about 11:15 to 11:20 p.m. when they passed the Rambler on their way back to Benicia, just moments after their frightening encounter with Gasser and Connolly. Investigation uncovered their car clock was 7 minutes fast. Thus it was right around 11:08 p.m., more or less, when they passed the Rambler. This now jives better with what Connelly and Gasser said about encountering a couple in a car at the Marshall Ranch and then leaving shortly thereafter themselves. Thus Gasser and Connelly must have left around 11:10 p.m., not 11:05 p.m.

Next pertinent witness was James Owen. He was driving to his nightshift at Humble Oil. Therefore like Medeiros he had been driving toward Benicia from Vallejo. He passed the turnout at 11:20 p.m. He saw the station wagon parked just where the Yours had seen it minutes before. However, Owen also saw another car parked parallel to the Rambler, about 10 feet to its right, on the passenger side. He could not identify it by model or year, but it was a dark car, not too big, not compact, and "no chrome," meaning little chrome bumper or flashings and ornaments. He did not notice anybody in either car or about the turnout.

One quarter of a mile down the road Owen heard what he thought was a gunshot. He had the radio on low so he wasn't sure.

About 4 minutes later Stella Medeiros would drive past, heading in the same direction as Owen, toward Benicia.

Thus there is a gap between about 11:10 p.m. when the Yours passed and 11:20 p.m. when James Owen passed. It is within this narrow margin that the killer found the turnout. Within the following 4 to 6 minutes (Owen to Medeiros) the killer not only had to get the kids out of the car, engage in a scuffle and kill them both, he had to escape without passing another car. (No car had passed Medeiros between the turnout and her ranch, which was two miles down Lake Herman Road toward Vallejo.)

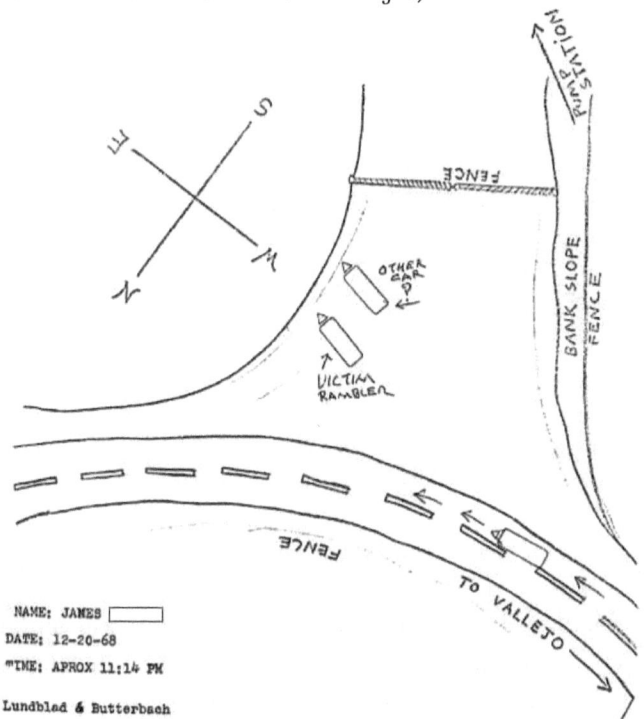

What James Owen saw, map from the Solano Co. Sheriff's report.

Owen unquestionably saw the killer's car parked next to the Rambler. Given the timing and the events that must have followed, it seems highly unlikely that the crimes could be committed in less than 1 minute. This is the least amount of time to allow the killer to head back to Vallejo and not be seen by Stella Medeiros driving to Benicia. (Lundblad drove the route from her ranch to the turnout and timed it at 2 ¾ miles and 3 minutes). However, the most likely scenario is that the killer drove off to Benicia and was sufficiently ahead of Stella Medeiros that she could not overtake him even at 70 miles per hour.

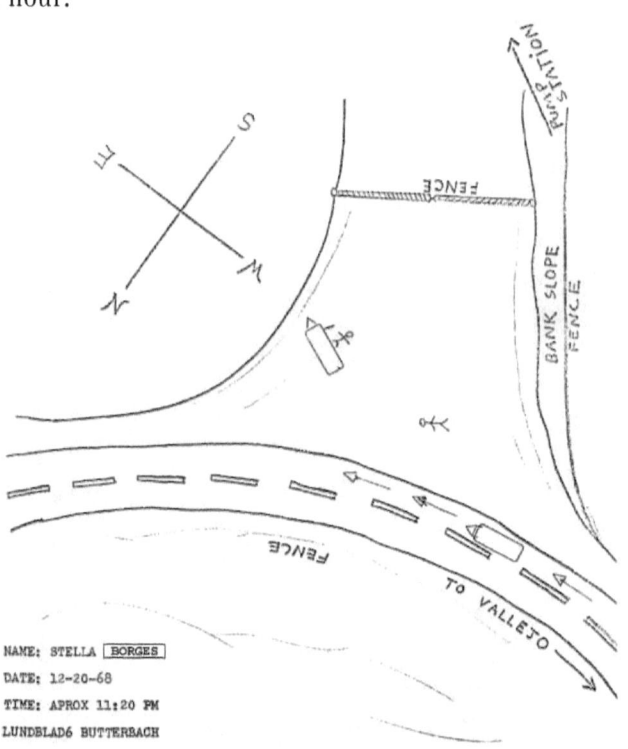

What Stella Medeiros saw, map from Solano Co. Sheriff's report.

Such details helped narrow down the time frame in order to account for the whereabouts of any suspects, but as the investigation proceeded little else was supporting the revenge theory. The group of Xmas party kids all had alibis. Nothing turned up on a drug dealer, and such a dealer would not have known where to find the couple that night anyway. Ricky Burton was ruled out. He had been at home watching a Bob Hope special on TV.

Finding no leads that could possibly indicate any personal revenge, Lundblad was beginning to believe a "crazed killer" was the only option remaining. "Cruising" now became a clue. The killer would have to cruise the road for a while waiting to find the right moment someone was at the petting spot.

Witnesses had already been offering information. On December 22, young Bill Crow had come forward about a curious encounter on Lake Herman Road on the 20th. It had occurred earlier that night at the very same turnout. Between 9:30 and 10 p.m. he pulled over to adjust the engine on his girlfriend's (Helen Axe) sports car. They had been cruising along together and he wanted to test the fuel mixture. At this moment a blue car, possibly a Ford Valiant, came from Benicia and shortly after it passed them it stopped in the road. The bright reverse lights came on and it started to back up. Crow jumped in his girlfriend's car and they dashed off to Benicia. The blue car turned around and sped after them. Crow said there were two men in the car, both Caucasians. At no time did they try and overtake him. When he turned off to Benicia they continued on Lake Herman Road to Highway 680.

Soon this encounter began to appear not so sinister as it first sounded. Two guys were out that night dragging their blue Chevy 409, and it is more than likely they were the two who decided to check out if they could pace Crow's natty racer.

More significant to the argument that the killer was a stranger cruising the road is the fact that Lake Herman Road was not in the average sense a backroad. It connected with Columbus Parkway and was thus a link with two major backroads. These roads led to 2 major attractions— Lake Herman and Blue Rock Springs Park— and between them they connected to 3 major highways. The upshot is the killer could have been anybody who had grown up around here. He did not have to know Faraday and Jensen. He merely had to know these roads.

By the New Year, Leslie Lundblad had the overall context of the crime before him. From the position of the bullets in the Rambler it was clear that the killer wanted the cooing teens out of the car. He did not wish to shoot them in the car or even risk wounding them inside. He wanted them out. He came to murder and he wanted to experience it personally and up close.

Furthermore, it takes more than proficiency with a handgun to create that "remarkable grouping." It takes a cold-blooded killer who can remain calm in a murderous situation. He shot a boy on his back, execution style, and then held his hand steady and hit a fleeing target— just a 16 year old girl in a miniskirt. The speck of gunpowder by one bullet hole, the bloodstained path between where the killer had stood and where she finally fell, testify to how he shot at her right away and continued to hold aim until she dropped.

Who could possibly have been on this major backroad at this time of night, near Christmas, and have been prepared to do this?

Several months went by and still nothing. The *Vallejo Times Herald* would condemn a "murderous maniac" as responsible. It declared the young couple had been "sadistically gunned down."

As summer 1969 approached, the Summer of Love was two years old. The establishment was growing more and more leery about the antiestablishment movement and the direction younger society seemed to be taking. So far, hippies were merely looked upon as harmless dropouts. They were peaceniks protesting the Vietnam War. But the idea of casting off the fetters of past morality and established norms was very disturbing. It could motivate extremes in other people. Criminals are also nonconformists. Was this era emboldening psychopaths? The murders of Faraday and Jensen could have been the result of some drugged-up wacko doing his "thing," as it was now called.

As high summer drew nigh, the case was basically shelved as a motiveless murder of the winter before. This was now July— warm summer temperatures and the excitement of Independence Day celebrations around the bustling San Francisco Bay.

3

SILENCE OF THE PEACOCKS

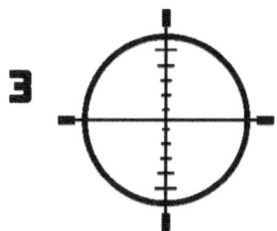

FIREWORKS BURST OVER THE SHIPYARDS AT MARE ISLAND IN SAN Pablo Bay and rain down over a regatta of sailboats in the estuary. The detonations lit the sky. The house tops of Vallejo glowed many colors and then retreated back into dark silhouettes. Cheers rose with every burst; awe cooed with each fabulous sequence of explosions. Sparklers sizzled in driveways. Whistling petes shrilled through middleclass neighborhoods. Barbeque smoke and its flavor— hotdogs, ribs, hamburgers, Americana— mixed with the heavy smell of cordite. It was late night 4th of July in Vallejo— the summer of '69!

Vallejo was a blue collar town, but it was also a city on the bay, which gave it a little more opportunity for pageantry. Vallejo always sponsored a boat regatta and a massive firework display. There was little fancy in Vallejo, but it was an old town tied to the ship building yards at Mare Island, the Navy, and to a way of life inseparable from the rustic fringes of the San Francisco Bay Area.

At an opposite to the tempo of courageous men, ships and the sea, there were the surrounding grassy foothills. One of Vallejo's major landmarks was Blue Rock Springs Park. Giant and ancient eucalyptus flourished by the springs, and oaks dotted the surrounding brown hillsides like giant green umbrellas. As a therapeutic destination, the springs went back in popularity to the 19th century. Aptly named Springs Road was the main road eastward from Vallejo. As the city expanded, it did so along Springs Road. It was now modern and developed with businesses— space-age gas stations, Mr. Ed's Drive-In, car washes, storefronts, and off here the new suburban neighborhoods.

Modernity, however, ended where Springs Road met Columbus Parkway. The latter was a paving of the old dirt road that had led to the springs. Its chief use now was a back way to the highways or to go to the huge park built around the springs. It was a beautiful country jaunt in the day. Take a left at the end of Springs Road onto Columbus Parkway and dash up and down the rolling, brown hills like a dragonfly, whisk under the canopies of tall eucalyptus and then as the road sank into the cleft of the hills, there under the densest canopy of eucalyptus was the parking lot to Blue Rock Springs Park. The lot was but a wide spot in the road, deep enough to fit two rows of cars.

The slopes of the foothills here were green and manicured. Winding paths led to stands of towering eucalyptus. Up the shoulders of the hills an old wooden porch house was used by the caretaker. Peacocks nested up here. They sat on beds of dried eucalyptus leaves and mewed over the vista. Pools of natural spring water were deep green. Their bottoms were impenetrable to the eyes because of the glassy reflections of giant eucalyptus. One pool was spanned by a wooden walking bridge. It was rustic and meant to be rustic. Even the parking lot was rustic. It was edged with uncut, raw boulders. It was a country park, sporting an old style redwood timber sign with the park name painted in golden yellow.

Beyond the park Columbus Parkway held nothing. The road climbed a slope of the dry foothills and eventually came down toward nothing but a convenient half cloverleaf in Highway 80 on the outskirts of northern Vallejo, the main highway from the Bay Area to Sacramento inland.

At night the area had a foreboding air. Darkness clutched the road under the canopies of eucalyptus. Within the curve of the road, in the cleft of the bosom where the parking lot was located, a car would sink into an abyss, its headlights plunge in a tarry pool. There was a lamp in the park near the parking lot. It stood out like a weak lantern pestered by the shadows of the eucalyptus leaves dancing with the foothill's bay breezes.

Centered over the park, this aerial looks toward Vallejo, showing Columbus Parkway traced in eucalyptus. Vallejo Historical Museum.

Festivities were ongoing this night, so that the park was neither quiet nor foreboding. But as it grew late the partiers had thinned out. Columbus Parkway and the park grew lifeless and dark. The brown hills became tope behind the lace of country night. The clusters of trees were black silhouettes that strengthened their clutch over Columbus Parkway, plunging it into eerie shadows. Soon the plaintive cry of the peacocks faded.

Yet in Vallejo rockets still sailed into the sky and burst in electric colors. Kids spun their sparklers in hand, and parties were only beginning.

At 11:30 p.m. it was still early for Darlene Ferrin. She was one of the most popular people in her set in town. Vivacious is putting it mildly. She was a captivating character with a lively personality. This made up for her somewhat gnomish looks. She was only 5 foot 4 inches tall, but she was a firecracker herself. At 22 now she had already been married twice and divorced once. She was a popular waitress at *Terry's* on Magazine Street, and had more than a few admirers who came into eat there just to see "Dee," as her friends called her. Frankly, she was flighty, always late and often a flake. But her bubbly, unpretentious personality kept friends close.

Dee radiated in her bright blue print slacks and white daisy patterned top. She sped down Springs Road in her brown, sporty Corvair coupé. In keeping with her character she had kept her friend Mike Mageau waiting. . . and waiting. She was supposed to have picked him up at 7:30 p.m. so they could go together to see a film in San Francisco. Things, as always with Dee, had happened. She gave him a heads-up earlier that she might be late, explaining she had to take her younger sister Christina to the Miss Firecracker pageant. She would call him later. This was the last he had heard from her. Mike thought the world of Dee. Home alone because his dad was staying at a motel and his twin brother Steve lived with their mom down south, he waited by the phone for hours instead of enjoying this festive day. Now at 11:30 p.m., Dee finally arrived at his home on Beechwood, near Springs Road. Figures!— just as the day was almost over. He rushed out and jumped into the passenger side of her sporty Chevrolet Corvair.

As usual Darlene was also without embarrassment over having made Mike wait. It was too late for them to go to San Francisco. She now said she wanted to get something to eat. They headed to nearby Mr. Ed's diner on Springs Road. Suddenly, impulsively perhaps, she told Mike she wanted to talk. How about if they went to Blue Rock Springs Park? It wasn't far. Her location of choice wasn't surprising. It was her favorite meditating place. She turned around on Springs Road and headed to the nearby outskirts of Vallejo.

This sudden turn of events revealed why the extrovert Dee was always late for events. Right now she was supposed to be out getting fireworks for a late night party. Her husband Dean had called and told her to try and find some. After they closed at *Caesar's*, where he was the cook, he was going to bring people home and give a party. After Dee had come home, she tidied up a bit and then walked out on her babysitter, telling her she was going to look for fireworks and would be back by 12:30 a.m. Instead she finally went to meet Mike.

Apparently the fact Dee was married and had a baby girl did not bother the young 19 year old Mike Mageau, at least as little as it bothered Dee. This was 1969 after all, two years after the Summer of Love. Dee liked the beat that came from the antiestablishment pulse— break the norms and don't assume the most negative thing about anybody acting outside that norm. But the mainstream reaction to Dee's lifestyle nevertheless would still have been worse than the one embodied in the lyrics of one of the top 10 songs of the year before—"Harper Valley P.T.A."

Dee was as much a reflection of the counterculture as she was, by type, part of the cause for the receptive attitudes around San Francisco. Her life was certainly not the typical mainstream life of a 22 year old wife. Nor had it been. Her reputation for excitement must have been such that the young Mike Mageau had a definite impression of her and geared his introduction accordingly. When they had first met, he had said he was wanted by the FBI, thinking this would make her like him.

But Dee had liked him anyway, though he had some peculiarities. He thought he was too skinny. As a result he dressed to build himself up. For instance, despite the summer's tepid air from the bay he had dressed tonight in 3 pairs of pants, 1 t-shirt, 1 long sleeve shirt, and over these 3 sweaters.

In this combination— her thin but lively flower print and his built up stork's physique— they sailed down Columbus Parkway in her brown Corvair, windows down and radio playing the currents hits. Under the clutches of the canopy of eucalyptus, into the starlight, and at last they plunged into the cleft of the bosom where the solitary orb of light floating in the ink marked the lamppost at Blue Rock Springs Park.

The Corvair's headlights swept the golden letters of the painted redwood sign, steadied, closed-in and stopped. Dee parked at an angle, her headlights obliquely lighting the sign. She didn't park in

Above, the only known photo showing the parking lot as it looked in the late 1960s. Cars are parked along the narrow parkway and crammed within the small parking lot. The inset closes on the parking lot and by coincidence the Mustang is essentially idling where Ferrin had parked that night. (Vallejo Historical Museum.)

a stall. No one was there. There was no point in being picky. Dee was never picky. She turned the headlights off and the sign went dark. She turned off the engine and kept the radio playing softly.

There wasn't much time to say anything before a couple of cars came rolling in. Teens cheered, laughed, set off some firecrackers, and rolled back onto Columbus Parkway and into the clutching shadows of the eucalyptus canopy.

They had not been alone long when yet another car came from the direction of Vallejo. It pulled in next to Dee on her driver's side, only 6 to 8 feet away. The driver was alone. He turned off his headlights and sat there. Considering she was parked crooked, it was bold to mimic her angle.

Mike and Dee looked over.

"Do you know him?"

"Oh, never mind," she replied.

He joked how she knows everybody, but she didn't elaborate.

No matter anyway. The headlights on the strange car came on, the engine started and it pulled out and drove off back to town.

It was a queer moment, but Dee knew many odd people. After all, she liked the far side. Mike didn't pursue it.

Only minutes later a car returned, this time pulling up behind them and slightly to an angle. At first, they thought it was the same car. They looked over their shoulders at the blinding headlights. It might be a policeman. The cop on this beat checked the lot occasionally. A powerful flashlight came on and started to move up to Mike's open window. Now Mike was sure it was a cop.

As the light came to the window he looked over his shoulder. He saw a beefy guy; under 6-foot tall he estimated. He had a blue short-sleeved shirt on. He carried one of those big handheld flashlights in his left hand. Mike leaned back and reached around to get his wallet. It was a fortuitously timed act.

A shot burst forth. Mike felt burning pain in his neck. He jumped back. Dee clutched the steering wheel in surprise. Two more shots pumped out, piercing through her right arm and then through her left. Another shot spit out. She slumped from a bullet in her ribs. Mike was flailing about. From behind the blinding splatter of the flashlight, another shot hissed out. His hip burned with pain.

The bright flashlight beam streaked off the car. Footsteps casually thumped away. Blood trickled and dripped down the interior, lit only by the surreal angles of light slicing through the windows from the assailant's headlights. As the shooter passed before them, the headlights cast his lumbering shadow over the gruesome scene in the Corvair.

Mike let out a scream of agony, mixed with anger.

The shadow stopped, steadied. The flashlight beam streaked over the car again, sparkling off the rear window and illuminating the blood streaking down the interior paneling. The footsteps were returning. Mike panicked. He started jumping about in the backseat. The flashlight splatter stopped at the side window. From behind the splatter two more shots burst out. His shoulder burned in back and then his leg. Two more shots burst out at Dee. She was slumped over the wheel and took the shots in her right back without any attempt to block them.

The splatter of the flashlight beam dashed off the car again. Moments later the killer's shadow lumbered over the dripping blood in the Corvair as the villain passed in front of his headlights again to the driver's side of his car.

Mike reached out and unlocked the passenger side door. He fell out. The assailant's car had just backed around. For a brief moment he saw the attacker in silhouette. A big face. He let out a wail of pain on the tarmac. The attacker hadn't heard him. The brake lights snipped off and the car surged forward. Mike saw the back of the car and noticed it seemed to be a lighter brown than Dee's, but of a similar model. The assailant's car drove off and turned left onto Columbus Parkway— back to Springs Road and Vallejo.

Just moments later, a truck came coasting up from the other direction, that is, from the right, down from the rise in Columbus Parkway from the north, from the direction of Highway 80.

Roger, Jerry, and Debbie were a little more radical looking than the mainstream. They were morphing into mainstream hippies, which was largely just veneer for teens their age. Presently they were looking for one of Jerry's girlfriends. They came this way from Vallejo to see if she was at the park. Debbie, the oldest at 19, was driving. She stopped on the road and they looked up to the dark Corvair.

On Columbus Parkway, looking at the park and parking lot (obscured at the low point in the road by the stand of trees) from the direction Jerry, Roger, and Debbie came. (Vallejo Historical Museum.)

(The parking lot slanted up at an angle, so that Columbus Parkway was noticeably below the apex of the lot.) They debated for a moment whether the girl they sought was in the car and whether they should pull in and look. At this moment, what must have been only seconds after they arrived, the Corvair's lights came on and so did the left blinker. They saw a young man roll out from behind the right side and heard him scream. They pulled in.

Roger jumped out.

Mike Mageau lay in the fringes of their headlights. Blood burbled from his mouth: "We've been shot! Get a doc. Quick!"

Jerry had barely come forward when Roger bolted back. Jerry wanted to stay, but Debbie and Roger blurted "No way!" They assured Mike they would get help quick. They ripped out and sped toward Springs Road. They sped through the clutches of the eucalyptus canopy. Emerging into starlight again, Lake Herman Road

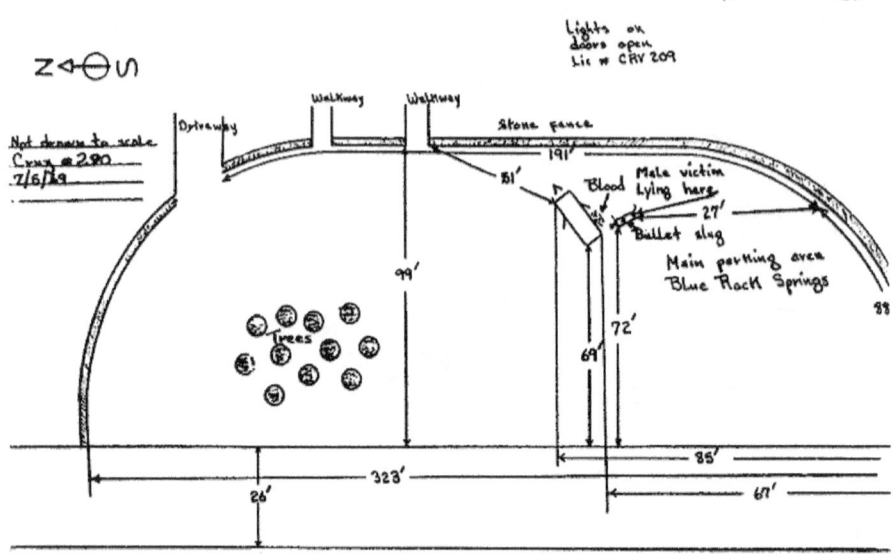

Map from the Vallejo PD report, showing the exact position of Ferrin's car in the parking lot. A grove of eucalyptus once stood in the left-center of the lot, now removed. Below, photos from the Vallejo Historical Museum showing the lot in the 1960s.

cutoff was soon on their left. They noticed a car's taillights receding away as it headed to Benicia. They couldn't tell what type of car. They squealed right onto Springs Road. Soon they squealed onto Castlewood Drive (not far from Beechwood) to Roger's house.

Frantic about the shooting, Debbie tried to explain to the police. Neither Roger nor Jerry had time to look into the car to see Dee Ferrin at all, so Debbie had little to screech over the phone except there had been a shooting at Blue Rock Springs Park. As such, the police were unsure of the extent of the carnage that awaited them.

At 12:10 a.m. all units heard the broadcast. Closest were officers Meyring and Lindemann in Unit 119, and in Unit 130 officer Richard Hoffman. Each turned around and went screaming onto Columbus Parkway, heading to the park.

Hoffman was the most surprised by the report. He had just checked the park about 15 minutes before (around 5 minutes to midnight). No one had been there.

Now just by the clubhouse of the new golf course (on the opposite side of the parkway), oncoming headlights emerged from the canopy of darkness that hung over the road by the park. A gray late model Caddy passed them heading toward Vallejo. Meyring and Lindemann do a squealing U-turn and hit the overhead lights. Hoffman plunged forward into the darkness. His headlights bounce up and down as he took the gutter at quick speed. Then the headlights swept a young man rolling in a pool of blood by the rear of the parked Corvair.

Hoffman rushed up. Mageau is retching in pain. Blood is flowing freely from his mouth. In such severe pain, he could say little as Hoffman knelt by him. He only said they had been shot and didn't know who it was. Hoffman then got up and looked in the open window of the Corvair. Dee Ferrin was breathing, but only shallowly. He could see the holes in her arms and one in her side a few inches below her right armpit. He went around to the driver's side. He saw no more bullet holes, but recoiled at the amount of blood splattered about in the car. Angered by the scene, Hoffman impatiently awaited other units.

Headlights quickly appeared through the stand of eucalyptus. It was a plain car racing in. It pulled up behind Hoffman's car. Out jumped Sgt. Roy Conway of detectives. Hoffman confirmed both victims had been shot. Both were barely holding on. He suggested that Conway go back and tell Meyring and Lindemann the details, since they had stopped a suspicious car. Conway acknowledged and, after seeing the carnage for himself, pulled out.

At that moment Officer Doug Clark pulled in from the Highway 80 direction.

Hoffman was administering aid to Mageau, so Clark quickly went to the driver's side to help Ferrin. Amidst the dripping blood from the ceiling, he reached in and carefully felt her pulse. It was weak. She was breathing very shallowly. She tried to say something. It was the barest articulation. It was "I" or likely "MY" for Mike Mageau.

Soon Conway was back. He had made sure that the youth driving the Caddy had been arrested.

The scene about him was bloody and unfathomable. What on earth had happened here on this festive night?

Altogether there would be 4 detectives moving about but staying out of the way of the ambulance drivers, gurneys, and forensic men measuring and taking pictures. The new arrivals had been Sgts. Ed Rust, John Lynch, and Ken Ordione. Amidst the flashing lightbulbs and blinking red lights they would decide who would take the case. Rust and Lynch would be assigned.

The solution to the case may prove easier than at first thought. A message had just burst over the car radios. A man had called the police station and confessed to the crime. The voice on the phone had admitted that the gun he had used was a 9mm luger. Bright brass shell casings on the ground were pulsing with reflections from the rotating red light of the ambulance. They had already been identified as 9mm. Conway was eager to get back.

If any of the detectives thought this would prove an easy case, such thoughts were dashed by the fact the phone caller had also admitted to having killed "those kids last year." Before he hung up, his voice had lowered ominously. "Goodbye," he had said in a taunting way, indicating there was more to come.

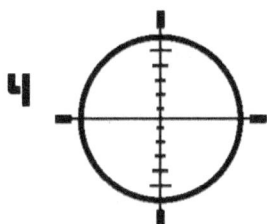

MURDER SAID EASY

What a bloody, edgy world this was becoming. Music had been preaching the end. Napalm prophets had strummed their message on a guitar. Barry McGuire's song about being on the eve of destruction was about 4 years old now, but it seemed even more prophetic. As background the song would have fit perfectly the dystopic atmosphere of the Vallejo police station. Yet there was no beat of music. Phones rang. Dispatches were coming through. Teletype messages pecked out. The lyrics were ingrained. It was one of those earwig songs that come to mind at moments like this.

Early morning doesn't carry with it the philosophic moods of twilight. It is an unnatural time for the pace of daily routine. It is a taboo time. A police station in the early AM hours lends a chilling feeling. It is with this mood that Debbie, Roger, and Jerry sat with Sgt. Ordione and relayed dramatically what they had experienced.

Nancy Slover was still at her station. She was the police operator who had taken the "confession call" and jotted down the message when it became apparent the caller was in earnest.

> I want to report a double murder. If you will go one mile east on Columbus Parkway to the public park you will find the kids in a brown car. They were shot with a nine millimeter luger. I also killed those kids last year. *Goodbye.*

From his monotone tempo she had the feeling the caller was reading or had memorized the brief statement. When she had tried to interrupt to get clarification, the caller raised his voice and spoke over her, continuing with his declaration. By contrast this is also what made his "Goodbye" sound sinister. Slover said he had lowered his voice and put a taunting inflection to it. Thus it indicated someone who both enjoyed what he had done and was implying more to come. Try and catch me. Otherwise there was no accent or anything remarkable in his voice.

Underscoring Slover's impression is the careful wording of the caller's statement. The caller did not confess to the Blue Rock Springs shooting outright. He did so only implicitly in the last sentence by saying he had also killed Faraday and Jensen last December. The statement does, in fact, seem designed to not alert a police operator that the killer was on the line until the last sentence. Due to the careful wording, there was little reason for Slover to ring the desk sergeant until the call was essentially over. This she did, but by the time he picked up his extension it was too late for him to hear anything. The caller had hung up.

If the statement was as rehearsed as it had impressed Slover, the caller certainly betrayed knowledge of how a police operator would react if he had started with "I just killed. . . "

Yet the caller didn't mind saying the words: "I killed those kids." It takes a lot to say that word, in that context.

The call had been traced. It had come from a phone booth on the sidewalk by Joe's Union Gas Station at Tuolumne and Springs Road in Vallejo.

As the booth was being processed for latents, the street looked desolate. A few neon signs glowed from a bar here and there. Joe's had closed at 8:25 p.m. so the staff could enjoy the 4th fireworks. The bloodless halogen lights set in the metal canopy over the pumps revealed only abandonment. They must have cast merely a fringe of fuzzy light as far as the booth on the sidewalk. There was little chance there had been witnesses.

But something was happening right now at the police station that shed light on the confession call. It was 2:35 a.m. Dee's husband Dean Ferrin and her employer Bill Lee had just come in to the police station. Dean quickly informed them that they had already received two phone calls at home in which it was clear someone was on the other end but wouldn't speak. There had only been breathing. Then the caller hung up. (This would be compounded later in the morning when Leo Suennen Sr., Dee's father, admitted that at 1:30 a.m. that morning he too had received such a call.)

Hang-up calls are disturbing, especially in a case where a confession call had been made. "Coincidence" is hardly the most reassuring explanation. The hang-up caller must have known the shooting had occurred and also knew Dee Ferrin enough to know something of her family. (There had been no news announcement of the shooting.) Thus from this moment forward Vallejo PD would begin to suspect that Ferrin's killer had known her and in addition to the confession call he had also made these calls.[1]

There was no question the confession call was legitimate. A crank listening in to the police channel would have known that both victims were alive at the time the call was received. As it stood now, only Ferrin had died. She had been pronounced dead on arrival at the hospital. Aside from the police on duty, there was nobody else but the killer that knew the shooting had occurred. The confession caller was obviously the killer, and his erroneous belief he had killed both victims underlined how quickly he had committed the act and fled. This fit the crime scene data and Mageau's painful statement.

Right now Mike Mageau was fighting for his life in ICU. More than one doctor was attending him, the chief surgeon trying to get bullets out of his back and leg. He had been shot four times, whereas Ferrin had 16 holes in her. Though shot 5 times, she had been riddled by entrance and exit holes. Just those two shots that had pierced her arms had created 8 holes in her.

Every sound in a morgue seems final. Every echo seems to lead to an empty vault. The bland, swinging doors close and the echo leads nowhere. The walls are some faded pale green. It is supposed to be anodyne, but the antiseptic aura of a morgue is a utilitarian one. It is not like a hospital, where the purpose is toward preventing death.

---

[1] The narrative is going chronologically. We are in July 1969 here, and no other time or information is influencing the narrative.

Everything in a morgue is utilitarian toward disposal. The surgical tables are stainless steel, cold but clean. All the hardware is stainless steel. Lights on overhead elbow joints lend no warmth— the cold steel simply sparkles. Life is gone. Sterile function takes the beat.

Bodies lie under sanitary sheets of that ugly pale green. A little tag is wrapped round the big toe of the cadaver. It's not even a body now. A shell. The shell is to be processed. It is pushed along on what look like large stainless steel dinner dollies. There to the morgue table they go; a squeak of the wheels, a heft onto the table. Underneath are the channels and the drains for the flow of blood and bodily fluids. Men in masks lean over and logistically "hmmm" before they start with the scalpel.

Such was now the end of vivacious Dee Ferrin.

Before Dr. Satoshi Shirai could even do the coroner's job he had to play detective and measure the bullet entry and exit wounds to get an idea of trajectory. The angle between them was very apparent. He dictated the following into a microphone:[2]

> General: Well developed, well nourished, fully built. Scalp hair is light brown, but dark towards the roots. Irises are blue; pupils equal at 0.5cm. Both eyelashes are false. Rigor mortis is 4 plus. Body is embalmed.
>
> Wounds: There are nine bullet wounds of entry, seven exit wounds, and two bullets recovered from the body, internally. Right arm shows two entry wounds; one at five and one half inches above elbow on right lateral side, going through and fracturing the humeral shaft and exiting anteriorly and medially at one and one quarter distal to elbow. The other is behind forearm, three and one half inches above the wrist, chafing the skin from right to left. Left arm shows two entry wounds; one is medially located in upper arm at three and one quarter inches above the elbow and exiting the opposite side. The other is medially on the forearm located two inches above the wrist, going through and fracturing the radial and ulnar bones, and exiting above and laterally at three inches above wrist.

---

[2] The autopsy had been conducted in the funeral home, its facilities used as the morgue.

There are five entry wounds on the right half of the back, mainly on the posterior thoracic cage. From down upward, the first is located half an inch right of T-12, through posterior margin of T-12, the liver, stomach, and exiting through left rib number eight, laterally, on left mid-axillary liner. The second is located three and one quarter inches right of T-10, through posterior margin of T-1- and T-11, the liver, spleen, and bullet is recovered medial margin of left rib number nine. The third is located seven and a half inches to the right of T-7, about posterior axillary line, through the right lung, lacerating posterior-apical area of left ventricle of heart, the left lung, and exiting through the left rib number 7 laterally about the mid-axillary line. The fourth is located two and one quarter inches to the right of T-4, through 4th rib, the right lung, the anterior shaft of right second rib, where the bullet is recovered in subcutaneous tissue here. The fifth is located back of the right shoulder, through the soft tissues, the subcutaneous tissues of the anterior chest wall, and chafing the anterior margin of the sternum at level of 4th rib, and exiting to the left side of left breast, slightly above the level of nipple.

No scalp injuries or skull fractures.

The heart, both lungs are within normal limits, except for hemorrhages around the course of the bullets. The GI tract (track), appendix, liver, pancreas, gallbladder, spleen, kidneys, ovaries, and uterus (not pregnant) are within normal. The stomach is filled with undigested foods. The bladder is filled with clear amber urine. There are no tumors or abnormalities of the organs. The thyroid and adrenal glands are not remarkable.

There are bloody fluid [sic] in the thoracic cavity (200cc. each) and abdominal cavity (300cc.).

Dr. Shirai wrote the obvious conclusion under <u>Immediate Cause of Death</u>: "Multiple bullet wounds to chest and abdominal organs." The attendant finished up and the body was rolled slowly into the cold refrigerator unit and the box door shut.

Hospital rooms are about as humorless as the morgue. The ICU room is painted warmer colors, but the atmosphere of tragedy keeps anyone from embracing it; that terrible limbo that does not exist in a morgue. Here people are fighting to survive, their loved ones praying desperately for them. Despite how intense the battle is, the only movement in such a ward is glowing green lines on dark screens. They beep up and down or shrill a terrible, frantic warning.

I.V. bottles and tubes hung about Sgt. Ed Rust as he sat next to Mike Mageau's bed. The 19 year old was pale. The drip of blood from the bottle to the tube was the only thing maintaining any color in him. Half of his face was covered in a bandage, sealing the bullet hole in his neck. The blood had been cleaned out of his mouth. His bloodstained clothes had been taken for photographing as evidence. He lay here now covered, stitched, heavily drugged, the residue of what was to have been a late night romp on the glorious 4th of July.

Ed Rust's voice is the only sound to disturb the rhythm of the monitors' electronic beeps. Dr. Scott said he could have a short time to talk to Mike. The purpose was obvious: "State the facts."

Mike repeated as best he could the day's events and how they came to be at the parking lot. He recounted how the car had pulled up earlier and sat next to them on Dee's side for about a minute. He qualified that Dee was popular, and how when he asked if she knew this driver she just replied "Oh, never mind." Then the car pulled out. Mike now told Rust:

> ... A white man drove up in a car, got out, walked up, shined flashlite [sic] inside and started shooting. Man was older than me, window was down. After stop shooting I got out of car. I tried to get people to come over but they drove off. After finally 10 minutes, the Policeman came.

Understandably, Mageau's memory was patchy. Such was expected at this moment, but Rust nevertheless had to ask for a general description of the shooter. He wrote it down as follows:

> Subject appeared to be short, possibly 5'8", was real heavy set, beefy build. States subject was not blubbery fat, but real beefy, possibly 195 to 200, or maybe even larger. Stated he had short, curly hair, light brown, almost blond. He was wearing a short-sleeved shirt, blue in

color. Cannot remember if it was light or dark blue. States he just saw the subject's face from profile, side view, and does not recall seeing a front view. States there was nothing unusual about his face, other than it appeared to be large. Michael stated the subject did not have a mustache, nor was he wearing glasses or anything. He could not recall anything unusual except that he had a large face. Michael reemphasized that he really did not get a good look at subject other than his profile. Also, it was dark out and it was hard to see the subject.

Michael states that he could possibly recognize the responsible if he had a profile view, as this is the best view he had of the subject. Stated subject was a white male, approximately 26-30 years. Was unable to judge real well what his age was. States he feels sure the subject wanted to make sure they were dead. This due to the fact that he returned and shot each one of them twice again after the first shooting.

Ed Rust came away feeling that Mageau could not identify the shooter. Essentially it came down to a thick, beefy guy, big face, under 6 feet tall, maybe under 30 years old. He wore dark clothes. He carried a powerful flashlight.

Not much to go on, but in general this description gave some advantage to the detectives in their process of elimination of persons of interest. And all of these POIs, as they are called, were taking form in a peculiar, to say the least, corral of potential psychopaths in orbit around the life and times of Dee Ferrin. It was becoming undeniably clear that if anybody in town could have known a crazed killer, it was Darlene Ferrin.

Aside from those hang-up phone calls, a few suspicious things had been discovered that caused Vallejo PD to believe that Ferrin had actually known her killer.

One, it was very suspicious that the confession caller also confessed to the murders of Faraday and Jensen. A very different weapon had been used there and their killer hadn't bothered to confess afterward. This sounded like the caller was trying to draw attention away from any notion Dee Ferrin had been specifically targeted.

Two, Mike Mageau's statement to Ed Rust contained a blatantly false comment that looked like he was covering up their actual motive for being at the park. He had told Rust that after they got together that night they were going to go eat because they were both hungry. Instead Dee suddenly wanted to talk. The result was that they went to the remote Blue Rock Springs Park. (I followed this re-creation in the narrative reenactment in chapter 3, but in truth the facts contradict it.) The autopsy showed that Dee Ferrin had just eaten a full meal, and it was not even digested yet. Thus Mageau was confused or they had gone somewhere first and had eaten and he did not want to admit they went to the park afterward for romantic reasons. . . or very possibly for something far more dangerous.

Dee was indeed a small time weed dealer. A workable theory came to mind. A pass-off may have been the motive for going to the park this late— and the reason Mageau had to lie about why they went. Her supplier could have been a jealous suitor who thought Dee was fooling around with this snot-nose 19 year old. Instead of the drug pass-off, he starts greasing. If not that, then there were other potential jealous suitors.

Vallejo PD was turning up lots of clues. If anybody in Vallejo could have provoked a jealous killer, Vallejo PD quickly realized it too was Darlene Ferrin. To put it mildly, the exuberant lifestyle of the bon vivant of the blue collar crowd could have set off far more than one man to take vengeance. The life and times of Darlene Ferrin would inspire almost every direction and misstep the budding Vallejo PD investigation would now take, until almost the entire investigation was one massive tangent trying to expose someone who had known her and who was capable of acting out his jilted canteen ardor with blue steel.

Though already on her second marriage at only 22 years old, Dee Ferrin still "dated" other men. Mike Mageau was an example of her tastes, and he seemed a little off the beam. Friends promoted her as merely being impetuous and this brought her into the orbit of wild and crazy events. Whether the wild side was her taste or merely the byproduct of her character, there was more to her past than most people have at 22 years old. Another story said she had seen a murder in the Virgin Islands while on her honeymoon with her first husband. When he, John Philips, was finally contacted he confirmed no such thing. However, he said the reason for their breakup was that she had "other men" in her life already at 19 years old.

After the initial canvassing of her life, Vallejo PD believed jealousy of some sort was involved. After all, Dee, a *married woman*, was parked with a guy, *not her husband*, at a known petting spot when they were shot. The killer could be someone hidden in her past or lurking about in the shabby present of her workplace.

The last seemed more probable when Vallejo PD discovered that Dee really had a stalker. He was associated with a white car and inopportune phone calls. This jasper was of great interest, but nobody knew his name. They only knew him by sight. He watched her at the restaurant and appeared at her house once bearing gifts from Mexico. He, whoever he was, sounded like a good fit. But there were other candidates with more solid information on them— i.e. Vallejo PD actually knew their names.[3]

There was George Waters— an appropriate name for an habitué of the Kat Pad and past denizen of the Krazy Kat and The Viking, all three swill joints between Vallejo and Albany, another ship building town down the coast across the Carquinez Strait. At 29 years of age he fit Mageau's age estimation. He was stocky, about 5 foot 8 inches tall, just like Mageau had described the shooter. He also knew Darlene beyond being just an admirer of her waitress talents. While guzzling it down one night, he took it further. He said *he was* the shooter.

On July 11, 1969, Sgt. Barber walked into the Kat Pad. In daytime an exotic bar is a different world, low key, dirty in the unwelcome light, out of place to its function. Barber quickly learned that George had worked a variety of jobs. He had worked at Mare Island, the shipbuilding center. Before his nightshift it was his custom to come to the Kat Pad and quaff a dish of bourbon. Then about 1 a.m., after work, he would stop in for a beer. He started coming to the Kat Pad in February 1969, having moved on from his last job near Albany. He soon became attracted to the manager, Linda. In between her managing the dive, she doubled as the exotic dancer on the bar. One evening after an especially inspiring time watching her gams contort about in front of him, he followed her out and seized her, threw her on top of the hood of a parked car and tried to get "fresh," to put it euphemistically. She grabbed his hair and boxed

---

[3] Again, the narrative is going chronologically. We are in July 1969 here, and no other time or information is influencing the narrative.

him with her fist. He backed off. She told him never again! She told Barber that at that time he had driven a '54 Chevy, white over green or blue. Another customer was in the Kat Pad while Sgt. Barber scribbled the details. He had owned the Krazy Kat and remembered George in Albany. George was a blowhard. He claimed he was rich but drove the old junker because he didn't want to show off.

None of this surprised Barber. He was there asking because Vallejo PD already had some squirrelly info on George or, better put, sound info on squirrelly George. His name had been put forward immediately on July 5 by Dee's married sister, Linda Del Buono. The surroundings had been rather dramatic. It was only about 7 a.m. in the morning. Ed Rust and John Lynch had just returned to the parking lot to look for clues when Linda and her husband Steve pulled up. Dee's shot-up and bloody Corvair was still sitting there.

Linda faced them and declared: "George visited Darlene frequently, was very emotional, and would get all uptight when Darlene didn't pay too much attention to him."

Interest in George Waters nevertheless had only been general until Barber filed his report from the Kat Pad. Well, George looked more suspicious now that the bar crowd had chattered.

Rust and Lynch left Vallejo at 8 p.m. the very night that Barber came back from the bar. They got to Yountville and approached George. George had a little different story to tell. He used to go into *Terry's* late night after the bars closed and have breakfast. He called her Deedee. He said that he used to give her a ride home when her shift ended. This is how he realized they had a '51 pink Chevy truck to sell. This is the only time he ever met her husband. "Denies ever threatening Darlene, but does state that many times he did tease her and make her angry." This was followed by his dry and anticlimactic appraisal of her as a "very capable waitress." She had lots of friends. He didn't know any by name. Last time he saw her? George said it was in May, when he stopped by at *Terry's* with his wife. He kidded with her but she was quiet. Then he somewhat unadvisedly admitted he knew her nightlife too. He knew that she usually went to the Coronado with friends.

George was a curious case. He was genuine bozo matter, but there was nothing to tie him to the crimes. For only doing odd jobs, George could afford a number of cars and residences. In the last year alone he had owned the blue on white Chevy he was known for at the Kat Pad. He had bought Dean's pink '51 truck. He owned a Bonneville, with a Benicia address on it. He seemed to have lots of contact with bars from Albany to Napa. Rumors continued to trickle back to Vallejo PD that Dee was a petty drug dealer. Waters would make a great contact or supply man.

Over the following days Rust and Lynch continued to collate the leads on various suspects. But there was a lot they had to figure out from what they already had. For instance, George Bryant Jr. had come into the station the evening of July 5 (around 7:55 p.m.). He was the 22 year old son of the Blue Rock Springs Park caretaker. They lived up in the old wood porch house. Around midnight he had been lying in bed on his stomach, looking out the window just enjoying the tepid night breeze. He then heard a gunshot. It was a much louder sound than the firecrackers he had heard during the merriment about 30 minutes earlier. There was a pause now. Then there was another loud report. "After another short pause he heard rapid fire of what appeared to be gunshots. He then heard a car take off at super speed and it burned rubber and was squealing its tires as it sped along the road." Young Bryant wasn't sure of the direction, and he didn't check since it was the 4th of July, as he thought it was just some celebrating.

When this would be compared to Mike Mageau's statement it would be hard to fit together. By mid-July he had recovered enough to make a full statement. He now said that he had not heard a gunshot. Rather his neck suddenly began to burn and he realized he was shot. The bullets continued to come out with a spitting sound, as if there was a silencer on the gun.

Bryant could never have heard a silencer muffled gunshot from where he was. The house was about 800 feet up the slope of the park from the parking lot, and there were stands of huge eucalyptus between the house and parking lot. Nevertheless, the spacing of the sounds he had heard coincided with Mageau's statement that the killer returned and shot them four more times.

By the time Mageau was *compos mentis*, the double shooting and murder of Ferrin wasn't top news anymore in Vallejo. As in the world, so it was in Vallejo. News broadcasts followed the momentous flight of Apollo 11 toward the moon. On July 16, 1969, it had taken off amidst special broadcasts from coast to coast. There was probably no television set that was not tuned-in to the launch. Its progress was updated on radio broadcasts and each evening on the 6 o'clock news on ABC, CBS, and NBC. Astronauts Buzz Aldrin, Neil Armstrong, and Michael Collins were now household names.

Then on July 20, 1969, "one small step for man, one giant leap for mankind" took place. John F. Kennedy's challenge to put a man on the moon by the end of the decade had been met. It was not just a new age in philosophy. For the establishment it was proof the Space Age *was* the future. Stanley Kubrick's 1968 masterpiece *2001: a Space Odyssey* was replaying in the theaters. The age of the *Jetsons* was here in more than just the era's architectural concepts and in the spindly "futuristic" plastic furniture designs.

The triumphant re-entry and splashdown of Apollo 11 on July 24, 1969, was more momentous news and it pushed to the backseat the other routine events like Vietnam War protests. Coverage continued for days. Richard Nixon visited the men while in decontamination aboard the carrier *Hornet* and declared, in the usual hyperbole of a politician, that they had brought the world closer together.

Routine investigation into Dee Ferrin's murder had continued over the whole of the month. Leads still went nowhere, however. Jealously/Revenge had been and shakily remained the obvious motive. Everything on the police report was entered under that heading on the title page. By the time of the astronauts' triumphant return, however, the report had swelled to dozens of pages, many entries just brief annotations on the day's investigative events, none of which had opened the door to a viable suspect or, for that matter, closed the doors on some of those on the suspect list.

By the end of July, Vallejo PD's Chief Jack Stiltz was still in a quandary about the motive in the Ferrin murder due to the difficulty in uncovering all the bizarre characters around Dee Ferrin's daily schedule. Then on August 1st things changed. Someone was eager to prove they had killed "those kids" back in December and Dee Ferrin too. Vallejo PD wasn't expecting what followed.

GAMESTER OF DEATH

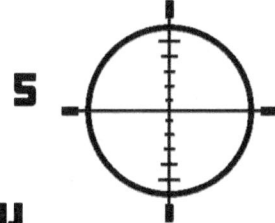

By the end of July, that momentous July, the tumultuous 1960s had about half a year left. It was finishing on a dichotomous teeter-totter. Counterculture was sweeping through the nation preaching the innocence of early man in communes, love-ins, and at skinny-dipping holes. On the other hand, the establishment had finally crossed the threshold of Science Fiction into Science Fact.

News had now come back to earth, literally. Yet no current story was particularly outstanding. In fact, otherwise intriguing news seemed flat by comparison to the moonwalk. The shooting at Blue Rock Springs Park was not only old news, it was forgotten news. . . and it had always only been local news. No lead from the life and times of Dee Ferrin had taken the investigators anywhere but to the suspicion that she had been murdered by someone who knew her. As a result there was a division between investigators whether there was a link between her murder and the Faraday/Jensen murders. In those murders, of course, the investigators came to the conclusion that a crazed maniac was responsible and not a jilted, jealous lover.

On August 1, the *Vallejo Times-Herald* received a disturbing letter in the mail. It was a confession. In truth, it was really more of a declaration. Along with it there was a cryptogram— a cipher written in code letters. The letter was written with a felt pen in a hasty freehand. At a stark contrast, however, on a separate piece of paper the cryptogram was neatly, very neatly hand-printed with the same felt pen. This was written by someone who didn't mind beginning a letter with the sentence "I am the killer. . ."

Dear Editor— I am the killer of the 2 teenagers last Christmass at Lake Herman and the Girl last 4th of July. To prove this I shall state some facts which only I + the police know Christmass 1 Brand name of ammo Super X 2 10 shots fired 3 Boy was on back feet to car 4 Girl was lyeing on right side feet to west 4th of July 1 Girl was wearing patterned pants 2 Boy was also shot in knee 3 Brand name of ammo was Western Here is a cipher or that is part of one. The other 2 parts have been mailed to the S.F. Examiner + the S.F. Chronicle I want you to print this

[continued on back of page]

> Cipher on your front page by Fry. Afternoon Aug 1-69. If you do not do this I will go on a kill rampage Fry night that will last the whole week end. I will cruse around and pick of all stray people or coupples that are alone then move on to kill some more untill I have killed over a dozen people.

It didn't take long for the editor of the *Vallejo Times-Herald* to confirm with the editors of the *Examiner* and *Chronicle* in San Francisco that they each had received a letter, each similar to the one the *Times-Herald* had received. Each also received a cryptogram. Each was made of the same odd symbols though the sequence of these symbols was different. Obviously, they were all written with the same code and concealed different statements; or just as the writer had implied they carried different parts of a single statement.

Naturally, the San Francisco newspapers also quickly verified with Vallejo PD and Solano Sheriffs that such murders had occurred as claimed by the writer of the letter. Each newspaper then made copies before turning the letters over to the police.

The newspapers didn't receive the letters until too late to meet the deadline on Friday August 1. None were going to be rushed anyway. Newspapermen were and are a cynical lot. Each newspaper knew they were being maneuvered, but if this letter writer really was the killer these murders were a résumé that put a punch behind his threat to go on a rampage. They had to consider what to do.

The San Francisco *Chronicle* was first. On August 2, on the *second page*, they published the cryptogram and the story. The Sunday (August 3) editions of the *Vallejo Times-Herald* and the San Francisco *Examiner* published their parts.

Vallejo Chief of Police Jack Stiltz was skeptical. He wasn't sure that the killer and the letter writer were the same person, and quickly qualified this to the press. He declared that anybody who had contact with the crime scenes or knew someone who had contact could have picked up the information that the letter writer had presented as proof he was the killer.

Of course, Stiltz was not going to elaborate the reasons for his caution. But his views implicitly reflected Vallejo detectives' majority belief that Ferrin was murdered by someone who knew her and there was therefore no link to the savage Faraday and Jensen slayings. Stiltz knew that the investigation by the VPD had uncovered a number of innuendos, shall we say, regarding Darlene Ferrin's unusual past and then-current lifestyle, plus the fact more than a few of her friends were wackos. Ephemeral to her circle were a number of cops. This is expected with a waitress. Some cop could have let something innocently slip that spiraled to the bottom of Ferrin's secret admirer list, and one of these cranks was responsible for the bizarre "confession" letters.

On Monday, August 4, it was obvious the kill rampage had not occurred despite the fact the newspapers did not meet the deadline and the "frunt" page demand. The San Francisco *Examiner* had a reporter in Vallejo who now filed a special report: "Vallejo Mass Murder Threat Fails." The article republished all three cryptograms together. In it Jack Stiltz's skepticism was given high profile, culminating in: "The police chief urged the writer yesterday to send more letters with more facts to prove his connection with the crimes."

Meanwhile behind the scenes the failure of the "kill rampage" only strengthened Stiltz and Vallejo PD's theory that Ferrin knew her killer and the letter writer was just a crank. . .Yet there was debate in the department, and rightly so. There were reasons to be shaken by the lengths the writer had gone to get published. Three cryptograms precisely and painstakingly drawn out for no less than 3 major newspapers underscored how much time and care this nut had devoted to just a macabre "hoax."

Cipher sent to the Vallejo Times-Herald.

Cipher sent to the S.F. Chronicle.

Cipher sent to the S.F. Examiner.

Furthermore, the letter writer had shown himself cleverly manipulative and ingenious. A written confession and threat would not have gone far. Curiosity, however, is a far greater manipulator. That cryptogram was intriguing. Each newspaper got a cipher of 8 lines of 17 symbols. There was no way to tell which newspaper had the first part and which had the last part of the cipher. This was the cipher writer's calculated way of making all three newspapers print his story and their part of the cryptogram. One paper might refuse, but with three newspapers involved one was going to print it and the others would have to do likewise. This was not your average stunt. The writer was interested in enticing more than in deceiving. He was also interested in manipulating far more than Vallejo.

The upshot of the letter writer's manipulation was that it had paid off. The residents of the Bay Area had opened up their newspapers over the weekend to be greeted by the details of a grisly boast of murder and then to be intrigued by the block of neatly designed symbols inviting all and sundry to try and decipher the message to reveal what the self-declared murderer was concealing. By Monday, the *Examiner* had already labeled him the "Cipher Killer."

There was a major difference in the 3 letters, one that reflects the writer's self-importance. The final hook in the letter to the *Chronicle* enticed the people to believe his "idenity" lay within the cipher. In the other 2 letters the writer said he wanted them to print his ciphers on the "frunt" page and if they didn't he'd go on a kill rampage. Before the kill rampage threat in the *Chronicle* letter, he inserted: "In this cipher is my idenity."

How long had this writer taken to devise his cipher and write those 3 letters and 3 cryptograms? It had almost been a month since the Blue Rock Springs Park shooting. Had it taken him that long? Or had he waited to mail them because the momentous news of the moonshot would have upstaged him?

Considering all the effort he had put into this "stunt," it is evident the writer wanted clear title to the murders and undivided attention to his cryptogram. Given this, there was a good chance the writer would respond to Stiltz's request for more information.

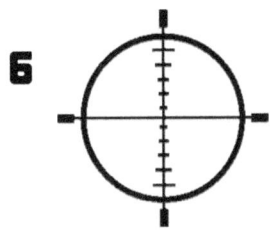

6

GOOD TIMES IN VALLEJO

ON AUGUST 7, THE SAN FRANCISCO *EXAMINER* RECEIVED ANOTHER envelope addressed to "The Editor" written in that blue felt tip pen. It was easy to pick it out of the pile of daily mail. The Letters Editor sliced it open and unfolded the paper. It was 3 pages! After the trite "Dear Editor," the writer introduced himself. It wasn't anything so generic as "I am the killer." It was a preamble: "This is the Zodiac speaking"— the language of introducing a divine oracle. The writer of the previous confession letters was, in fact, responding to Jack Stiltz!

(All misspellings are ZODIAC's)

> In answer to your asking for more details about the good times I have had in Vallejo, I shall be very happy to supply even more material. By the way, are the police haveing a good time with the code? If not, tell them to cheer up; when they do crack it they will have me.
> On the 4th of July:
> I did not open the car door, The window was rolled down all ready. The boy was origionaly sitting in the frunt seat when I began firing. When I fired the first shot at his head, he leaped backwards at the same time thus spoiling my aim. He end-ed up on the back seat then the floar in back thashing out very violently with his legs; thats how I shot him in the knee. I did not leave the

cene of the killing with squealling tires + racing engine as described in the Vallejo paper,. I drove away quite slowly so as not to draw attention to my car.

The man who told the police that my car was brown was a negro about 40-45 rather shabbly dressed. I was at this phone booth haveing some fun with the Vallejo cops when he was walking by. When I hung the phone up the dam X@ thing began to ring + that drew his attention to mc + my car.

Last Christmass

In that epasode the police were wondering as to how I could shoot + hit my victoms in the dark. They did not openly state this, but implied this by saying it was a well lit night + I could see the silowets on the horizon. Bullshit that area is srounded by high hills + trees. What I did was tape a small pencel flash light to the barrel of my gun. If you notice, in the center of the beam of light if you aim it at a wall or celling you will see a black or darck spot in the center of the circle of light about 3 to 6 in. across. When taped to a gun barrel, the bullet will strike exactly in the center of the black dot in the light. All I had to do was spray them as if it was a water hose; there was no need to use the gun sights. I was not happy to see that I did not get frunt page coverage.

What's this "Zodiac" business? It went unclarified in the entire letter, so that it made little impact. The misspellings were crude, the language that of a pompous thug. The ending was that of a cheap, taunting crank.

After the *Examiner* made a copy, they gave it to Vallejo PD. Stiltz still mulled over it. Most of the letter was unsubstantial bragging. How could they verify if he had driven off quietly? The statement about Mageau's changing positions in the car was the only thing that could be checked, but still a crank with police contacts might have picked up this information.

Although there was still hesitation to believe the letter writer was really the murderer, there would soon be no hesitation to accept that he took an awful lot of time to develop his game. The cryptogram had proven real. It was soon decoded by a Salinas couple, a school teacher Don Harden and his wife Bettye. He had sat down and worked hours and hours on the cipher and soon Bettye sat down with him. Wisely, she assumed the words "kill" or "killing" would be in a message written by someone who boasted of murder. They began to look for double symbols that would indicate double letters, like "l" in "kill" and "killing." They made their breakthrough and soon the message began to take form in front of them. On August 8, Don and Bettye were sure they had it down correctly.

I LIKE KILLING PEOPLE BECAUSE IT IS SO MUCH FUN IT IS MORE FUN THAN KILLING WILD GAME IN THE FORREST BECAUSE MAN IS THE MOST DANGEROUE ANAMAL OF ALL TO KILL SOMETHING GIVES ME THE MOST THRILLING EXPERENCE IT IS EVEN BETTER THAN GETTING YOUR ROCKS OFF WITH A GIRL THE BEST PART OF IT IS THAE WHEN I DIE I WILL BE REBORN IN PARADICE SND ALL THE I HAVE KILLED WILL BECOME MY SLAVES I WILL NOT GIVE YOU MY NAME BECAUSE YOU WILL TRY TO SLOI DOWN OR STOP MY COLLECTING OF SLAVES FOR MY AFTERLIFE. EBEORIETEMETHHPITI

When it was published, the whole Bay Area read that Simple Simon statement. Not surprisingly there was no revelation about the killer's true identity. Instead what emerged was his motive. It was at a stark contrast to the punk language of his letters. He now asserted some bizarre occult motive.

Despite stating he would not divulge his name, the idea persisted that his identity was indeed in the cryptogram. This made the last incoherent line EBEORIETEMETHHPITI of far more public interest than the potential dangers inherent in his gleeful bragging. Perhaps it was another code, some shift in the meaning of the symbols? It could therefore be his name. Various suggestions (in Letters to the Editor) said it was an anagram. Robert Emet the Hippi became the most popular— a reflection of how the killer's occult motive seemed to fit so well with the mainstream's impression of the strange counterculture.

Vallejo PD inquired of the FBI about the belief that the slain of a warrior would be his slaves in the hereafter. Even if this was just a ruse, this statement might be a clue about where the writer/possible killer had traveled before. Finally, all that could be ascertained by the Feds was that a primitive tribe in Mindanao in the Philippines held that view.

At first glance, this might indicate a Vietnam veteran. Clark Air Force Base in the Philippines was the biggest staging area for logistic support for Vietnam. The nearby town of Angeles catered to the base and even had a notorious Red Light District. A US serviceman might easily pick up this information here. He might even have gone Section 8 and was now back in America.

Unfortunately, this was not the only place to pick up this information. Beat and hippie religions had corralled many esoteric views and incongruously put them together, from Aztec religion to eastern mysticism, to form their Lego house philosophy. A stroll through the Haight's shops or a chat in the guru soup kitchens could have provided equal inspiration for the killer's arcane claims in cipher.

Significantly, this nutjob's letters had been posted from San Francisco. Therefore it was not a stretch to assume he had more than a passing acquaintance with the Haight. It also meant that if he was the killer he drove some distances to commit his crimes.

Needless to say, the bragging cryptogram had generated a lot of news, most of it surrounding trying to guess the writer's real name from the last garbled sequence of symbols. As a crime moniker, however, "ZODIAC" didn't register. A catchy newspaper handle seemed more appropriate— the "Boastful Slayer."

Citizens were warned about traveling the backroads of the Bay Area. This was the official advice. The rest of the advice was more philosophic and consumer driven. A crazed killer who liked to shoot people for trophies was too exotic not to inspire social commentary on radio shows. The commentary naturally revolved around where civilization was going with this counterculture movement. Was this bragging killer just another byproduct of a society casting off the fetters of morality?

Motiveless thrill murders committed on average citizens (as opposed to tenderloin slayings) were not new but they were becoming more bizarre. Just August 3 two girls, Debbie Furlong (14) and Kathie Snoozy (15), had been brutally murdered on a hillock park (Foothills Park) in the new Almaden Valley development in San Jose, south of the Bay Area. Their killer had gone berserk and stabbed them a combined 300 times.

Just as the decoding of this "Zodiac's" murder-gram was published in Bay Area newspapers, Los Angeles was rocked by the maniacal murders of starlet Sharon Tate and her guests at her Cielo Drive house overlooking Beverly Hills. The next night another couple, Leno and Rosemary Labianca, were butchered in their house in Hollywood. Using the blood of the victims, the killers had written on the walls or door at both residences. They denounced them as "Pigs" or declared "Rise"— the motto of Black Panther militants. "War" had been etched into Leno LaBianca's stomach.

The "Cipher Slayer's" stunt of publicity was just a drop in the August bucket of blood. It helped to send shudders down the mainstream spine. No home seemed safe in Los Angeles. A knife-wielding maniac was loose in San Jose. The streets of the Bay Area were a potential shooting gallery now.

By mid-August all macabre news had to stand aside. More than one news sensation had arrived.

Filling TV screens was the momentous ticker tape parade in New York on August 13, 1969, for the astronauts of Apollo 11. Michael Collins, Neil Armstrong, and Buzz Aldrin were now out of decontamination and being adored by a rejoicing public. Shredded ticker tape rained down on them and the cheer of the crowd followed them. The first men on the moon had safely returned.

Back to Earth, an introduction more than one newsman could give tongue-in-cheek, the networks began commenting on the unexpected phenomenon that was Woodstock. On August 15, 1969, the roads to Bethel, New York, had become jammed with traffic until it became a massive parking lot. News choppers showed us a green hillside of bright moving colors before a stage built like a yellow jungle gym. Hundreds of thousands of youth came to the rustic farm to attend the 3 days of "Aquarian" peace and love and music. It became the Summer of Love squeezed into a weekend. It would come to define a generation only because now, two years after the Summer of Love, the crowd at Woodstock showed the mainstream had caught and modified the vibe. Counterculture was now a nationwide movement of the Baby Boomers. Some 400,000 youth covered the grasslands and rolling hills. The extremism of the Haight and Beat religion was not at Woodstock. No gurus in Nehru collars. It was the genuine festival of music for the mainstream. . . and they had piled in. It was not a culture now. It was a generation. As Scott McKenzie's *San Francisco* had become the herald for youth to come to San Francisco for the summer festival "Love-In," so had the 5th Dimension's chart topper *The Age of Aquarius* in spring set the tempo for the mainstream.

The era specially designed for Dee Ferrin had come—Aquarian philosophy and no limits. However, Dee was gone. When finally released from hospital Mike Mageau would flee Vallejo and vanish for years, fearful like all others in Dee's crowd that somehow the maniac killer knew her and those around her. He would be unavailable to clarify anything Ed Rust or John Lynch would come up with in terms of suspects.

By the end of August only the Tate/LaBianca murders were still national news, not just because of the star power involved but because of their gore. Locally in the Bay Area the "Code Killer" was no longer news. It had been close to 2 months since he had killed.

As it would turn out, the decoding of the cipher was the last that the press or police would hear from the murderer that summer. People still called the newspapers to inquire whether the "Cipher Slayer" had been caught. But old news is old cabbage. The ZODIAC faded quickly. In fact, "Cipher Killer" was still used more in print than the handle he gave himself. The letter writer had used "ZODIAC" only in the *Examiner* letter, and by the end of August too much world news and lurid murders had reduced him, under any handle, to forgotten news.

CEREMONIAL BUM

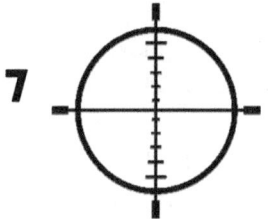

7

KNOXVILLE ROAD SNAKED ABOUT THE BARREN SHOULDERS OF THE dry foothills, a thin line on the cusp of the valley lake known as Berryessa. Like a Scottish loch, Lake Berryessa is long. Any oasis of civilization, whether it was a lone coffee shop or boat ramp, was connected only by narrow Knoxville Road following as closely as possible the entire western side of the lake.

Lake Berryessa was and was not remote. There was a wide spot in the road known as Spanish Flats, and a Park Ranger headquarters. It was supposed to be an outdoor rustic area preserved by the government, which means it was intended to be visited but not made to be used. The few buildings and docks served the seasonal boaters. A coffee shop serviced the travelers. Law might be around, but it must have only been a few Rangers. The Sheriff had jurisdiction, but their main headquarters was 30 minutes away in Napa. The closest real medical facility was in Napa too. Simply put, this was a vacation area for the sportsman, church groups, school fieldtrips, and a day trip for those who came to target practice in the hills. There was one other group, and it was rather unique to any outdoor land preservation area. A boutique town across Pope Valley called Angwin was home to Pacific Union College. Young couples frequently came to lounge lakeside and romance each other.

Altogether Lake Berryessa was a popular summer destination, but in late September it was not a busy place. Though the grass was still summer's gold ochre, the vibrancy of summer was long gone.

Knoxville Road was not etched into the hills so high that it afforded one a bird's eye view of the sapphire lake. As Bryan Hartnell drove along in his old 1956 Karmann Ghia, the lake only fleetingly peeked through stands of old oaks. With him was his former flame Cecelia Shepard. About midway along this road there was an area of the lake most frequented. It was this area that Bryan was trying to find. He slowed here and there. Between walls of saplings they tried to spy the location.

Bryan finally gave up and pulled over on the right of the road. A wide spot, a footpath by a stile, indicated there was a pathway down the grassy inside bowl of the valley to the lake. Here the two got out, got their blanket, and carefully walked down the slope to the trodden game trail. Along this narrow path they strolled amidst the tall but bowed summer chaff until they reached the peninsula.

Like fingers reaching out from foothills into the lake, boney peninsulas serrated the shoreline of Lake Berryessa. In between each peninsula there was a deep and narrow fjord. The water was dark green and deadly still. The steep shoreline was bland, ugly dirt. Parallel striations marked the yearly rise and receding of the waterline, each little etched line marking a past water level. Despite being nothing but dirt, it was called the "beach." Above the waterline scraggly straw-like dry grass covered everything.

Across the green lagoon to their right Mackenzie Point butted into the lake and was thick with a scalp of oak. To their left a hillock capped in a lush grove of oaks overlooked a little cove. Beyond it was their destination. It was a knuckle on this long finger-like peninsula.

This knoll was crowned by three oak trees. Two stood aside each other and faced the lake. Under these two green canopies, at the demarcation of seedy brown grass and dry, ugly "beach," Bryan and Cecelia now spread their blanket.

It's an unusually quiet place, Lake Berryessa. The valley was a bowl of strange, faded echoes, and now with a base of flat, calm water, the area seemed in suspended animation. Ducks paddle and beat the water a hundred yards out; yet their sound can gallop along the shoreline and nudge a drowsy couple with surprise.

This was the day, late afternoon of Saturday, September 27, 1969. Lulled by the silence, between the wistful thoughts of autumn repose, the couple quietly reminisced. You wouldn't think that a 20 year old guy and a 22 year old gal would have much to reminisce about, but at that age it seems a lifetime has gone by since high school. They were no longer an item. Bryan had a girlfriend in Oregon, but he and Cecilia were still friends. When she came up from southern California to visit a friend at Pacific Union College, where Bryan was now attending, they got together for the day.

They were still nestled under the twin oaks at around 6:15 p.m. when the faintest sound of footsteps on the dry chaff disturbed the solitude. Bryan's eyes were closed as he relaxed on his back. His thick glasses lay beside him, by his Playboy Joke Book.

"You have your specs on," he said softly to Celia. "Why don't you see what the deal is over there?"

She raised her head from his shoulder and saw a man near the furthest, solitary oak tree. "Oh, it is just some man."

"Is he alone? What's he doing?"

"Well, he just stepped behind the tree."

"What's the idea of that? To take a leak? Well, keep looking and tell me what happens—"

Celia squeezed Bryan's arm in a sudden burst of alarm. The man had come out from behind the oak tree and was approaching them. "My God!" she cried. "He has a gun!"

Bryan rolled over and grabbed his glasses.

The man walked unflinchingly toward them, an automatic pistol in his right hand pointed at them. A black hood covered his head.

Bryan's first thought was that he had only .75 cents. The thief wasn't going to get much, so that they might just as well indulge the unique experience of being robbed.

At 6 foot 6 inches Bryan is not a man easily intimidated. To him this was a robbery, nothing more. He didn't really stop to consider the strange nature of the black hood. The top of the hood was square, as if the black cloth draped over a graduation cap. The whole hood seemed generally square. It had eyelets and over these was clipped a pair of clip-on shades. The front piece of the hood hung down near to the man's waist. On it was neatly sewn a white circle with crosshair.

The hooded gunman stopped at a safe distance, still pointing the pistol at them. He was chunky, big, but under 6 foot tall with a paunch. Not blubbery fat, but beefy. His shoulders were rounded.

Closer now, it was clear the hood was quite intricate and theatrical and, because of this, it was frankly quite at a contrast to what it

adorned. The gunman looked more like a mismatched country bum.

This paunchy assailant wore a thin cotton jacket, almost like a windbreaker or jogging jacket. His pants were tight at the waist ruffling out old style pleats, a style not seen in pants since the late 1950s. His gun belt was obvious and it tightly hugged his waist, a holster on the right and a long knife, like a homemade bayonet, in a scabbard on the left. Yet another contrast was his dark high-lip shoes. His pants had cuffs. They were a bit high water and they tickled the top of his shoelaces. He wore tight black gloves, but it was the dark blue steel automatic pistol in his clutching and extended right gloved hand that held their attention the most.

"What do you want?" asked Celia.

"Now, take it easy," calmly said the hooded man. "All I want is your money. There is nothing to worry about. All I want is your money."

"OK, whatever you say," assured Bryan. "I want you to know I will cooperate so you don't have to worry; whatever you say, we'll do. Do you want us to come up with our hands up or not?"

"Just don't make any fast moves," replied the hooded assailant. "Come up slowly."

Bryan and Celia pushed off with their hands and remained on their knees. Despite the assailant's eyes sunk behind dark clip-on shades, Bryan could tell he had watched them keenly.

"But we don't have any money," Bryan clarified. "All I have is seventy-five cents."

"That doesn't matter," replied the assailant coolly. "Every little bit helps." There was a pause. Then the assailant offered: "I'm on my way to Mexico. I escaped from Deer Lodge Prison in Montana. I need some money to get there."

"You're welcome to the money I have, but isn't there something else I can do for you? Give you a check or get more for you?"

"No."

"I can give you my phone number and you can call me."

The paunchy, hooded figure just stood there statuesque, pointing the gun at them.

"I want to get in contact with you," continued Bryan. "I am a sociology major and maybe I can even offer you more help than you think you need."

"No."

"Well, is there any other thing you need?"

"Yes. One more thing. I need your car keys. Mine is hot."

Bryan reached into his pants pockets. Pulling out nothing, he started patting his back pockets. "I guess in all the excitement I don't remember where I put them. Let's see. Are they in my shirt?" He patted his chest pockets. "In the ignition," he thought out loud. He looks around. "On the blanket? Say! Would you answer a question for me? I've always wondered. On TV movies and in an article in the Reader's Digest they say that thieves really keep their guns unloaded. Is yours?"

Time was being wasted, and it was reflected in the assailant's excited response. "Yes, it is!" His tone quickly returned to manner-of-fact again. "I killed a couple of men before."

So far, the assailant had been hard to hear. His black hood had no mouth hole and he spoke in an even voice. It was not particularly distinctive except for some kind of cadence, some way of speaking that Bryan thought he had heard before but could not now identify.

"What? I didn't hear you," said Bryan.

"I killed a couple of guards getting out of prison." He warned: "I'm not afraid to kill again."

"Bryan, do what he says!" cried Celia.

"Now I want the girl to tie you up" With his left hand the assailant reached around and pulled out from behind him precut white clothesline. He tossed it.

Celia started tying Bryan's wrists behind his back.

"This is really strange," observed Bryan casually. He continued with small talk. "I wonder why someone hasn't thought of this before. I'll bet there's good money in it."

The assailant paid no attention. After Celia finished, he directed her with a wag of his gun back to her spot. He then holstered his gun and approached. He tied up Celia's wrists and retied Bryan.

Bryan remained observant. As the assailant was tying them he got a look askance. Through those clip-on shades he could see some of the assailant's hair was dark brown and greasy. The hood was meticulously made. It had seams at the four corners and had been carefully sewn. The white gunsight was also neatly sewn on.

Bryan asked: "What was the name of that prison?"

The assailant didn't respond.

"No, really," Bryan continued. "What did you say the name of it was? I'm just curious."

Finally the assailant begrudgingly replied: "Deer Lodge."

Finished tying them, he stood back behind them. "Now I want you both to lay face down so I can tie your feet."

"Come on," protested Bryan, "we could be out here for a long time and it could get cold at night."

The assailant growled: "Come, get down!"

"Listen, I didn't complain when you tied our hands, but this is ridiculous!"

"I told you—"

"We aren't going anywhere," Bryan protested again. "Anyway, I don't think that is necessary."

The assailant stepped around Bryan and drew his pistol and pointed it at him pointblank. "I told you to get down!" he snarled.

Bryan let himself fall forward. He heard the assailant holster his gun again. He then heard him stepping about their legs. The assailant then tied their ankles, pulled up their legs, and then strung the clothesline around their wrists and pulled their ankles and wrists together (hogtie).

Bryan kept a keen eye on Celia and the assailant as he hogtied her. To Bryan, it seemed as if the assailant was tense.

Bryan: "Your hands are shaking. Are you nervous?"

The reply was: "Yes, I guess so," but this was offset by a casual chuckle.

"Well, I suppose I'd be nervous too," replied Bryan.

Finally, the assailant was finished. He stood up. Bryan could feel him hovering over them.

Bryan asked: "Now that everything is done, was your gun really loaded?"

"Sure, it was." The hooded assailant stepped around to Bryan's side. He drew the gun from the holster and pulled the magazine out from the butt of the handle. He showed Bryan up close one of the bullets.[4]

The assailant then reloaded the magazine, holstered the gun and stepped around behind him. Before Bryan could say anything else he heard "chomp" sounds in his back. He realized he was being stabbed. He went rigid, into shock and after 6 stabs feigned death.

Cecilia was hysterical. She started screaming and writhing to get free. Then the assailant descended on her and started stabbing her back. She continued to writhe and then rolled over. The hooded assailant continued to stab her. The more she struggled, the fiercer he became. He kept plunging and withdrawing his long knife. She finally went limp.

The assailant stood up and just walked away.

They both began speaking right away to each other, but it seems the assailant didn't hear them. He continued to walk away over the summit of the knoll and then descended out of sight beyond that

---

[4] Bryan Hartnell estimated it was the bullet of a .45 caliber.

great solitary oak by which he had first appeared.

As soon as they felt safe, they started screaming. Celia got her hands loose and finally untied Bryan.

A boat was out on the lake, about midway from the shore. Bryan got up and both of them kept screaming at it. The engine idled and then cut. The person on the boat looked over. He is Ronald Fong. However, despite them screaming more and more for help he didn't come closer. He waited. Soon he cruised in closer. The situation became obvious when he noticed how bloody they were. He gunned his motor and dashed off.

Fong's boat cut a frothy white wake as he sped to Monticello, the main docking area. There he reported what he saw to Archie and Elizabeth White (owner of the boat repair shop). They got on the payphone and called the Rangers. Sgt. William White (no relation) picked up the intercept at 6:55 p.m. and rushed to Monticello.

Meanwhile Bryan staggered along the trodden footpath. Instead of trying to get up the slope to the shoulder, he staggered along the dirt access road. He was draining blood like sweat. It streaked down his back and soaked his pants. He continued to stagger and finally coming close to a cyclone gate his vision long having dimmed, things finally went black.

Sgt. White screeched to a stop at Monticello and bolted out. Together the three Whites— Archie, Elizabeth, Sgt. William— and Ron Fong got in Archie's speedboat and dashed across the lake to the scene.

There they arrived to find Celia Shepard on her elbows and knees, rocking back and forth in great pain. She was drenched in blood, back and front, especially around the groin. It was clear she had been stabbed many times. Celia kept rocking while Elizabeth White tried to calm her. "He was a man with a hood," she said in pain. "His face was covered. He wore black pants." She kept repeating: "It hurts, it hurts."

Soon they heard a pickup pulling up. It was Park Ranger Dennis Land. Bryan Hartnell sat in the passenger seat, shivering, turning white, and fading out again. Land had come by the access road and found him spread out on the ground. He picked him up and called for backup and for an ambulance.

Sgt. William White tried to get information out of them, despite their pain. Celia Shepard could say little more than what she had already said. White went over to the pickup. Bryan Hartnell was able to say a little more. He said a man with a hood and dark clothes approached them behind an automatic pistol. He said he had escaped from a prison and "I'm going to have to stab you." It was clear that Bryan was fading out. He was rambling, saying that he had asked to be stabbed first.[5]

As twilight carried the tormented colors of red fading to blue-gray, the Piner Company ambulance arrived after its long drive from Napa. The drivers got both gurneys over the levy and slid the victims inside. Celia was unconscious. Bryan faded in and out. He kept repeating the events, in nightmarish agitation.

The ambulance finally lunged forward and pulled out, its red lights twirling over vacant, dusky hillsides. Up Knoxville Road, in sight of the access gate, Rangers pondered over something bizarre on the passenger door of Hartnell's Karmann Ghia.

---

[5] When *compos mentis*, Bryan did not reaffirm this but stated the attacker only started stabbing without warning. This was in an interview with detective John Robertson.

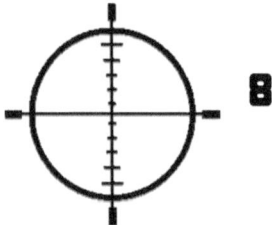

CAR DOOR SCORE

AT 7:40 P.M. THE RANGERS WERE STILL SECURING THE SCENE BY THE Karmann Ghia. At this precise time officer Dave Slaight was receiving a call on the switchboard at Napa Police headquarters.

"Napa Police, Officer Slaight."

"I want to report a murder; no, a double murder," said a calm, young man's voice. "They are two miles north of park headquarters. They were in a white Volkswagen Karmann Ghia."

The line was silent. Slaight could hear casual but distant voices passing in the background; perhaps also traffic.

Slaight finally asked: "Where are you now?"

The voice was barely audible, as if the receiver was not close to the caller's mouth anymore. "I'm the one who did it."

Now Slaight heard the receiver being set down— not hung up but set down and the line left open. "Is anyone there?" he asked. "Is anyone there?"

Slaight quickly dialed the Sheriff's office since it was their jurisdiction (he had immediately assumed it was Lake Berryessa). While doing so he thought he heard feminine voices come over the line. They were very faint, as if walking past in the background. This would indicate a downtown area.

After he informed the Sheriff's office of the call, he dialed the operator and asked if the call could be traced. The operator confirmed that it came from a 255 prefix phone booth, but that is all she knew right now. She did offer that the caller had refused to give the number when asked. Slaight deduced the obvious: that the caller had called her and asked for the police department number.

It was about 8:30 p.m. Sergeant Ken Narlow, the Napa County Sheriff detective, arrived at Queen of the Valley Hospital in Napa. The ambulance was still on the long drive back to Napa. He stepped from the receiving desk to await his partner, Dick Lonergan. He had taken only a few steps when he was called back. The Sheriff's operator was on the other end. He was now told a phone call had come in from a man confessing to the crime. The gist was a basic confession call, but they traced it to the exact phone booth.

Forensic man Sgt. Harold Snook walked up at that moment. Narlow immediately told him about the call and that it had been traced to the booth at Main and Clinton in downtown Napa. Just as immediate, Snook left to go process the booth.

Moments later Dick Lonergan came in. They had no choice but to pace and wait. Neither had much more information, certainly nothing that said how bizarre the crime was. But there was one tidbit the Rangers had sent over the radio to Napa. The assailant had busted out of jail. Therefore Narlow hoped the phone booth was a quick solution. A con's fingerprints would be on file; if there are prints and they match up, they have their man.

The corner of Clinton and Main in downtown Napa was dark except for the fuzzy halo from the streetlamp. It illuminated the brick walls of Napa's historic and oldest building. In the large parking area behind it, owner Mike Black had built the space age, modern Napa Car Wash. Affixed incongruously to this historic 19th century building was a stark contrast of 1960s lathed stucco. This was a narrow set of offices that managed the carwash. Here the phone booth stood by the stucco wall.

Hal Snook parked down the street and walked to the parking lot. A police officer was guarding the area. He confirmed that he had arrived quickly at the scene and, now shining his flashlight beam on the dark booth, the circle of light showed it had not been disturbed. Snook saw that the receiver was still off the hook. Both then shined their flashlights around, looking for any clues.

Meanwhile, Narlow and Lonergan paced the gurneys as the victims were rushed into ER, where Drs. Caulkins and Seibert started attending them immediately. Narlow and Lonergan followed in and hoped for some information. When the blankets were pulled back, all were surprised by how brutal this was. Blood soaked their clothes, trickling out from under temporary bandages. Both were in critical condition. Another doctor was being summoned. The doctors told Narlow and Lonergan to get out.

There wasn't much for them to do. Lake Berryessa was about 30 minutes away along a thin, dark country road marked only by reflectors here and there. Whatever evidence awaited them, none of it was as important as the eyewitness accounts. So they waited.

Flashlight beams crisscrossed for the last time. The sidewalk, parking lot, and the gutter revealed no tracks. Snook got his dusting kit and went to the phone booth. He noted the receiver faced south; mouth piece was almost under the phone and the earpiece near the edge of the shelf. The openings faced east. In other words, the caller had held the phone with his left hand. Not surprising since most people dial with their right hand. Moreover, given the location of the booth in relation to the street, this was more convenient for the caller's safety. This allowed the caller to keep his eye on Main Street and the sidewalk to see who passed while he spoke.

Time passes slowly in a hospital corridor. Narlow and Lonergan still waited. Finally, the doctors said they could talk to Bryan. He was the most stable of the two. At 9:37 p.m. they were allowed a brief chat.

Hospitals are cold places. It is not a temperature that registers on the skin but in the centers of living. An x-ray room is particularly anodyne. The machine makes its noise. Voices echo in the Spartan surroundings. Nurses are always calm. Doctors are utilitarian. Bryan lay on the steel table in fear of his life, drugged up and in shock.

The detectives leaned over and smiled at him. Their faces were a friendlier sight than the cold white glare of the overhead light set in the ugly, dull ceiling.

Before they could say anything, a nurse peaked in. Narlow was wanted on the phone. Lonergan proceeded with asking questions.

In such a state like this, Hartnell was only capable of repeating the most significant details. It was clear from his description that the appearance of the assailant was striking. The first detail he gave was the most disturbing. He said the man wore "a black ceremonial type hood, square at top." The attacker was heavyset, about 200 to possibly even 250 pounds. Though he approached with a gun, he stabbed them with a long knife. The gun was an automatic; the knife appeared homemade with a black handle. His clothes were dark.

Headlights coasted about the dark two-lane road. With every bend, they swayed off sapling brush on one side and chiseled hillside on the other; occasionally white wood posts glowed with little reflectors on them. Finally, on the right side there was nothing but a black morass— the valley lake. Narlow and Lonergan pulled up at 11:54 p.m. and walked past the roadblock. They were curious as to why Rangers grouped around a car on the right hand shoulder of the road. Rangers Dave Collins and Dennis Land approached. Best check out the passenger side door of the Ghia, they said.

Flashlight beams glide over the scrawled, slanted printing. The other dates had no meaning, but the overall meaning was clear. This was a ledger of death.

From the footprints, which their flashlight beams now coasted over, it was evident the perpetrator had come up from the lake by the foot stile. The slope down to the lake was sunk under the heavy night. The round beams of their powerful flashlights were eventually suffocated in the expansive darkness— a narrow path descending amidst the brown grass into the void. Ranger Land said he'd take them down via the access gate where he had found Hartnell.

As Land drove them along the rough dirt road, the headlights bounced off dried grass and here and there groves of oaks, the canopy of shadows underneath as uninviting as a graveyard. The hard dirt walking path came into view. They stopped and got out. Their flashlight beams coasted over the trail and quickly yet another footprint impression came into focus.

Narlow was now cautious. He didn't want them walking around in the darkness and possibly spoiling other evidence. The entire area was sealed off. They would return at first light.

Hal Snook's headlight beams finally caught sight of the rear lights of parked Ranger cars. Collins stood there and waved him forward. Snook had arrived there at 12:20 a.m. September 28.

In like manner as with the detectives, Collins referred Snook to the passenger side door of Bryan Hartnell's 1956 Karmann Ghia.

As a forensic man, Snook immediately thought logistically. It was written in black marker. There must be a finger or a palm print somewhere. As for the meaning, he drew the same conclusion as Narlow and Lonergan. This was but one installment in a series of attacks. His flashlight coasted over the footprints.

Hal Snook writes dispassionately: "Reporting officer observed footprints leading from the foot stile to the passenger side of the Karmann Ghia, where suspect had to approach to letter the passenger door of the vehicle. The footprints measured approximately 13 inches in length and 4 ½" at the widest point of the sole; heel width 3 ¼ inches and heel length 3 1/7 inches."

Tire tracks behind the Karmann Ghia were another matter. The span between them measured 52 inches, from center of tread to center of tread, but the tires were only 5 and ½ inches wide, with a narrow line down the center of one of them. This indicated a retread.

After Snook dusted the car for prints, Ken Narlow gave him the victims' belongings, which Dennis Land had taken from the beach. These were: 1 multicolored blanket; 1 army type field jacket; "several lengths of" bloodstained white clothesline; 2 Fourex condoms sealed in packets in box; and 1 Playboy party joke book.

For the rest of the early morning they assisted Hal Snook in casting the footprints by the Karmann Ghia. At first light (7 a.m.) they went down the hillside with Snook, Captain Don Townsend and Sgt. James Munk. They followed the perpetrator's footprints as best as was possible, marking particularly good ones for photographing and then casting. A green bottle, probably not related, was found behind the large oak tree where the assailant had first stood. Snook took it for testing. Soil samples were also taken from behind the tree and at the scene of the attack. Eventually they made it to the actual crime scene by the "beach."

To his chagrin Narlow noticed that Dennis Land had essentially raked up the crime scene in order to gather the evidence he had given him the night before. However, some good footprints were found nearby. They showed how the perpetrator had advanced and stood in the area between the oaks. Snook placed cardboard over them.

Lonergan and Narlow hadn't been at the crime scene long when Sgt. Munk got a message from park headquarters. A doctor and his son had seen someone yesterday in the late afternoon. They thought it may be important. This could be the first break in an otherwise bleak looking case.

At Spanish Flats coffee shop they soon heard the story. Dr. Rayfield and his son David were about 5 fjords (lagoons) north of the crime scene in the late afternoon when his son saw a white male adult strolling the hillside. He described him as 5 foot 10 inches, heavy, dark trousers, long-sleeved shirt, blue with some red in it. He carried nothing. He was just strolling about. When this man saw David, he turned and walked up the hillside, in a southerly direction, to Knoxville Road. Dr. Rayfield told them that they had not seen another car parked on the road before they arrived.

Ken Narlow returned to the scene of the crime by the beach. He walked about, curious over the peculiar nature of the stabbing. Both victims were still alive at the hospital, but it was clear from what he knew that murder and nothing else was the intent of the attacker. The writing on the car door connected it to others, and the significance of the dates had been uncovered. These were attacks in Vallejo that the "Cipher Slayer" had boasted about to the newspapers. Except for attack "by knife," the victims fit that nutcase's *M.O.*: a young couple at a rural area.

He knelt and considered the early autumn day. The only sound was from the forensic guys still casting the footsteps of the attacker. Why did the killer wear a hood? If he intended to kill them, why wear a hood? This was a quarter of a mile from the road. Why go this far from the safety of a quick escape?

Late afternoon, Narlow and Lonergan heard that the Dean of Pacific Union College could have some vital information. There were 3 interesting, very interesting and potentially crucial witnesses.

It is from the interview with three young coeds that Ken Narlow would get a significant description of a man prowling the lake. Putting together their individual recollections, their account is as follows. The 3 coeds arrived at Lake Berryessa around 3:30 p.m. and parked at a roadside parking area on Knoxville Road. As they were heading down to go sunbathe at the "beach," a Chevrolet, sky blue in color, pulled into the lot. The car was quite noticeable because of the way the driver had parked it. They had come from the north, so that they had parked facing south. The driver, a young man, had come from the south, pulled in, drove past their car and then backed up until his rear bumper was almost touching theirs. They also noted that the taillights were long/rectangular and not round, which indicated a newer model car. The girls also took note because it was not the car that a young man would be driving. The driver remained in the car. They descended the pathway to the "beach."

At about 4 p.m. they looked up while sunbathing and noticed the man was about 50 feet away at the tree line. He looked away when they looked at him. He was 28 or 30 years old, heavyset, about 6-foot, short-sleeve pullover sweater; a t-shirt stuck out from under in back. Dark trousers. His hair was dark and parted on the left and appeared styled— an older fashion. He hung around for about 45 minutes and then went back up the hillside.

What was especially important is that they pinpointed the area where they had been. It was about 2 miles north of the A&W stand on Knoxville Road. This placed them very close to the north of where the attack would occur to Bryan and Celia.

Attacking and killing 3 girls didn't fit the *M.O.* of the nut who had been killing in Vallejo. If this was the maniac, just why then had he hung around so long? The detectives had a very good idea. The three coeds confirmed that a couple was also nearby at the "beach"— Wayne and Denise. In fact, when the 3 coeds had pulled up they had recognized Wayne's car already parked across the road in another parking area.

Organizing their notes that evening, Narlow and Lonergan issued the statewide All-Points Bulletin of the collective description of the suspected perpetrator. Narlow sat there and considered the sketch Bob McKenzie (*Napa Register*) had drawn based on the three coeds' description. Was this their man? Moreover, was this the nut in Vallejo known as the Cipher Slayer? Why did he move north and change his *M.O.*?

Sadly, on September 29 at 4 p.m. Cecelia Shepard died. Despite being stabbed over 20 times she had died of only two major wounds, which they could not completely repair. It seemed Bryan Hartnell, although still in critical, would pull through. Six wounds are deadly, but the killer had not hit any major organs or blood vessels, most

likely because it was difficult to get an unobstructed line of strike on Hartnell's back with his arms tied behind him in hogtie fashion. Celia's mistake had been in resisting and turning over.

At 7:45 p.m. that evening the only bright news came in. The killer's shoeprint turned out to be traceable to the Air Force. Narlow and Lonergan went and spoke to Travis Air Force Base's flight line mechanic Bassel Jones at his house in Napa. He showed them his chukka shoes. As Narlow compared the sole of the shoe, which matched exactly the plaster cast he held, his expression grew hopeful that this clue would solve it. Suddenly, however, he was disheartened. Jones told them they were standard issue at Lackland AFB, where *all* cadets are trained. They are used as "wing walkers." As such, all Air Force personnel had them at one point. Equally, civilians at the bases can get a requisition.

They then drove to Travis AFB where they met with ranking personnel. Then, in turn, they were introduced to a special agent of the Air Force. "Wing Walkers" were indeed standard Government Issue, but they didn't keep any on hand at the base supply. However, they were told the Base Sales Store would carry them. They then followed the agent to the Sales Store and eventually found the shoes in question. With a greater selection of sizes at hand, they were able to match the plaster cast to a size 10.5R. "It was determined through Air Force records that they were unable to furnish officers with the specific data regarding the sales of this shoe. . ." However, they discovered that over the last 13 months 100 pairs of Wing Walkers of the size 10.5R had been sold. It didn't get better. The type of shoe was manufactured by International Shoe Company in Philadelphia and then shipped to the main depot in Ogdon, Utah, before being shipped to bases upon requisition. The shoe in question was not necessarily purchased at Travis AFB.

Logistically speaking— a dead end.

Narlow and Lonergan were particularly anxious for their next destination— Vallejo. There they met with Sgt. Jack Mulanax to compare data. The Napa duo naturally had lots of clues and evidence Vallejo didn't have. Still, except for the addition of the Air Force size 10.5 Wing Walkers it all tended to confirm what Vallejo had already suspected. Actually, the best corroborating information Napa had was the weight of the Cipher Slayer, which Hal Snook had determined from the depth of the footprints. The guy was indeed heavy, about 210 to 220 pounds. Mike Mageau had said the perpetrator was a beefy guy with a big face. But Mageau had been a sketchy witness at best for Vallejo. Napa's evidence was more concrete. It confirmed the "Boastful Slayer" was heavy.

On Mulanax's part, he confirmed for Narlow that the decoding of the cryptogram was accurate. Together they confirmed the matching of the handwriting on the car door with in the letters received last August. There was no question this was the same guy. This was doubly confirmed by the hood. Narlow had a good description of it now. Sgt. John Robertson had had a long talk with Bryan in ICU. Hartnell described the emblem sewn in white on the chest of that bizarre black hood. It was the same as the Code Killer's gunsight signature on his bragging letters. This was clearly the villain who had called himself the ZODIAC.

Crime scene photo of David Faraday's Rambler in the turnout. The dark pool of blood is evident.

One of the bullet holes in the Rambler which forced David and Betty Lou to get out and face their assailant. Below, forensic photos detailing two of the .22 caliber shell casings recovered from the turnout.

The turnout on Lake Herman Road, as seen in 2012 (top, August; bottom, December 19). Author's photos.

At the turnout, looking toward Benicia (2012)

Looking at the turnout. The gate used to be flush with the telephone pole. The "No Trespassing" sign is graffiti'd with the zodiac symbol.

The original Blue Rocks Springs parking lot is now only the first section of the expanded parking area. The sidewalk is basically where it had joined with Columbus Parkway, which is now a large 4 lane road. The car is parked where Ferrin had parked that night, at the same angle.

The author's car is parked where Ferrin had parked that night.

The parking lot (distant) as seen from the caretaker's house. Here is where the peacocks roost.

Contemporary sheriff photo showing the knoll and the 3 oaks. All 3 oaks have since fallen. Sheriff's photo.

The crime scene from the hillock overlooking the knoll. Author's photo.

At the precise spot of the crime scene— the remaining tree roots of the last oak to fall mark the spot.

Astride the knoll, looking back up to Knoxville Road— the long walk back for ZODIAC. Author's photos.

Looking up to the road, where ZODIAC had to walk up to letter the car door. Below, Knoxville Road where Bryan Hartnell had parked. Author's photos.

9

ZODIAC

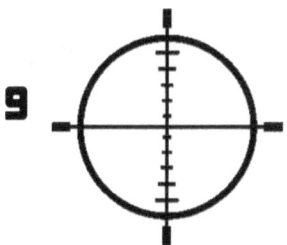

On October 2, 1969, outtakes of Cecelia Shepard's funeral gained coverage on local Napa and East Bay TV news. Along with the image of a hearse, pallbearers and mourners, there was an insert presenting Napa's sketch of a person of interest.

In print, Captain Don Townsend cautioned: "This may not be the killer, but we would like to talk to the fellow." The expressed reserve was not the only reason the composite had little metropolitan impact. Two months is a long time for news, and the rural outback of Lake Berryessa is far away from the hubbub of San Francisco. Print news did not give much circulation to the story, other than to confirm that the maniac who had briefly intrigued the Bay Area two months before with his cryptograms about "I like killing people" was still prowling the boondocks.

Nevertheless, for the first time we have a face for the Code Killer. The reports and events at Lake Berryessa give us our best and longest glimpse at him before and during the act, and despite Townsend's caution the sequence of events underscores this sketch is to be taken seriously. In order to appreciate this juncture in his bizarre crime spree it is best to break the narrative and take our first detailed look at the killer that had taken form.

In terms of appearance, there are three sketches of this heavyset, young man. Yet although they differ in intricacy, overall they show great continuity.

Of these sets of sketches, the single sketch shown on TV is worth

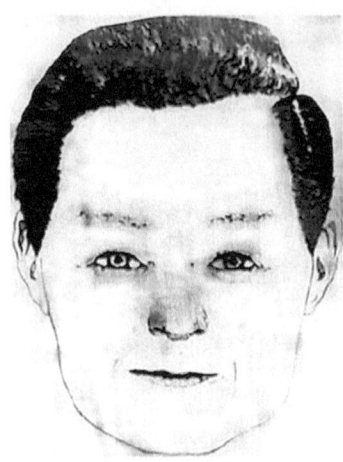

Napa sketch of the heavyset, young man seen by the 3 coeds, and then broadcast on local TV October 2, 1969.

the most. It is the one based on the descriptions given by the three coeds. They had the longest look at the "suspicious man," and due to his behavior they remembered him well.

Not only can we have a degree of certainty that the features of this composite are in general accurate, we can be relatively certain that this man is indeed the ZODIAC and not an aimless visitor who lurked about the hills for hours. It is not just in that he was heavyset and wore dark clothes; nor in that he was young and could own the young voice Dave Slaight heard confess. Certainty is found most of all in his actions. He came down to do more than just sit and obliquely watch the coeds. He remained for a long time. No other witnesses reported this heavyset man doing this except here, most likely because at no other location was a viable couple within reach and yet presently safe because witnesses were close at hand. Denise and Wayne were some distance from the coeds, and they matched the ZODIAC's type of targets. He may have lingered in hopes the coeds would eventually leave and he would be alone with the couple.

Perhaps yea or nay to the last supposition, but it is a fact that a heavyset man answering a similar description continued to prowl the hillsides in the general area until 6:30 p.m. The difference is that by this time he wore a long sleeve shirt.

The sequence of events, especially the encounter by David Rayfield, places a heavyset man very close to the crime scene not long before the attack. Ken Narlow dismissed Dr. Clifton Rayfield's account because of Rayfield's estimation of time. Narlow also interpreted Rayfield's account to mean that the sighting happened just after he and his son had arrived. Years later, however, David Rayfield would speak out and give a far more consistent account. David asserted they had not just arrived. At the time he saw the stocky man he was wandering around the hillsides with his .22 rifle whereas his father was fishing by the lake. (This better explains why his father never saw the man.) This explains why the Rayfields saw no other car when they had arrived; obviously they had been down there for a while when David finally saw the heavyset man. The way Narlow had written up the account it had sounded as if the Rayfields had just arrived and were presently walking down the hillside. This suggested the 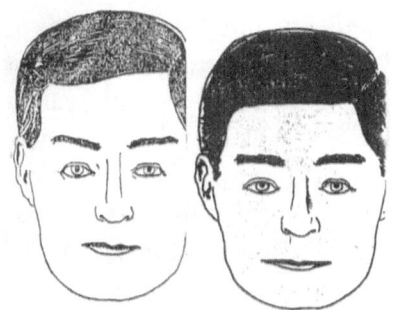 stocky man was already there. It was the doctor's statement that they had seen no other cars parked on Knoxville Road which had dissuaded Narlow from believing the man David saw could have been ZODIAC. Without a car Narlow did not believe this heavyset man could have gotten to the crime scene in a short time. In fact, if David is right the man could have parked after them on the road and, if ZODIAC, was presently walking down the hillside looking for the occupants of the Rayfields' car to see if they were a young couple.

Unfortunately, inference and interpretation are what we are left with for these two encounters. No sheriff or ranger seems to have gone to the location where the three coeds encountered the heavyset man in an attempt to find the distinctive imprint of the Wing Walkers. Finding them would have ended the argument. Nor did anyone go check the area where David Rayfield had seen the man in order to see if they could find the same shoeprints or tire tracks along the shoulder indicating ZODIAC had parked along this area. Narlow's lack of follow-up resonates in another way. David never described age, hair style or even hair color. Thus he only gives us a heavyset man without a face wearing a very different shirt.

Confirming that David and the coeds had seen the perpetrator would not only have ended the debate in Napa that this sketch was the ZODIAC but also in Vallejo where nothing but a brief and profile glimpse by Mike Mageau had given the Vallejo PD the barest outline of the ZODIAC being heavyset with a big face.

There is one other point of unity, however, between the heavyset man and ZODIAC. The three coeds noted that the strange young man had styled dark hair. Hartnell saw brown hair through the perpetrator's eyelets, which means his bangs were long enough to go with styled hair.

With all of the above added together it is a legitimate induction at this juncture to propose the suspicious young man represented in the sketch was the killer. This was the ZODIAC. This was the letter writing braggart. He had finally materialized. He was a misfit; someone who took the whole afternoon to find a viable target amongst the lounging, normal, happy visitors to the lake.

Although by this time he had only used the moniker "ZODIAC" once, its use combined with the sketch and his behavior at Lake Berryessa come together to reveal much about the "Boastful Slayer."

For starters, he was an average looking guy and not a hippie. Obviously, he also took his alter ego 'the ZODIAC' quite seriously, seriously enough to design, sew, and wear that bizarre theatrical hood. Put into focus, the context is truly disturbing.

Up until this point the ZODIAC's crimes had looked spontaneous, even sloppy, the *M.O.* of a random drive-by shooter. But the attack at Lake Berryessa reveals that careful, calculating mind that had written out those nasty cryptograms so neatly. The exposed location at Lake Berryessa was not convenient and the attack was not spontaneous. ZODIAC had labored on creating a hood to shield his face, which means he intended a daylight attack. He took the unnecessary risk of walking a quarter of a mile from where he had parked. He could have gone to a lovers' lane and shot another couple in the dark of night. But he didn't. He seems to have intended knifing a couple (or *needed* to knife a couple), and this required a remote location and distance from a road where he could spend sufficient time to bind them. This was not possible at a drive-by lovers' lane.

The 'ZODIAC' was no longer just an alter ego in print. Because, and only because, the victims survived (Shepard only initially) to give an account of that hood we have to confront the fact there was truly some bizarre motive for the murders, a motive that puts some body into the strange claims made in the gleeful but simple grammar of that horrid cipher. His letters were meant to be seen, his cipher meant to be cracked. But the hood was not something we were to know about. The victims were not meant to survive. This hood was not a part of his publicity game.

Bryan Hartnell later described it to Sgt. John Robertson in detail. It was intricate, with sewn seams on all 4 sides, with a long front bib, back bib and separate shoulder flaps, the front bib prominently embroidered with the crosshair symbol.

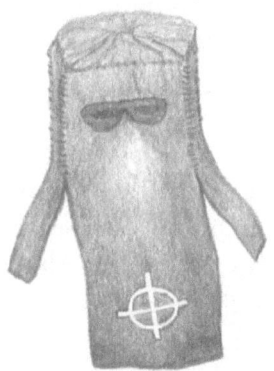

The argument that ZODIAC wore it because he wanted to frighten his victims and then feed off their fear, however, falls flat. A ski mask would have been sufficient for those needs. Someone wears a ski mask and points a gun in your face and there is no misunderstanding what they want. In this case, Hartnell didn't know what to make of the hood. Moreover, instead of feeding off their fear by jumping out and declaring he was the deadly ZODIAC, he tries to calm them into believing he merely wanted money and car keys. After they were bound, ZODIAC engaged in no ceremony. There was no build-up or attempt to frighten them. He merely started stabbing. He got it over quickly and casually walked away.

The hood, in fact, was pointless because ZODIAC made nothing of it. Therefore, most perplexing of all, this hood truly meant something to the "Cipher Slayer" of the Bay Area. He labored on it as much as his ornate cryptogram with the childish syntax of how he liked to kill people.

Writing on Hartnell's car door is another act that tells us much of ZODIAC's character. He desperately wanted public ownership of these murders, *all* of them. When last heard from two months before, his quick response to the *Examiner* showed that without carefully planning his thoughts he just tended to brag. His letter's point was to prove that he the letter writer was one and the same as the killer. As most was unverifiable boasting, it hadn't entirely done its job. There was still a question in the public mind whether the letter writer was the killer, thanks on a large part to Jack Stiltz's vocal reticence. Here on the car door of the Karmann Ghia the ZODIAC removed all doubt. It is immediately evident that the hand printing on the door matches the hand printing on the letters— proof that the letter writing ZODIAC was at the crime scene.

ZODIAC's tendency to brag was not just incidental in his response to the *Examiner* on August 4. A few days later the Hardens broke his code revealing the cryptogram was essentially nothing but gleeful gloating. Boasting doesn't exist in his 3 confession letters because their purpose was to prove he was the murderer. They set the stage to entice people to uncover his ultimate motive with an intriguing cipher. Thus his ultimate purpose *was* gloating. "I like killing people because it is so much fun. . ."

The *Examiner* response and the cryptogram show that the killer had a propensity to brag from the beginning. And from his entire "idenity" stunt the ZODIAC's sense of self-importance is palpable. He thought his murders were something exceptional and exposing his identity was worthy of metropolitan interest. This was the hook by which he concluded his first letter to the *Chronicle* and with which he opened his response to the *Examiner*. Crack this and you have me.

Ownership to these rural murders was so important that he acted quickly to respond only when his authenticity was questioned. Otherwise he took his time. The Lake Berryessa attack, for instance, was almost two months after his last letter.

Put together with the details of his attacks and a frightening but contradictory image emerges. . .one that can only be explained by a cold-blooded killer becoming enamored with each new layer of thrill he encountered, evolving sometimes right in front of our eyes.

The best example of this evolution is found in his 3 simultaneous "confession letters." As he progressed with writing them his self-importance grew. The first two began similarly— those to the *Times-Herald* and the *S.F. Examiner.* "I am the killer." The *Chronicle*'s was more ominous. "This is the murderer." Killer and murderer are not the same thing, and those words are not interchangeable. Murder does not just reflect taking life as "killer" does; it reflects the *desire* to take life. The letter to the *Chronicle* alone ends with the "idenity" hook. It would seem that the *Chronicle* letter was written last of the three. As the ZODIAC wrote he grew more inflated with the exultation of what he was saying. Within a short span of time he went from "I am the killer" to "This is the murderer." In a day or so: "This is the Zodiac speaking," as though he was introducing an authoritative oracle.

What was evolving before us in print was his presentation, but a careful killer's mind had always been behind it all. At first glance his confession calls seem a demented thrill seeker's way of needlessly confessing to the police. On the contrary, they too reveal an equally prepared mind at work.

Vallejo	Napa
I want to report a double murder. If you will go one mile east on Columbus Parkway to the public park you will find the kids in a brown car. They were shot with a nine millimeter luger. I also killed those kids last year. *Goodbye.*	I want to report a murder; no, a double murder. They are two miles north of park headquarters. They were in a white Volkswagen Karmann Ghia. I'm the one who did it.

The calls reveal how ZODIAC chose his words carefully. In contrast to the letter confessions, he never begins the call with "I just killed" likely because he feared that the operator could possibly start a recorder. Instead ZODIAC reports the basics and then in his last line confesses to having committed the crime.

A careful mind, yes; but was it a demented occult mind? It is when trying to understand motive that continuity is lost and convolution begins. A careful, premediated mind is seen in the preparations ZODIAC had to take, but the excuses he employs poorly fit. Only in print had he invoked some highly dubious occult fringe benefit. From the looks of his victims, his occult claims didn't have to be taken seriously unless he wanted nothing but teenyboppers in the afterlife. And Napa's sketch supported Mageau's sighting: this was no hippie gone bad. From the point of view of someone simply wanting to "collect slaves" in some occult delusion, why were confession calls even necessary? Why the letters? Why the cryptograms? Why the bragging? Just forget those stupid, bragging letters and that ridiculous cryptogram. Just look at his actions, not his own publicity stunt. Red herrings, the whole lot.

But now this. Now this strange ceremonial hood.

How to explain all this?

The short answer is that all this was done because it was indeed thrilling just like he said. Put in perspective, he was a psychotic killer who believed his alter ego was worthy of comic strip super villain grandeur. He was part pool hall thug and part comic strip arch villain. QED= he's one crazy SOB. This is the short answer. It is too soon for the long answer.

One thing was real: ZODIAC's persona had become important to him. He went from being a heavyset, plain man who didn't take credit for his murders to one who then did; by phone and then by letters and an elaborate cipher. At last, he became that exotic alter ego in real life. Everything in his crime spree, in fact, seemed to be escalating with one purpose: terrorize the whole Bay Area.

The recent anodyne news coverage must have been disappointing for one with such an ego. Attacks on the fringe of Vallejo hadn't carried too much of a punch in the big city. Now two months later he had finally struck again, proved it was him by writing on the car door, but naively thought that an attack in an even more remote area like Lake Berryessa would be enough to command San Francisco. From wherever his lair was, ZODIAC must truly have been disappointed with the paltry news coverage. To fulfill his goal to hold the Bay Area in terror-suspense, what could he do now?

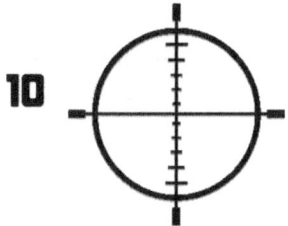

ANTE IN THE GAME

It was a crisp Saturday night, October 11, 1969. Downtown the streets of San Francisco were only moderately busy. Horns honked sporadically, as always. There is something innocuous about the car horns of San Francisco. They are short little notes, as if a loud piano was pecked. They are seldom angry. They are just inevitable. The hiss and roar of the muni buses is a sound taken for granted, a rather strange note added to the tonal orchestration.

About 9:35 p.m., Paul Stine, 29 year old college student, part time cabbie, part time insurance salesman, was a part of the orchestration of night sounds. He had just come back from one fare and parked back on Geary, near Mason. At 9:45 p.m. he gets a dispatch to go to 500 9th Avenue. A fare also approached. The man was heavyset, under 6-foot, and he was wearing old style rust-brown pleated pants. In contrast, he wore a casual and fashionable dark blue windbreaker jacket. It looked like he had a crewcut. He wore thick black rim glasses— altogether a bit unusual for a guy looking in his 30s. But then this was Lower Nob downtown.

The man got in the cab. In a monotone voice the paunchy fare ostensibly said: "Washington and Maple."

Nice, very nice part of town to go— Presidio Heights. How convenient that this guy hailed him at Geary and Mason. It was an easy route to the POSH neighborhood and it was on the way to Outer Richmond and 9th Avenue.

Stine pulled out and turned left at California Street. It's a 3 mile ride west down California to P. Heights. The traffic was light. On the way It's not far from the Heights in nearby Inner Richmond. When he got to Maple he turned right. At this time of night there was no traffic, but at Presidio Heights there's a stop sign at every block. It becomes a tedious, slow drive.

Kids are having a party on the upper floor of the large house at the corner of Washington and Cherry streets. About 9:55 p.m. they look out and see a parked taxi cab across the street. A chunky guy is sitting in the front passenger's side, going through the cabbie's pockets. They see him wiping down the inside of the cab on the driver's side with a white cloth. They see him get out and wipe off the passenger side door by the handle and then walk around and with what looks like the same white handkerchief wipe off the door on the driver's side. He then casually walks down the sidewalk on Cherry Street. He soon fades from the fringes of the cone of light from the streetlamp and melts into the darkness.

The kids call the cops.

At 9:58 p.m officers Frank Peda and Armand Pelisetti screech to a halt behind the cab. It sits there silently near the halo of light from the streetlamp. The passenger side door is swung open. As they cautiously approach, they see the lights on across the street and silhouettes in the windows. The kids haver in the street near the cab. The father walks out the front door and tells them what had happened.

> R/Os immediately checked the interior of the cab and found the victim to be slumped over the front seat with his upper torso in the passenger side, head resting on the floorboard, facing north. Ambulance was summoned Code three, and other units were requested for an immediate search of the area.

One of those units was officers Don Fouke and Eric Zelms. They are speeding west on Jackson, one street north of Washington. As they are approaching Maple, Fouke notices a thickset white guy in baggy, rust-brown pleated pants and blue windbreaker jacket lumbering down Jackson toward Maple. The paunchy figure has his hands in his jacket pockets and he is keeping his head down. As they speed past, the man appears to turn north onto Maple. (Maple ends here at a wall set behind thick hedges, shrubbery and trees. Beyond a small gateway there is a 4 foot drop to West Pacific Street.)

A car-level view almost precisely from where Fouke saw the lumbering man approaching and turn left (our right) on Maple.

For some strange reason the police dispatcher had reported that the suspect was a black male adult. Therefore Fouke paid little particular attention to the white man. They turned left on Cherry and arrived at the crime scene. Here they learn the suspect was actually white. Fouke realized he may have seen the killer. They tear out, turn around, turn left on Jackson, a quick right on Arguello and then a quick sharp right onto West Pacific. With their searchlights energized they cruise down the long parkland boulevard.

The piercing beams of their powerful searchlights streak the tall brick wall on one side, but in the other direction deep groves of ancient and huge cedars create an impenetrable canopy of darkness. A quarter of a mile down the road the Julius Kahn Playground crouches in shadows.

Soon other units join the pursuit. The Presidio became a dynamic display of dashing searchlight beams slicing about like sabers through the underwood and over the grassy sweeps.

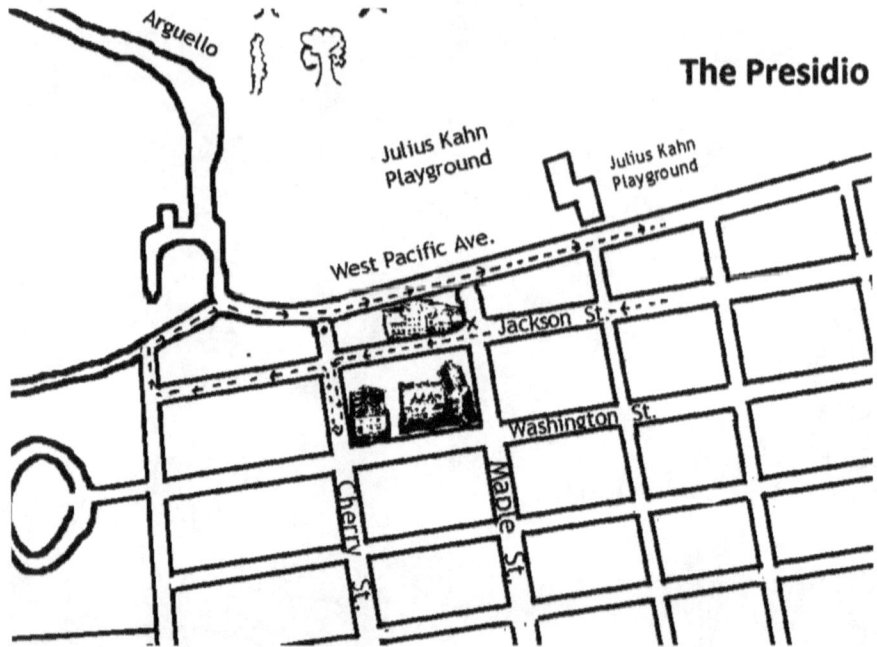

Dotted line traces Fouke and Zelm's approach down Jackson to the crime scene, and then back up Cherry to West Pacific. X marks where Fouke saw the lumbering figure.

Meanwhile the detectives, Dave Toschi and Bill Armstrong, arrived at the crime scene. There wasn't much official looking about Dave Toschi. His curly hair was full and careless. His casual appearance was augmented by his cord pants, easy fit loafers, open collar shirt, and his rumpled raincoat. Bill Armstrong's crisp suit and graying neatly cut hair marked him as the average appearing detective, something formal and official out of *Dragnet*.

Peda and Pelisetti kept back the crowd of murmuring onlookers. Squad car overhead lights blinked silently. Flashbulbs pulsed quietly. The police photographer carefully stepped around the blood. Police radio transmissions crackled over car radios.

Toschi stood by the passenger side of the cab. He shook his head mournfully at the tragic sight. The dead, limp arms of the victim dangled out over the gutter. Blood trickled down and dribbled into the gutter. A few more steps and he looked in.

The cabbie was on his back on the front seat. The top of his head craned back almost resting on the sideboard. His head and face were covered with blood, his hair so soaked it dangled with dripping blood. His eyes were closed. His bloodstained glasses were in place.

Toschi logistically considered the scene. The dark powder burn was still visible amidst the drying crimson blood. The perpetrator had put the gun up behind the right ear and fired pointblank. He must not have been expecting the mess. Blood had burst throughout the inside. Now his eyes spied a glint of light off shiny metal. A spent shell casing was on the passenger side floorboard. He slid his pen into the open end of the casing. It took but a moment under his scrutinizing eye to determine it was a 9mm casing.

The victim's bloodied shirt was in a curious state. It was rumpled up revealing his bare stomach. Toschi deduced the killer tore at the pants pockets to get the wallet and change. Curiously, however, the keys were gone from the ignition. Perhaps under the body? Toschi would wait until the forensic guys were through.

Botched robbery, Toschi thought. He took notes and drew a crude illustration of the crime scene.

On the surface it looked like the driver had been murdered by what must have been an amateur, but when the coroner and his men finally arrived and slid Stine's body out, things changed. No car keys could be found. Easy answer: the killer must have taken them by force of habit when he turned off the engine. But now it was clear that the back of the cabbie's shirt was torn and a big swath was missing. Easy answer: the perpetrator ripped the shirt to clean his bloody hands. Yet. . . across the street, the kids would soon inform the investigative duo that they saw the killer wipe off the cab inside and out— apparently getting rid of his fingerprints— and he used a *white* cloth. Yet Stine's shirt was gray and white striped.

Influencing the interpretation of a cab robbery gone bad was the fact a cab robbery had occurred within the week before and *only* a couple blocks over on Arguello. In this instance the robber had told the driver to stop one block further than his original requested destination. There he put a gun to the driver and robbed him, eventually locking him in the trunk of his own cab.

The investigative duo induced the same thing had happened here. It sounded like the same perpetrator was involved.

Things were still sketchy the next morning when the *Chronicle* ran a short story under "Cabbie Slain in Presidio Heights." The article reported that the suspect was seen to "dash" up Cherry Street. "Later reports indicated someone was seen running into Julius Kahn playground in the Presidio, and all seven police dog units were pressed into the search."

As San Franciscans glossed over the article, Toschi and Armstrong were backworking the clues. They would spend most of the day (October 12) uncovering exactly where the pickup must have occurred. The cab meter had read $6.25 at 10:46 p.m. (after they had arrived). Based on the rate, it must have read about $1:25-$1:50 at the time of the crime— (about 9:55 pm). Along with other clues, they were able to backtrack Stine to the Lower Nob Hill area and eventually to Geary and Mason as the place where he had picked up his killer.

Forensics felt good about a few of the latent prints they lifted. On a crossbar inside the cab, they had lifted two prints in blood. This definitely seemed to indicate they were the killer's. Another bloody print was found on the passenger door's outside handle area.

While this promising information was being compiled, a police artist sat with the kids and together they doped out what the killer looked like from their upstairs angle.

On October 13 the composite was finished and then issued with a handbill. The killer was clean cut but lifeless. No composite ever shows a particularly inviting personality. This one, however, had a tint of personality— a calculating, haughty coldness. Unfortunately, it also made the killer look skinny. The handbill deferred heavily to the *M.O.* of the serial cab robber who had struck in the area the week before. It read:

> Suspect takes cab in downtown area at 9:30 p.m. and sits in front seat with driver. Tells driver destination is Washington and Laurel area or area near Park or Presidio. Upon reaching destination, suspect orders driver to continue on at gunpoint into or near Park area where he perpetrates robbery. In one case victim was shot in head at contact. Victim's wallet and I.D. in the name of Paul L. Stine and Taxi Cab keys missing.

Publishing the sketch, the *Chronicle* reported:

> A composite drawing of the suspect wanted in the Saturday night slaying of Yellow Cab driver Paul Lee Stine has been released by Homicide inspectors William Armstrong and David Toschi.
>
> The suspect who got $10 or $11, is described as a white man, 25-30 years old, 5'8" or 5 feet 9 inches tall, weighing 150 pounds. He had reddish brown hair which he wears in a crew cut, and was wearing heavy-rimmed glasses and a navy blue or black jacket at the time of the slaying.
>
> Stine, of 1842 Fell St., was 29 years old. He had been working 9 p.m.-5 a.m. as a Yellow Cab driver for the past several months to pay his way through San Francisco State College, where he was a PhD candidate in English.
>
> He was also a part-time insurance agent.

Behind the scenes, the coroner basically confirmed what Toschi had seen for himself. Stine had been shot in the head pointblank. Ballistics, on the other hand, suggested something intriguing. This murderer probably used a new Belgian Browning 9mm pistol.

Elimination prints accounted for most of those fingerprints forensics had lifted from the cab. (Peda and Pelisetti insisted they had kept people back and didn't allow anybody to contaminate the crime scene.) This meant that those bloody prints must be the killer's. Comparisons didn't match any perp, so this cab robber was new at it— new with a new gun.

The detective duo had refined the clues perfectly. The problem is the evidence didn't go anywhere. They would have 7 weeks for something to break before their plate would become full with new cases. (They were on an 8 week shift— one week being the detectives-on-call, the next 7 weeks following up on those cases.) Unless he struck again and they got more evidence, chances were slim he'd be identified.

. . .But something should have nagged here. Early theorizing did not take into consideration one curious act by the killer. The killer came to Presidio by cab from downtown, at least 3 minutes away. How did he get away? Was his car parked somewhere up here? This means he parked here and walked all the way downtown just to get a

Handbill issued by SFPD on October 13, 1969.

cab and return in the quiet of night. This would seem to indicate a very careful beginner in cab robbery. All this for pocket change?

This very evening, however, October 13, 1969, SFPD's view would change. This was no ordinary cab killing. The shirt hadn't been ripped spontaneously to clean the perp's hands. It was a token. Right now it sat on the publisher's desk at the *San Francisco Chronicle*. It had come with a boastful letter. The envelope was scribbled with a basic address: "S.F. Chronicle, San Fran. Calif. Please Rush to Editor." But the return address was unique. It was the crosshair symbol. Carol Fisher, Letters Editor, had opened it. Out fell a small square — ripped not cut— of bloodstained gray and white striped fabric. When she unfolded the letter, it read:

This is the Zodiac speaking. I am the murderer of the taxi driver over by Washington St + Maple St last night, to prove this here is a blood stained piece of his shirt. I am the same man who did in the people in the north bay area.

The S.F. Police could have caught me last night if they had searched the park properly in stead of holding road races with their motorcicles seeing who could make the most noise. The car drivers should have just parked their cars + sat there quietly waiting for me to come out of cover.

School children make nice targets, I think I shall wipe out a school bus some morning. Just shoot out the frunt tire + then pick off the kiddies as they come bouncing out.

Shocked, Carol took it in to the editor. No one knew at the *Chronicle* what Stine had been wearing, but the editor could recognize the printing. It was the same as the printing on that bizarre murder rampage threat letter back on August 1. The killer also called himself "the ZODIAC" in his response to the *Examiner* a few days afterward.

ZODIAC had arrived in San Francisco at last and not just to mail a letter. This was news! Before it was taken to Toschi and Armstrong, the *Chronicle* made a copy of the letter and envelope. The editor had agreed not to print it yet in order to give the SFPD time to prepare to deal with the threat, but it was going to have to come out eventually. Thomas Cahill, Chief of Police, and the *Chronicle*'s editor and staff, knew that a state of alert was unavoidable.

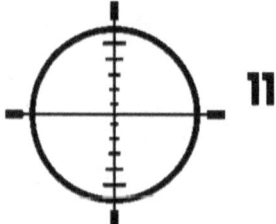

AUTUMN OF ANGST

THE *SAN FRANCISCO CHRONICLE* STORY BROKE ON THE MORNING of October 15, 1969. "'Boastful Slayer' Letter Claims Writer Killed Cabbie, 4 Others." It was perhaps the perfect title. Few readers would have connected with the handle "The Zodiac," but they remembered the sensational "Boastful Slayer" or "Code Killer" of last summer. The title and article now connected all the killings and brought San Francisco into the center of it all. It also laid the foundation for all news in the Bay Area, and the killer's choice of the *Chronicle* made it a part of the scoop. What a scoop! The newspaper's part in the revelation was something that all other newswires had to carry.

Bay Area newspapers were scrambling to get the files of all the murder cases. No reporting was too in depth, but it was obvious that the spans between the attacks were getting shorter and that the strike areas rippled far from where the killer had begun in Vallejo. He was dubbed The 'Zodiac' Killer, a "psychotic killer" who could strike anywhere over the whole Bay Area. Local affiliates were preparing to go nationwide.

As the detectives of record, Toschi and Armstrong were working the basic procedures done in any murder case, but with the sniper threat against school buses Chief of Detectives Marty Lee knew it had to go beyond the book. He had appointed 10 men to be the Zodiac Task Force. Their duty would soon be to thump the sidewalks and shakedown every stoolie, prostitute, leech and chiseler there was. Showing them the composite, the detectives would ask 'who's the local loner with a kink?' Another valuable question: 'which one got a haircut recently?'[6]

Much more expediently, Lee and the others had to brainstorm what to do about the sniper threat. Preparing for a sniper is almost impossible, and they had only a day before a planned press conference. They went over the school bus routes. The tallest buildings along the routes had to be sorted out and a police sniper placed on top. In addition, janitors of tall buildings would have to be told to lock all back entrances.

The task force assigned plainclothes cops to follow buses and report anything suspicious. They were also being placed at significant cross streets where a bus would have to stop and therefore be a more vulnerable target. If a bus should be attacked, Chief Cahill and Captain Lee settled on a plane. The drivers were to just keep going even with a tire shot out. ZODIAC could shoot the driver first and strand the bus, so the presence of an alternate driver had to be arranged.

San Francisco was only a small part of the threat. Suburban routes would be more dangerous, and rural ones the worst. Without the immediate need to escape, as in the city, ZODIAC could afford to take some time at a remote hillside with a high powered rifle. Sheriffs would be traveling behind each bus in the outlying counties.

There was no reason not to believe ZODIAC would go to this trouble. His crime spree had proven he had quite an arsenal of guns— a .22, two 9mm, possibly a .45 automatic. He no doubt also had a rifle. That hood at Lake Berryessa also indicated he was a real "psychotic killer" who devoted a lot of time to his occult motive.

By October 16 it was time to go public with the full threat. Marty Lee sat there before the cameras and read the final paragraph from ZODIAC's letter. The citywide alert was now officially initiated.

Naturally the first question from the press audience was: "What are you doing to protect the school buses particularly in San Francisco from attack?"

Marty Lee was cautious. "In San Francisco we have been since the first day, since the reception of this note, and up to now and

---

[6] I do not know if this was asked, but it is an obvious clue. Toschi and Armstrong had gone to Napa and compared the composites. They were also shown the footprint cast, indicating ZODIAC was around 215 pounds.

continuing, we have a number of plainclothes officers following buses in the morning and in the evening."

After being asked about progress in identifying "the ZODIAC" since last Saturday, Lee stonewalled. "We are learning more all the time, but I will put it this way: there is no one suspect that we're focusing on at this time."

In regard to the profile ZODIAC fit, Lee was only able to accentuate the danger. He declared: "I believe this man is a psychopath, very, very seriously mentally deranged. He appears to have no conscience at all. No remorse after any of the acts. Certainly no reason or even alleged justification for anything that he does. Several of the shootings have occurred without a single word to anybody; just merely to walk up and start shooting. This man is a serious problem to us. He's very, very sick and a very dangerous person."

Lee admitted that a task force was set up and that there had been a meeting between detectives and psychiatrists. The news outlets had already reported that the department had spoken with astrologers. The astrological angle, in fact, was dominating the news reports, where the 'Zodiac' Killer had been given an alternately catchy moniker of 'Astrological Assassin.' Is there a connection with astrology and has the department followed this clue?

A bit shy about the topic, Lee replied:

> I personally haven't any great faith in that science, if that's what it is. . .We have made two or three inquiries of people in that business to gain information on what particular signs might mean. In fact it was just a day or so ago that we learned that little symbol of the circle with the cross in the center of it; what they told us is that it symbolizes the center of the universe. And this is called the sign of the zodiac. Little things like that we can learn. We can learn if there is any, any significance as far as the zodiac is concerned in the dates of these killings. It might be possible that this man follows some certain pattern in that direction. We don't know yet.

Snippets of the press conference were in print the next day. Naturally they concentrated on the most garish points— "Police seek astrologer's help in murder spree." Articles introduced the poisonous post scriptum in ZODIAC's letter with: "'Zodiac' concluded his note with a chilling threat— 'School children make nice targets,' he wrote. 'I think I shall wipe out a school bus some morning. Just shoot out the front tire and then pick off the kiddies as they come bouncing out.'"

The City braced itself. Curfews went into effect around the Bay Area. In a rural county like Napa, the police and sheriffs were spread thin to protect the school buses. Counties as far south as Santa Clara were put on alert.

Only a few days after the Bay Area alert went into effect, the "Zodiac Seminar" was held in the Hall of Justice. Most every jurisdiction had representatives there. Included among these were Naval Intelligence (they had verified the Hardens broke the code and were ready to crack any other that might come in), the FBI, the Postal Inspector, the Highway Patrol, and even Arlo Smith, the Deputy Attorney General of California. All sat grouped before a large blackboard on which was drawn in white chalk the zodiacal symbol used by the killer. This was enough to merit network pick-up.

No network news was as popular as CBS; no anchor as influential as Walter Cronkite. On October 20, 1969, he broke the news from coast to coast in the gravitas of news anchors of the time. Over his shoulder on the screen behind him was Napa's composite.

"The search goes on in San Francisco for the man known as the 'Zodiac Killer.' The elements involved today include a psychiatrist, astrologers, and police guards for school buses. Terry Drinkwater reports":

"'School children are nice targets,'" Drinkwater's voice narrates over the scene of a sheriff's car escorting a school bus. "'I shall wipe out a school bus some morning. Shoot out the tires and then pick off the kiddies as they come bounding[sic]out.' That was the threat of the Zodiac Killer," declared Drinkwater. "Now every day police cars follow the buses which would be likely targets. Officers armed with shotguns take the threat seriously. The psychotic killer has already murdered five: One at a lovers' lane near a lake just north of San Francisco; three others in nearby Vallejo; the latest a taxi driver in San Francisco. The Zodiac Killer seems to crave publicity. He sent letters and cryptograms to newspapers and police, recounting his crimes, threatening more murders, and making Bay Area residents *very* edgy."

A close up of Captain Martin Lee flickered onto the screen. He spoke in a concise, professional tone:

> In his violent moments, or rather the violent periods he has been in, he's an absolutely ruthless, completely merciless killer. He calmly goes about his business; in one case telephoning the police, in another tearing a strip off the shirt of the dead body of an immediately killed victim. He doesn't get great excitement over it. He just thinks killing is just killing. So somebody like that is going to be a *very serious* problem for us.

"From witnesses there are two generally similar composite drawings," continued Terry Drinkwater. "He's around thirty, reddish hair, five feet ten, crewcut, but not much more than that is known. Today a meeting of law officers and psychiatrists from all over the Bay Area. They are weighing advice from astrologers on the theory that perhaps the killer who calls himself 'the Zodiac' may be planning his next victim based on astrological signs. Terry Drinkwater, San Francisco."

Amidst the glut of nerves and news reports, the Oakland Police Department received a call around 2 a.m. on October 22 from a man saying he was the 'Zodiac' Killer. He wanted to talk with F. Lee Bailey; if not him, then Mel Belli. He wanted one or the other to appear on the local and popular morning TV talk show *AM San Francisco* hosted by Jim Dunbar. He would make contact at the studio by telephone.

F. Lee Bailey was based in Massachusetts whereas Mel Belli was San Francisco's most flamboyant attorney. He was actually one of the most flamboyant and prominent attorneys in the country. He specialized in injury cases. Because of his long-winded court presentation of his clients' accidents, he earned the sobriquet Melvin Bellicose by insurance companies. His 722 Montgomery Street offices at Jackson Square were legendary. Carpeted in imperial red, the offices were adorned with historic roll top desks and apothecary jars from his grandmother's pharmacy business. (She had been California's first woman pharmacist.) A mock coat of arms greeted one as they walked into the building. Instead of noble insignia, a pair of crutches and dollar bills adorned the shield. On the scroll was written Rex

Tortius. That's what he had been dubbed— King of Torts. His flamboyance also got him nicknamed King of the Courtroom. "There may be better lawyers than I," he once said, "but so far I haven't come across any of them in court."

Belli's offices reflected his taste. They were in one of the oldest surviving buildings in San Francisco. Dating to the 1850s, they were an historical landmark with brick fronts and the old fashioned tall bay windows. At the center one he sat, so he could see out and all could see him. Buses frequently took tourists by the old buildings, the tour guides pointing him out. These beautiful brick buildings, opulently furnished, were the center of his pirating of corporate funds through injury lawsuits. After a large win he didn't hide his mentality about plundering large corporations. He flew the Jolly Roger from a flagpole and fired a signal cannon from a window sill. It was a worthy spectacle for the Barbary Coast.

He was at his home on Telegraph Hill when he got a call from Marty Lee. Mel Belli jumped at it. He was escorted down to the KGO studios. He already knew Jim Dunbar. Belli knew everybody. KGO was preparing for major news coverage. Reporters were behind the KGO cameras. The show aired 30 minutes early at 6:30 a.m. and kept rolling live as Dunbar and Belli engaged in small talk, frequently punctuated with explanations of why they were there so early and the importance of what they were doing.

Dunbar's Channel 7 talk show was one of San Francisco's most popular, and as every minute ticked by thousands and thousands more residents tuned-in to see if the infamous 'Zodiac' Killer would call. They waited to hear his evil voice.

Finally at 7:10 a.m. it came in. It was an alternatively plaintive, meek, and then threatening voice. He was young. He was also fearful that he was being traced. He would hang up abruptly. He called in numerous times, and 12 of these times it was recorded on air. During one of these Belli and he settled on a less ominous name than "Zodiac." He would agree to call him 'Sam.' Then again in a maniacal growl 'Sam' threatened to "kill all the kids" and hung up. The Bay Area gasped. But Dunbar and Belli remained calm. Soon "Sam" called again.

"Talk to us," invited Belli.

"Just talk to us," urged Dunbar. "Tell us what's going on inside you right now, please."

A halting voice responded. "I have headaches."

Belli asked quickly but gently: "How long have you had those headaches, Sam? I mean, a long time?"

"Since I killed a kid," replied the tormented voice.

"Was it before December you had the headaches?" asked Belli. There was care in his voice, but he sounded like an attorney looking for a loophole.

"Yes."

Belli continued as if interviewing a prospective client. "Were you in service, that you might have had an injury in service? Did you ever fall out of a tree or downstairs? Were you ever unconscious?"

A weak, indecisive voice: "I don't know."

"You don't remember," observed Belli. "Does aspirin do you any good?"

"No."

"Doesn't do you any good," Belli repeated.

"Sam?"— asked Dunbar

"Darn stuff never did me any good when I had a headache," humored Belli.

"Sam, let me ask you a question," said Dunbar. "Did you, uh, attempt to call this program one other time when Mel Belli was with us?"

Sleepily, the voice said: "What?"

"Did you try to call us at another time, oh, about two or three weeks ago when Mel Belli was with us," clarified Dunbar.

"Yes."

"And, well"—

"And you couldn't get through," interrupted Belli.

"And you couldn't get through— the phones were tied up. Is that it?'

Meekly: "Yes."

This was going nowhere.

Belli: "Sam, let me ask you this. There's some reason why you go to a particular doctor or a particular priest, and some reason why apparently you wanted to talk to me or Lee. Is it because you feel we have compassion for people who get in trouble, or is it you feel we can do something for you, or is it you feel that we have enough integrity that if we promise you something we'll stick to it—"

"Well, let's find out why he wanted to talk," Dunbar said impatiently. It sounded like Belli was using this for a commercial. "Why did you want to talk to Mr. Belli, Sam?"

Whimpering: "I don't want to be hurt."

Finally, in yet another call they were able to arrange a meeting between "Sam" and Belli. It was agreed upon to meet in front of the St. Vincent de Paul Thrift Shop on Mission Street in Daly City, the city immediately south of San Francisco.

The escort took place and there in the thrift shop on what is the main drag of Daly City, Jim Dunbar and Mel Belli waited. Covertly, police snipers were stationed about as protection. They awaited the infamous ZODIAC, the center of 2 weeks of intense press coverage. An entourage of reporters loitered at a distance down a side street. Not surprisingly it was a no show on Sam's part. After a couple of hours, the reporters were allowed to scurry up as the police unsecured the scene.

Mel Belli was firmly snug in his blue suit and prominent silk red tie; Jim Dunbar, tie loose and collar open showing his fatigue. They now confronted the reporters. The obvious question was, had ZODIAC been afraid to show?

"I assured him he wasn't going to be harmed," crowed Belli, "and I stood there, and I was a target for him, more than he was a target. I told him he wasn't going to be harmed and he wouldn't have been harmed, and that I guaranteed to him. And I would not have done that over the TV to the people of San Francisco and then had him harmed. I'd have rather gotten shot myself first than broken my word on that."

Much lower key, Dunbar declared: "I think we can say honestly that we acted in good faith on this. He requested some assistance and we tried to give it to him."

Reporter: "You both sound convinced that this is the man."

Belli and Dunbar together: "*No.*"

Dunbar added: "No, we're not convinced really. I'm not convinced. I don't know"—

"I'm convinced this is a kook," Belli interrupted.

Dunbar resists. "I don't know."

"I mean a sick man," qualified Belli.

"Yeah," Dunbar agreed. "Not well."

"Not a kook in the sense that he is perpetrating a hoax."

The media sensation of this cannot be downplayed. It played out live on one of the most popular a.m. shows, and then the Bay Area waited for the updates, being prompted now and again by radio news flashes, then in special preemptive news bursts throughout the morning. Again that night the day's events were resurrected on the evening news. It even went national again.

Walter Cronkite declared: "Famed attorney Melvin Belli accompanied by police and newsmen waited 45 minutes today to keep a rendezvous with San Francisco's 'Zodiac' Killer of five persons. The man who made the appointment never showed up. The meeting was arranged this morning when a caller identifying himself as Sam reached Belli on a KGO TV talk show. He said he was the 'Zodiac Killer' and needed help. Here's how it looked and sounded . . ." And national TV saw a clip from the segment on Jim Dunbar's show.

Another news sensation followed the next day, October 23, when Paul Stine's brother, Joe Stine, a mechanic in Modesto, California, announced that he challenged the ZODIAC to meet him in a duel. It was a bit odd, but it garnered enormous news.

Publicity for the 'Zodiac' Killer was phenomenal at this time, but it was also uncoordinated. Nationally, the networks showed the composite from Lake Berryessa, no doubt because the networks had picked this one up from the TV affiliates that had broadcast it locally on October 2 and 3. Locally in San Francisco the composite drawn from the memories of the kids across Washington and Cherry was the most prominent. This is the one newspapers carried nationwide. Unfortunately, the SFPD composite made ZODIAC seem quite skinny. It also was amended, meaning it was inaccurate.

This had happened on October 18, and the adjustment made the suspect look older. SFPD had not specified why the composite was amended; nor did they say what the source was for the amended features. But the truth is multilayered. The young age of the perpetrator was influenced by the first victim of the cab robbery. The kids had estimated that the killer was in his early 40s. Don Fouke finally came forward and essentially said the same thing. After Fouke looked at the composite he said the guy was older and thicker. The sketch was never amended to show that ZODIAC was much heavier.

Behind the scenes, Toschi and Armstrong had arranged for Brian Hartnell, Nancy Slover, and David Slaight, the three who had heard ZODIAC's voice, to listen to a replay of the recordings of *A.M. San Francisco*. None thought the voice of "Sam" was the one they heard when they had encountered the real ZODIAC.

Amended but remaining inaccurate as to weight.

Although 10 detectives worked the 'Zodiac' Killer case, Dave Toschi and Bill Armstrong began getting the most coverage. Wherever they went they were pulling down special mention in the news articles, billed as "The Zodiac Twins."

An examination of the ZODIAC's letters by the collective squad of detectives revealed some tenuous clues. One in particular was in ZODIAC's cryptogram, in which he said that "man was the most dangeroue anamal of all," a reference from both a short story and a movie entitled *The Most Dangerous Game*. In this plot a diabolical count named, interestingly, Zaroff, hunted people, having grown tired of hunting mere wild game. To a much more anemic degree this is what the ZODIAC was doing.

Yet ZODIAC's madness was not that of a sophisticated hunter, a fact clearly projected by that bizarre bit of headgear at Lake Berryessa. The impact of having worn that ridiculous hood truly hit home on October 24, 1969, in the most momentous week for ZODIAC news, when Napa's artist and Bryan Hartnell completed a full body sketch for what the ZODIAC looked like when he attacked him. By early November, all the other jurisdictions had seen it.

Taken altogether, there was division in the collective investigation as to just how smart ZODIAC really was. Wade Bird, a Vallejo police captain, had said: "I think he'll prove to be a genius who got so far out he went over the edge." Roy Conway thought him more of a spontaneous attacker who was lucky with publicity. Marty Lee continued to view him as a calculating, ruthless killer, but one that was really only a fat paperhanger with too much time on his hands.

Vantage point more than collective analysis had inspired the varied opinions. From SFPD's point of view ZODIAC was a clumsy killer, one who was so stupid he left behind fingerprints. Vallejo's experience indicated a spontaneous drive-by shooter. Napa Co. sheriffs thought they had a real wacko who read too much astrology.

More than the other jurisdiction, Napa had good cause to believe its opinion. The image of ZODIAC at Lake Berryessa is utterly outrageous, but which vantage point did it favor? It didn't necessarily bespeak of Wade Bird's view that ZODIAC was a genius. There was something common about the image, coarse and raggedy, offset by the neatly sewn comic strip hood.

However, there was nothing in the "cerebral theory" that required ZODIAC be a sophisticated killer or even a successful man in real life. Like others, Bird had been inspired by appreciating how much time the killer put into his publicity campaign. He had devised his own code and laboriously wrote it out with the neatness of a calligrapher. He could be festering in a basement by a hot water heater, for all that mattered, but he obsessed brilliantly on his publicity. . . and the intricate hood proved he obsessed on the image of his alter ego ZODIAC.

Naturally, the more in depth articles concentrated on ZODIAC's psychology. Psychobabble stoked the metropolitan anxiety by underscoring another attack was inevitable. Much of the autumn angst is both reflected in and disseminated by the tabloid *National Tattler* in its November article "Zodiac Murder Mystery" that it is worth a look. It quickly warns "that 'Zodiac' has not struck again. But psychiatrists believe he will, as soon as the homicidal pressures build

Napa's sketch of the ZODIAC at Lake Berryessa— about 5 foot 11 inches, paunchy, frumpy, pleated, high water cuffed pants, high lip Air Force shoes, but a neat ceremonial hood.

up and require an outlet." It presents a psychological profile: "The picture that emerges is of a bright man who is not too well educated, but who had dabbled extensively in astrology and the occult."

> The cryptogram he sent to the newspapers was composed of symbols taken from such varied sources as the Egyptian Book of the Dead, books on the legendary lost continent of Mu, primitive mythology, American Indian carvings, foreign alphabets and astrology and astronomy.
>
> Use of these symbols indicates the killer's pattern of reading and study. His extensive dabbling in the occult, psychiatrists say, indicates a great basic insecurity.

Continuing the psychological angle, the article goes on to tell us that it seems as if a "happy life has eluded him," so much so that he has plunged himself in "ancient and arcane" knowledge searching to find joy.

On a solid note, however, the article discussed how the investigators were looking at the cryptogram in order to try and detect some unconscious clue that would "directly" lead to 'Zodiac.' Specifically, the last undeciphered line (EBEO RIET EMETH HPITI) was declared to be four words and of "vital" importance since it didn't match the code. As the article reminds us, ZODIAC had promised that when the code is cracked "you will have me."

Psychologically, this scrambled last line was viewed as ZODIAC secretly desiring to get caught, a phenomenon amongst "psychopathic killers" supposedly seen before. "Repressed hostility can only be drained off by killing, in Zodiac's tortured psyche, yet a strong sense of guilt leads him to thinly disguised attempts at surrender."

After presenting the case for ZODIAC's childhood (by the psychological profiling standards of the time) it was declared to have been a deprived one, lonely and above all frustrated. Hence he resorted to subterfuge in expressing himself. This carried over into adulthood and this explained his use of a code to declare his motives (remember, his 3 confession letters never bragged nor gave a motive) and this explained why he switched his code in the last line so that it could not (yet) be deciphered and his identity revealed.

Subterfuge, or the theoretical need for it, naturally meant there must be a deeper code within the letters and cryptograms. "Decoding experts believe that the misspellings in Zodiac's cryptogram may be intentional, and that together with the last four, unintelligible words they contain essential clues to his identity."

Psychological profiling basically made the article delve into the significance of the Lake Berryessa attack, attributing the daytime attack to another subconscious desire by ZODIAC to be caught, his use of a knife to the desire for less "remote control" killing and use of penetration, of what you may well infer. ZODIAC had supposedly cut Cecelia Shepard with the sign of the zodiac on both breasts and in the groin— leading the article to indulge in a section on "perverted pleasures" where the link with the "Sharon Tate murders" was considered a possibility (according to the article Tate's body was mutilated in the same way). Finishing the psychological assessment, the article declared: "It appears Zodiac despises his victims— and primarily because he envies the pleasures he imagines them to have."

But more disquieting to public nerves the article noted how the time period between murders was decreasing. "The shorter time spans might be indicative of accelerating pressures on Zodiac."

The upshot for Bay Area readers was that this psychopath ZODIAC was a "twisted" killer who wouldn't stop, and as a shrewd criminal he would be hard to stop.

COMIC STRIP CRUSADE

While it is tempting to fall prey to the hysteria of the autumn of angst, we cannot imagine the ZODIAC sitting there controlling his game masterfully. To initiate the autumn terror he had sent only one letter confessing to Stine's murder. He had carefully engineered the final paragraph to incite panic, but to a large extent his publicity game thereafter had been aided by other grandstanders. In fact, since October 22 most of ZODIAC's publicity had been gratuitous. It reached crescendo with the *AM San Francisco* segment and then with Stine's brother stirring the pot by challenging him to a duel. During the media glut, ZODIAC need not lift a finger to be the ever-present villain.

During this time, however, he was not just sitting back idly enjoying a metropolis in fear. He was formulating another cipher. He carefully used his blue felt pen to draw the symbols in a long block on a single sheet of paper. He folded it and placed it in a greeting card. He included a macabre touch— a bloodstained piece of Paul Stine's shirt. It was a curious act since it was no longer necessary to prove he was the killer. But considering the difficulty he had in convincing Jack Stiltz back in the summer, he probably felt it was a wise gesture. He wrote on the envelope "Please Rush to Editor."

It was a chilly Saturday, November 8, 1969, in the City. The chunky villain opened the drop on the mailbox and let it scoop in the card. He probably used a drive-up postal box on the corner of the postal stations. At such a location there was no one to see him. He drove on, no doubt quite satisfied he had played another calculated hand in his game of death. Curiously, the villain appeared at a mail drop again on Sunday. He slipped in another letter.

Both postings arrived at the *Chronicle* on Monday November 10. The "Rush to Editor" scribble looked familiar. When the envelope was slit and the card removed, out fell a bloody swath of striped fabric. The greeting card had the illustration of a pen dripping ink. It carried the stock sentiment: "sorry I haven't written for a while, but I just washed my pen. . ." Opening it, a folded piece of paper fell out and landed by the bloody token. Inside the card there was the stock sentiment "and i can't do a thing with it." Around this was ZODIAC's nasty slanted scrawl in blue felt. In his comic strip way, he introduced his oracle:

This is the Zodiac speaking,

He barely got "speaking" to fit on the card. In a childlike way he curved it around to get it to fit. He then forewarned:

I though you would nead a
good laugh before you
hear the bad news
you won't get the
news for a while yet
PS could you print
this new cipher
I get awfully lonely
when I am ignored,

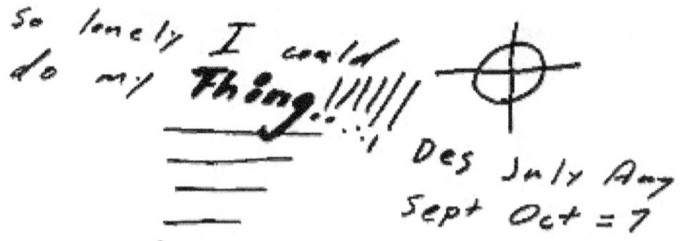

Childish and yet at the same time bloodlessly chilling with that casual ledger claiming two more victims in a tally by months. It takes more than just being a killer to frame a bloody token with the card's sentiment. This was someone with tongue firmly in cheek enjoying himself.

"**Thing**!!!!!!" underwent an evolution here. ZODIAC had originally written the word normally, starting with a small "t." When finished he went back and capitalized it. Tracing over it several times, he made it garishly bold.

If there was any doubt about the amount of time the 'Zodiac' Killer spent on his game it was vanquished when the piece of paper was unfolded. It was a new cryptogram. Instead of being in 3 pieces it was one big long block of symbols 17 across and 20 down.

The 340 Cipher, so named because it contains 340 symbols.

Surprisingly, another envelope turned up in the same pile— a 6 page letter dovetailing on the events of October 11. It began like the others with his pompous preamble: "This is the Zodiac speaking."

Up to the end of Oct I have killed 7 people. I have grown rather angry with the police for their telling lies about me. So I shall change the way the collecting of slaves. I shall no longer announce to anyone. when I comitt my murders, they shall look like routine robberies, killings of anger, + a few fake accidents, etc.

The police shall never catch me, because I have been too clever for them.

1 I look like the description passed out only when I do my thing, the rest of the time I look entirle different. I shall not tell you what my descise consists of when I kill

2 As of yet I have left no fingerprints behind me contrary to what the police say in my killings I wear transparent fingertip guards. All it is is 2 coats of airplane cement coated on my fingertips— quite unnoticible + very efective

3 my killing tools have been boughten through the mail order outfits before the ban went into efect. except one & it was bought out of the state. So as you can see the police don't have much to work on. If you wonder why I was wipeing the cab down I was leaving fake clews for the police to run all over town with, as one might say, I gave the cops som bussy work to do to keep them happy. I enjoy needling the blue pigs. Hey blue pig I was in the park— you were useing fire trucks to mask the sound of your cruzeing prowl cars. The dogs never came with in 2 blocks of me + they were to the west + there was only 2 groups of barking about 10 min apart then the motor cicles went by about 150 ft away going from south to north west

ps. 2 cops pulled a goof abot 3 min after I left the cab. I was walking down the hill to the park when this cop car pulled up + one of them called me over + asked if I saw anyone acting suspicious or strange in the last 5 to 10 min + I said yes there was this man who was runnig by waveing a gun & the cops peeled rubber + went around the corner as I directed them + I disappeared into the park a block + a half away never to be seen again. [must print in paper]

Hey pig doesnt it rile you up to have your noze rubbed in your booboos?
If you cops think I'm going to take on a bus the way I stated I was, you deserve to have holes in your heads.

Take one bag of ammonium nitrate fertilizer + 1 gal of stove oil & dump a few bags of gravel on top + then set the shit off + will positivily ventalate any thing that should be in the way of the blast. The death machine is all ready made. I would have sent you pictures but you would be nasty enough to trace them back to developer + then to me, so I shall describe my masterpiece to you. The nice part of it is all the parts can be bought on the open market with no questions asked.

1 bat. pow clock — will run for aprox 1 year
1 photoelectric switch
2 copper leaf springs
2 6V car bat
1 flash light bulb + reflector
1 mirror
2 18" cardboard tubes black with
shoe polish inside + oute
[For ZODIAC's diagram see page 134]

the system checks out from one end to the other in my tests. What you do not know is whether the death machine is at the sight or whether it is being stored in my basement for future use. I think you do not have the manpower to stop this one by continually searching the road sides looking for this thing. + it wont do to re roat + re schedule the busses because the bomb can be adapted to new conditions.

Have fun!! By the way it could be rather messy if you try to bluff me.

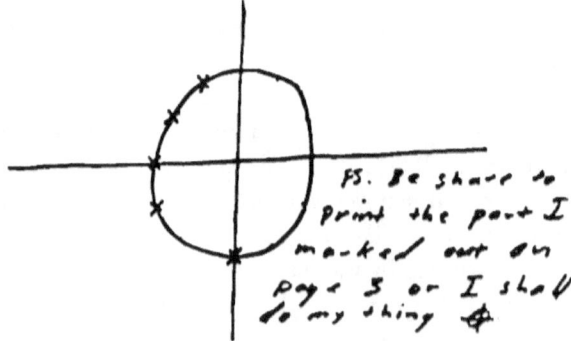

[PS. Be shure to print the part I marked out on page 3 or I shall do my thing.]

Apparently the x's mark strike points where he killed victims. If so, his deadly signature this time was in its way a map.

Almost as an afterthought the backside of the last piece of paper contains a paragraph in the *center* of the page.

> *To prove that I am the Zodiac, Ask the Vallejo cop about my electric gun sight which I used to start my collecting of slaves.*

[To prove that I am the Zodiac, Ask the Vallejo cop about my electric gun sight which I used to start my collecting of slaves.]

This little epilogue, completely out of place and incongruous, proves quite intriguing as a result. There was no need to prove he was the ZODIAC anymore. It suggests he may have drafted notes and reused an old piece of paper in this case. Or, as we will eventually discover, this could be one of the most significant clues, and perhaps ZODIAC's biggest mistake.

An analysis of the letter, however, was obviously not something the *Chronicle* was looking to print. The cryptogram was the big deal. ZODIAC had played a new hand in his game and ratcheted up the intrigue level.

Paul Avery, their crime reporter, broke the story the next day. "'I've killed Seven,' the Zodiac claims." Since the greeting card ledger indicated ZODIAC had killed in August, Avery harked back to the gruesome murders of Debra Furlong and Kathie Snoozy in San Jose on August 3, 1969. Collectively they had been stabbed 300 times at Foothills Park.

It could be that ZODIAC intended this link to be made. On the excessively large zodiac symbol signature he had marked an x on the bottom. If somewhere in the Bay Area is to be taken as at the center of the crosshair, then the southern x could easily be taken as representing San Jose.

For public consumption it was a timely boast. It heightened the fear in the Bay Area that ZODIAC was truly capable of killing school kids, the threat which was central to his success in causing the current terror mania.

With the publication of the new cryptogram, Marty Lee was once

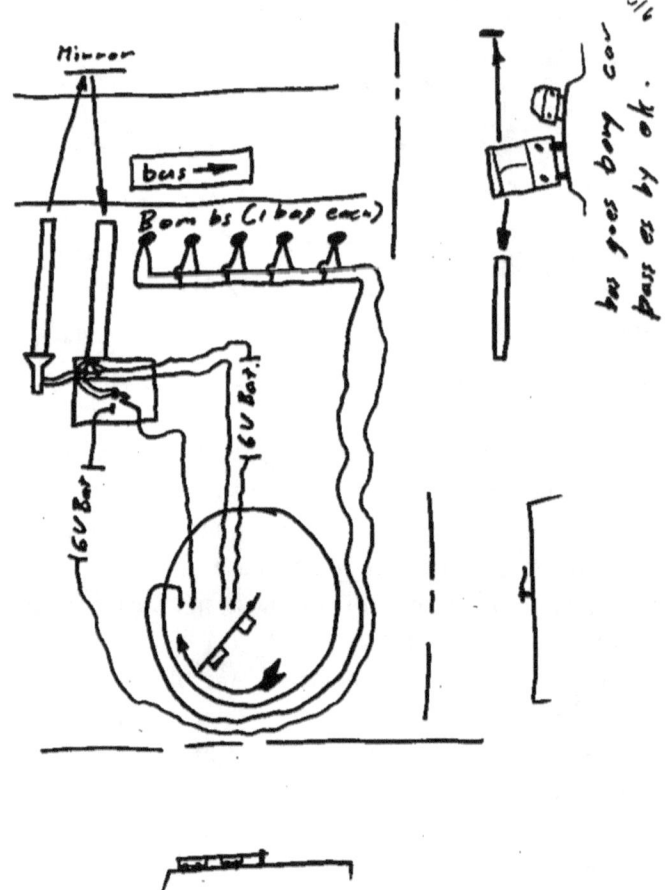

Page 5, where ZODIAC details in diagram his homemade bomb.

again at the center of an antsy press conference. It was Wednesday, November 12. Amidst the flashbulbs he had to field the reporters' questions. Lee wanted to qualify something.

> First of all he is described in all of the media as a nut, an insane person, a screwball and all of this sort of thing. And I don't go along with this. I think— and I have studied all of the letters; I think that this man is *legally* sane. We all know the difference; legal sanity, of course, being a knowledge of the difference between right and wrong, and also a knowledge that what one has done is forbidden and therefore taking of action of fleeing from the police. This man has certainly exhibited that much intelligence or rationality.

In almost tableau suspension, Bay Area residents had gathered around their TVs and watched the conference or listened to it on radio. The next day the *Chronicle* republished the cryptogram, this time besides Avery's new article: *"Zodiac 'Legally Sane.' Cop sure clues will snag him."*

Within the article Paul Avery asserts Lee's confidence that with 20 men working the case (all jurisdictions combined) it was only a matter of time before they had their man, and from the evidence they have gathered there will indeed be no doubt they have ZODIAC.

The public naturally did not know what Lee's certainty was based upon, and this may have been for the best for SFPD. For the physical evidence was, in fact, very thin. It only consisted of the bloody fingerprints in Stine's cab, hand printing in these nasty notes, and the ballistics indicating various guns. Without a suspect to match them to, however, fingerprints and handwriting are a reference in the case folder as vibrant as a fossil in a museum's archives. Napa and Vallejo didn't even have full faith in the bloody fingerprints. They thought contamination could have occurred.

What was Lee's faith based on? It must have been the fact that ZODIAC had used a *new* 9mm Browning. This alone could possibly *lead* to a suspect. Hand printing and fingerprints could confirm a suspect but not lead to one.

ZODIAC had taken exception to SFPD's claim that they were certain they had his fingerprints. He had actually made quite a point of refuting the claim. Was he right? Or was he the egomaniac Lee thought, one who couldn't handle the fact he had made such a simple mistake?

Truth didn't matter to ZODIAC. What mattered was maintaining his deadly evil genius image with the public. He never liked his publicity campaign's effect being minimized. When his claim to the murders was questioned by Stiltz, he wrote back quickly. To make his presence at the crime scenes incontrovertible he wrote on the Karmann Ghia side door— proof he had been there. Marty Lee had said that he believed ZODIAC had lied (in the October 13 letter) about being in the Presidio during the manhunt. Now in direct response, the ZODIAC clearly went out of his way to "mock the blue pigs" by getting specific, describing the cops as west of his lurking hideout and that only two dog teams came within hearing.

But ZODIAC wasn't the infallible evil genius. Not only did his crimes reveal his clumsiness, his bragging once again betrayed valuable clues. He confirmed that he actually was the man Fouke had seen. Whether or not he had actually seen the ZODIAC could have remained a source of debate had ZODIAC not pulled this stunt.

No doubt in response to ZODIAC's pompous claim (along with the demand it be printed), Don Fouke wrote his "scratch" to clarify the incident. It is dated on November 12, 1969.

> The suspect that was observed . . . was WMA 35-45 years old about 5'10", 180-200 lbs, Medium heavy build – Barrel chested – Medium complexion – Light colored hair possibly graying in rear (May have been lighting that caused this effect.) Crew cut – Wearing glasses – Dressed in dark blue waist length zipper type jacket (Navy or royal blue) Elastic cuffs and waist band zipped part way up. Brown wool pants pleeted [sic] type baggy in rear (Rust brown). May have been wearing low cut shoes.

The description is the image of Brian Hartnell's sketch of the ZODIAC at Lake Berryessa, only now with brown (though still obsolete) pleated pants and minus the black ceremonial hood.

Despite ZODIAC's taunting claims, Fouke and Zelms had never stopped and talked to him. In fact, his view was so fleeting that he admitted he didn't even know if Zelms had seen the suspect. He concluded by giving Zelms' name and badge number in order to facilitate a follow-up if his superiors desired.

ZODIAC's lie is self-exposing anyway. Fouke and Zelms had been told the perp was a Black Male Adult. Had they stopped, they would have asked him, 'Have you seen a black guy . . .?' Of course, ZODIAC didn't know this mistake had been made. Instead he invents a situation where he is asked about a "guy" acting strange. The truth is that ZODIAC had only seen two cops speed past and decided to use the encounter to mock the SFPD and demand they print it. It was a punk's way and language of embarrassing the "blue pigs."

There was little reason to believe anything ZODIAC said, one way or the other. His threat against a school bus is proof of that. It was calculated to instill terror, nothing more. Now he claimed it was purely a boast and the cops were stupid to have taken him seriously.

Which was the lie? Or was it all a lie? Essentially that was his goal—continue to harass and create doubt.

Marty Lee and the task force took ZODIAC to be a liar but the language of his letters to be reflecting his true persona—some fat but not that educated a man. They religiously looked for mistakes in his letters that could lead to him. Not lies— *mistakes*. The letters were studied in depth to see if ZODIAC betrayed some clue through the use of an expression or idiom. Some British English expressions had consistently crept into his language. For example, "kiddies" was thought to be British. In this light "clews" was also of interest. This suggested not a misspelling but the British usage of the word. It is a thin connection, but Fouke too had the impression the man he saw was of Welsh heritage.

On the other hand, ZODIAC's *spelling* mistakes were regarded as obvious frauds. With each new letter his spelling got intentionally worse, sometimes impossibly bad; for instance, "oute" for out. He got 'their' and 'there' right all the time, a problem this current generation has. He also paragraphed perfectly. All this indicated he knew how to spell and was overdoing the uneducated punk routine.

Then he knocked out with non sequiturs, such as at the end of his letter: "By the way it could be rather messy if you try to bluff me." Bluff how? No deal was being requested or arranged.

Was he being really smart or really dumb? He was clumsy at crime scenes. His bragging was uninformed and he needlessly gave away clues. And with his recent letters he was beginning to show a pattern of pointless lying. Nevertheless, he didn't leave traceable fingerprints on his letters. No one knew where he was based. Long distances spanned his crime scenes, but San Francisco was the center of his attention. What really was his game?

The ZODIAC was a boastful slayer, and he was proving himself a skillful player of terror.

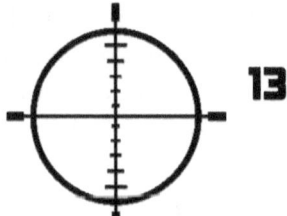

SKILLFUL PLAYER

Terror exists in the fearful anticipation, not in the mournful aftermath. ZODIAC knew this. His timing was betraying his intent to capitalize on everything he had done. A month after Stine had been murdered the publicity was winding down. At this time what did ZODIAC do? He sent another letter cold-bloodedly claiming two more victims. With this he had included his second cryptogram. Nothing had excited public interest as much as his original cryptogram and its decoding last summer. By early November it was the perfect move to make in his publicity game. It worked. It garnered him enormous attention and it kept the Bay Area edgy. . . and *very* interested.

School buses continued to be escorted, though the ZODIAC said he was never going to try a sniper attack— on a bus anyway. On the other hand, his recipe for the bomb was fairly legitimate. A sudden explosion anywhere near the roadside could cause a lot of damage. There was a *remote* chance the threat was genuine, and therefore the police units had to remain close by just in case.

Throughout the rest of November the Bay Area remained at a heightened state of alert. Yet the month ended without a killing, and nobody could break his latest cipher to give us a huge news flash courtesy of the ZODIAC. Once again, he was losing that precious commodity—publicity. As harsh winter came, the terror faded.

The ZODIAC now played his skillful hand. On December 20, he mailed a letter to the home residence of Mel Belli. Because Belli was currently away in Europe, his mail was accumulating at home. On the 27th his personal secretary took it down to his offices at 722

Montgomery. The back of the envelope read "Mery Xmass + New Year." It was first thought to be just a Christmas card.

When the envelope was opened by his assistant, a piece of Stine's bloodstained shirt fell out. It was proof, of course, that he, ZODIAC, wrote the letter inside; and specifically here it might have been necessary.

> **Dear Melvin**
>
> This is the Zodiac speaking I wish you a happy Christmass. The one thing I ask of you is this, please help me. I cannot reach out for help because of this thing in me wont let me. I am finding it extreamly dificult to hold it in check I am afraid I will loose control again and take my nineth + posibly tenth victom. Please help me I am drownding. At the moment the children are safe from the bomb because it is so massive to dig in + the triger mech requires much work to get it adjusted just right. But if I hold back too long from no nine I will loose complet all controol of my self + set the bomb up. Pleare help me I can not remain in control for much longer.

The ZODIAC had written in a very rigid style uncharacteristic of his hasty, slanted scrawl. (Over the course of the letter, however, he betrayed hints of his usual printing style.) But the bloodstained piece of Stine's shirt was undeniable proof that this was from the "Boastful Slayer."

But it is not the printing which immediately strikes one. The true contrast with ZODIAC's previous letters is that the "Belli Letter" in attitude dovetails on the personality of "Sam." This similarity was immediately noticed in Belli's office.

A legal associate flew to Munich and there gave Belli photocopies of everything. Belli was soon on the phone with Paul Avery at the *Chronicle*. On December 29 the story broke. Mel Belli and "Sam" were center stage again.

Paul Avery reports: "'He'll meet any time'— Urgent appeal by Belli to Zodiac.'" Belli declared that he would meet in secret anywhere, any place ZODIAC chose. The *Chronicle* also got a plug when Belli asked ZODIAC to write to him "in care of the Chronicle" to let him know what he has decided. In this way, Belli talked to ZODIAC through the article, expressing his heartfelt worry to the tragically inner-tormented murderer fearful of losing "controol."

Because of the letter there was every reason to believe that "Sam" and ZODIAC were indeed one and the same. There was also every reason to believe that ZODIAC would soon go berserk and kill again. In addition to Sam's desperate on-air attitude, the letter heavily, *very heavily*, reflected all the psychological profiling that had filled the pages of Bay Area newspapers and national rags like the previously mentioned *Tattler*.

As a result the year ended on a sensational note. The 'Zodiac' saga dominated the news, all of it another installment of the sensation that had followed the October 22, 1969, Jim Dunbar *AM San Francisco* appearance by "Sam." It was, if anything, more intense. After 'Sam' had failed to appear in Daly City, Belli had been certain he was just a "kook." Enclosed in the letter, Stine's bloody shirt was now proof that 'Sam' had been ZODIAC all along. The October scenario seemed justified and was relished in news blurbs. Belli was cast as the towering legal expert emotionally pleading with the psychotic killer to turn himself in, the man trying to stave the hand of death and help the plaintive, mentally disturbed and socially deprived mass murderer resist the "thing" in him.

It is not my desire to break the chronology of the narrative, but some points cannot be avoided here in order to appreciate this juncture in the ZODIAC's publicity crusade. There can be no doubt that the real ZODIAC was musing over the entire sensational affair he had intentionally just set in motion with his letter to Mel Belli. And equally there can be no doubt that he pulled it off intentionally in imitation of the biggest and most gratuitous bit of publicity he had received— the caller "Sam" episode—for it is a fact that ZODIAC was *not* "Sam."

This was proved within a couple of weeks, though this episode played out exclusively behind closed doors. "Sam" started calling the Belli residence on Montgomery Street. This fact was not uncovered until decades later when a cleared FBI Airtel report held an oblique reference to it. One of the calls had been traced. They were being made by Eric Weil, an inmate at the mental hospital in Napa. Belli had confirmed to SFPD that Weil's voice was the same as Sam's on the Jim Dunbar show. It is a fact that Eric Weil, that simpering weasel oddkin "Sam," was not ZODIAC.

Nevertheless, it is also a fact that the "Belli Letter" of December 20, 1969, was from the real ZODIAC. He had dovetailed on the tenor of "Sam" and tempered his language to reflect that miserable, plaintive jacket job. His ultimate purpose therefore was to prove he had been caller "Sam" on that frenzied October 22 on the *AM San Francisco* show and by doing so reignite the publicity and terror suspense he so desired. "Sam" had given him more publicity than he got for killing Stine and threatening school children. It is not a coincidence that he chose to reignite this particular episode.

Mockery, manipulation, tongue-in-cheek goading— the holy trinity of ZODIAC's macabre sense of humor. He sat back and enjoyed his game, launched merely with a letter and a clipping of his last victim's bloody shirt. This was skillful playing at publicity.

However, it seems he opted not to remain ensconced in the safety of his lair, wherever it was. For this "Belli Letter" he decided to risk being seen. The letter actually represented something far more sinister than realized at the time.

The ominous nature of the letter was contained on the envelope. This was not discovered until decades later. On December 20,

2008, Ricardo Gomez was conducting one of his San Francisco 'Zodiac' Killer site tours. He held up a copy of the envelope (long released by SFPD) to the address on Belli's old house on Montgomery. He then noticed that ZODIAC had copied the font style *exactly*.

Within the library of ZODIAC's nasty communiqués, the "Belli Letter" envelope had always been at a stark contrast to other ZODIAC envelopes. Normally, he wrote the address hastily and often abbreviated. By contrast, great care had been given to writing the address on Belli's envelope. It had a rigid style and the street number of the address was meticulously written in sans serif form, just like Belli's house address font. ZODIAC displayed great attention to detail and had a very steady hand. He was indeed a careful imitator.

In consequence, it is impossible to avoid the deduction: ZODIAC must have watched Belli's house. In his own little impish way he was inflicting a moment of terror on the famous attorney. The envelope was intended to let Belli know that he had physically watched his residence. It is an interesting way of stalking. There was no overt statement "I'm watching you" in the letter, the usual ink-bound stalker's way of inflicting terror. It was a far more subtle move in his chess-like game of terror.

Perhaps the ZODIAC had sweet visions in his mind of the news agog with footage of police snipers on the roofs of POSH Telegraph Hill, staged to protect the influential legal media star.

Unfortunately, ZODIAC's subtlety went unnoticed contemporarily and as a result there was no payoff in terms of publicity. Here on the envelope he had proved too subtle.

Today, this attempted stunt becomes a vivid clue to his calculating character. And in spite of the fact that SFPD did not recognize the potential of the envelope at the time, for the sake of context here it is necessary for us to keep ZODIAC's stunt in our minds. It helps us to understand a very calculating mind at work.

Months passed. The clock ticked forward into the new year. Nothing. No letters. No murders. Nothing. ZODIAC had strangely vanished.

Author's photo showing Washington and Maple, where the killing may actually have happened. Below, looking to Washington and Cherry.

Washington and Cherry— looking toward the crime scene. The cab had been parked near the curb where the car and van are now parked. Below, looking across the street at the angle from where the witnesses saw ZODIAC wipe down the cab.

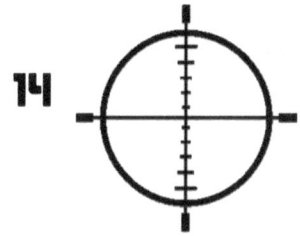

PAPER TIGER

A S SPRING WAS COLORING THE AIR WITH BEAUTIFUL FRAGRANT blossoms it had been 4 months and still no word from the killer who had delighted in calling himself the ZODIAC.

The elder generation continued to think the nation was going to hell in a wheelbarrow. The urban environment was becoming shabbier and littered with trash. Crime was rampant and it was bold. This was underscored on January 1, 1970, when only one hour into the new year Eric Zelms, Fouke's former partner last October, had been gunned down with his own police .357 magnum by three burglars when he caught them breaking into a pawn shop. The newspapers summarized: "There were 143 homicides in the city during 1969, about as many as in 1967 (58) and 1968 (90) combined."

Drug use was increasing. Bizarre crimes and militant actions were on the rise. Increasing disgust over Vietnam broke into fights between police and protestors. Soldiers returning from their tour of duty had balloons of urine thrown on them. Peace power and sit-ins collided with flag burning and clashes with police in full riot gear.

Souring the psychedelic idealism of the 1960s counterculture the most were the Manson Family murders. The nation now knew that those ghastly murders last August 1969 had been committed by a hippie cult and its guru arch killer— so much for hippies representing the peace movement. Now they came to represent more than a source of frustration. Hippies represented a movement of drugged-up, licentious deadbeats. Counterculture came to mean anything against the pervading norm of decent American middleclass morality. So far as the mainstream was concerned, this now included primitive cults and murder, Satanism and sacrifices. Such a thing as the gruesome Tate/LaBianca murders could happen again, to anybody, committed by those in a movement that harbored and empowered dangerous devil worshiping zombies.

Haight was becoming an urban scene and not a gem of enlightenment. The original flower children had moved on, leaving in their wake a Haight that was no longer Bloomtown but a decaying compost of deadbeats. When George Harrison of the Beatles finally visited the youth Mecca to experience some of the vibe of which he had heard so much he was visibly disappointed. He lamented there was nothing there but a bunch of dropouts.

Flower children had long taken to the countryside, and the 1960s had moved on from the bright innocence captured in Kodachrome. The 1970s were already becoming darker and soon to be nostalgic over the "good old days" when life seemed Technicolor and classy— *i.e.* any time before the counterculture.

In this new era ZODIAC reintroduced himself. His new letter was postmarked April 20, 1970. He, of course, introduced it with his usual grand declaratory preamble, but he quickly got to his reason:

> This is the Zodiac speaking
> By the way have you cracked
> the last cipher I sent you?
> My name is —
>
> A E N ✦ ⊙ K ⊙ M ⊙ ⌐ N A M

The implication, naturally, was that if SFPD had cracked the cipher of November 9, 1969, then they should be able to decode his name above, ostensibly written with the same code. He continued:

> I am mildly cerous as to how
> much money you have on my
> head now. I hope you do not
> think that I was the one
> who wiped out that blue
> meannie with a bomb at the
> cop station. Even though I talked

> about killing school children with
> one. It just wouldn't doo to
> move in on someone else's teritory.
> But there is more glory in killing
> a cop than a cid because a cop
> can shoot back. I have killed
> ten people to date. It would
> have been a lot more except
> that my bus bomb was a dud.
> I was swamped out by the
> rain we had a while back.

Sgt. Brian V. McDonnell was the cop to whom ZODIAC makes reference. Militants (ostensibly the Weathermen) had placed a bomb loaded with fence staples near the Waller Street station in Golden Gate Park on February 18. Several officers were wounded and McDonnell was fatally pierced by the staples. ZODIAC mentioning the crime was a deadly reminder that his bomb was very much possible and to be taken seriously. Accordingly he includes a diagram again of his revised death machine.

This letter was at a stark contrast to the "Belli Letter." He had no fear of losing "controol." The cunning manipulator was back to his original character— the punk taunting the police. The misspellings, especially "cid" for "kid," were overkill. Again, it merely revealed to what extent ZODIAC laid false clues. It has no real effect except to underscore he was better educated than he presented. Nevertheless more time had to be spent checking if all these misplaced letters in the misspelled words formed yet another message.

Of course, the ZODIAC knew his 340 Cipher had not been decoded. Had it been it would have been big news in the papers. He also no doubt knew that the cipher had lost importance now, even if it was decoded. Cunningly, he reintroduces its relevance by implying his "Name Cipher" is encrypted with the same code. Crack the 340 Cipher and you have me. He had shifted to his old hook yet again— uncover his true identity— as the bait to re-excite interest in him.

One week later on April 28 another joke card arrived at the *Chronicle* (postmarked San Francisco). On the front there was a cartoon of an Old West prospector on a donkey followed by another, much older prospector saddled on a dragon. "Sorry to hear your ass is a dragon," said the man on the donkey to the man on the dragon. It was ZODIAC's way of chiding SFPD for not yet solving his identity. On the front of the card he had written in his blue felt pen:

> I hope you
> enjoy your
> selves
> when I
> have my
> **Blast.**
>
> ⊕
>
> P.S. on
> back

Tongue-in-cheek, he declared on the back of the card:

> If you dont want me to have this blast you must do two things. Tell every one about the bus bomb with all the details. & I would like to see some nice Zodiac butons wandering about town. Every one else has these buttons like, ☮, black power, melvin eats bluber, etc. Well it would cheer me up considerably if I saw a lot of people wearing my buton. Please no nasty ones like melvin's
>
> Thank you

Coming just a week after his last letter, this bizarre card carried a little more punch. The ZODIAC was giving the appearance of being pushed closer to the edge— that building pressure mentioned by the psychologists, the pressure which could only be released by murder.

Yet nothing happened. ZODIAC vanished yet again.

More and more San Francisco was becoming the city of *Dirty Harry*— murder, mayhem, militants. A notable murder occurred on June 19. Officer Richard Radetich, only 27 years old, was double parked in the Haight-Ashbury (also on Waller Street), writing a ticket for a car with an expired license plate. It was a dark 5:25 a.m. Someone approached and fired 3 shots from a .38 through the window. Yet another young cop (Zelms was only 22 years old) had been murdered. No one took credit. It was someone doing their "thing."

On Friday June 27, only 5 days after Radetich's much publicized funeral, the *Chronicle* received another letter.

> This is the Zodiac speaking
>
> I have become very upset with the people of San Fran Bay Area. They have **not** complied with my wishes for them to wear some nice ⊕ buttons. I promised to punish them if they didnot comply, by anilating a full School Buss. But now school is out for the summer, so I punished them in an another way.
> I shot a man sitting in a parked car with a .38.
>
> ⊕-12   SFPD-0
>
> The Map coupled with this code will tell you where the bomb is set. You have antill next Fall to dig it up. ⊕

There then followed another string of code:

C △ J I ■ O ⋊ ⊥ A M ⊐ ▲ Ω O R T G
X ⊙ F D V ʊ ▨ H C Ɛ L ✣ P W △

From the tally at the end of the letter, ZODIAC was claiming 12 victims now. Considering the huge turnout (over 1,000 mourners) for Radetich's funeral, ZODIAC was obviously trying to get as much publicity as possible by implying (subtly, granted) that he had killed the young officer.

The letter was accompanied by a folded Phillips 66 road map of California.

The map proved of little use except that it highlighted Mt. Diablo— Devil's Mountain— as something significant in ZODIAC's mind. Despite being 30 miles east of San Francisco, Mt. Diablo looms over the entire Bay Area. From this perspective the Berkeley Hills, which stand opposite San Francisco's bay, seem to cringe in the shadow of the ill-nomen peak, even though they are miles from its towering form. It is especially visible from the turnout on Lake Herman Road, where it can be seen as a shade on the horizon.

The map and its zodiac crosshair over Diablo do, however, remind one of the earlier November 9 letter which ended with a large crosshair where ZODIAC marked x's along the circle. It seems now that Diablo could have been at the center of that deadly crosshair. Aligning that crosshair to magnetic north does line up a few of the x's with ZODIAC's crime scene locations. Yet in terms of a bomb's location, the Diablo code and map lead nowhere. . . unless that unaccounted x leads to the bomb.

If these clues have any validity, they merely imply more is to come. They are little installments; little cliffhangers.

And indeed the game continued a month later on July 24, 1970. ZODIAC sent a short letter.

> This is the Zodiac speaking
>
> I am rather unhappy because you people will not wear some nice ⊕ buttons. So I now have a little list, starting with the woeman + her baby that I gave a rather interesting ride for a couple howers one evening a few months back that ended in my burning her car where I found them.

The "woeman" ZODIAC refers to is the young mother, Kathleen Johns. Months before on March 22, 1970, Johns claimed she had been abducted by the 'Zodiac' Killer on a lonely stretch of the rural two-lane road designated State Highway 132. At that time she was driving with her baby from Modesto to the I-5/580 Interstate to head north to the Bay Area. At one point a car paced her and eventually the driver got her to pull over. The driver got out and told her that her wheel was loose. He did a Good Samaritan act and tightened the lugs. She thanked him and drove off. Soon it felt as if a wheel was about to fall off. Then it did. She screeched to a stop. He stopped again and offered her and her baby a lift to the Union 76 ahead, but instead he continued on and took her on a long, frightening ride through California's center valley farm and orchard land. During this ride he told her he was going to kill her soon. She finally escaped the harrowing ordeal and somehow appeared at 2:30 a.m. before the police station in Patterson, a dusty, scant populated ranch town about 30 minutes south of Highway 132. There in the office while she recited her convoluted tale to Sgt. Charles McNatt she saw the SFPD wanted poster of ZODIAC. She cried "That's him!"

Other than an article in the *Modesto Bee*, the news story didn't get much circulation at the time it happened. Now in July there was little reason for the ZODIAC task force to believe it. The facts didn't jive with what Johns had said. They checked. When her car had been found, it had been found abandoned on Highway 132 near the I-5 overpass. The car had been torched, but no tire had fallen off. (Much later, in assessing the account, Roy Conway said: "I'm at kind of a loss as how to explain it, but I don't believe that what she described even happened, let alone that the ZODIAC did it.")

From our vantage today, we can see ZODIAC using the same publicity pattern here he had used with "Sam." He had waited 2 months to capitalize on the Caller Sam fiasco with his own letter to Mel Belli. Now ZODIAC had waited months to dovetail on the Kathleen Johns incident. He seemed to keep such news reports in mind for future use when publicity had died down.

Two days later (July 26) ZODIAC mailed a much longer letter in which he elaborates on his previous two letters. Still drumbeating on his zodiac buttons, he gives clues on how to interpret the Phillips 66 map symbol and then goes into a refrain about the little list he had mentioned in the July 24 letter. This letter, like all the others, was also postmarked San Francisco.

> This is the Zodiac speaking
>
> Being that you will not wear some nice ⊕ buttons, how about wearing some nasty ⊕ buttons. Or any type of ⊕ buttons that you can think up. If you do not wear any type of ⊕ buttons I shall (on top of every thing else) torture all 13 of my slaves that I have wateing for me in Paradice.

He continues:

> Some I shall tie over ant hills
> and watch them scream + twich
> and squirm. Others shall have
> pine splinters driven under their
> nails + then burned. Others shall
> be placed in cages + fed salt
> beef until they are gorged then
> I shall listen to their pleass
> for water and I shall laugh at
> them. Others will hang by
> their thumbs + burn in the
> sun then I will rub them down
> with deep heat to warm
> them up. Other I shall
> skin them alive + let them
> run around screaming. And
> all billiard players I shall
> have them play in a dark
> ened dungen cell with crooked

cues + Twisted Shoes.
Yes I shall have great
fun inflicting the most
delicious of pain to my

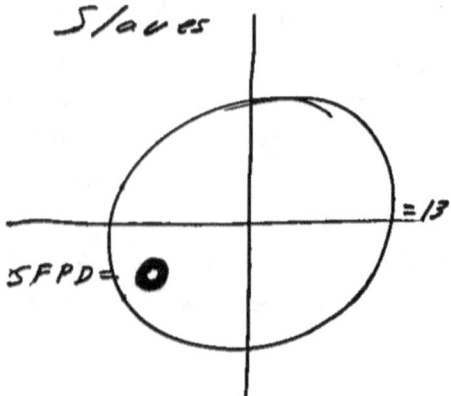

This part of the letter was yet another attempt to look as though he was but a demented, occult killer— quite a contrast to his April letters where he presented himself as a vicious punk threatening more militant attacks. Bizarre misspellings dot this letter, but "delicious" is spelled correctly.

The last lines are of most interest. "And all billiard players I shall have them play in a darkened dungen cell with crooked cues + Twisted Shoes." It's a specific type of rhyme. It echoes the refrains and the lyrics of the Executioner Ko-Ko from Gilbert & Sullivan's comic operetta *The Mikado*. And, indeed, ZODIAC now quotes the entire song. He didn't look at a libretto. He listened over and over again to the record as it clunked and whirled. This is obvious by the fact that some of his misspellings are not misspellings but his inability to pick up the accent of John Lamb Reed, the English actor who basically owned the part of Ko-Ko and sang the famous patter song in all recordings of the D'oyly Carte Theatre renditions.

Due to the length of the "little list" dissertation, it is reproduced in regular type below. Where ZODIAC strays from the original lyrics significantly, the correct lyrics will be placed in brackets.

As some day it may hapen that a victom must be found. I've got a little list. I've got a little list, of society offenders who might well be underground who would never be missed who would never be missed. There is the pestulentual nucences who whrite for autographs, all people who have flabby hands and irritating laughs. All children who are up in dates and implore you with im platt [and floor you with 'em flat]. All people who are shakeing hands shake hands like that. And all third persons who with unspoiling take thoes who insist [And all third persons who on spoiling tête-á-têtes insist]. They'd none of them be missed. They'd none of them be missed. There's the banjo seranader and the others of his race and the piano orginast I got him on the list. All people who eat pepermint and phomphit [puff it] in your face, they would never be missed They would never be missed And the Idiout who phraises with inthusastic tone of centuries but this and every country but his own. [Then the idiot who praises, with enthusiastic tone, All centuries but this, and every country but his own] And the lady from the provences who dress like a guy who doesn't cry [And the lady from the provinces, who dresses like a guy, And who "doesn't think she dances, but would rather like to try"] and the singurly abnormily the girl who never kissed. I don't think she would be missed Im shure she wouldn't be missed. [And that singular anomaly, the lady novelist — I don't think she'd be missed — I'm sure she'd not be missed] And that nice impriest that is rather rife [And that Nisi Prius nuisance, who just now is rather rife,] the judicial hummerest I've got him on the list. All funny fellows, commic men and clowns of private life. They'd none of them be missed. They'd none of them be missed. And uncompromising kind such as wachmacallit, thingmebob, and like wise, well—- nevermind, and tut tut tut tut, and whatshisname, and you know who, [And apologetic statesmen of a compromising kind, Such as — What'd'ye call him — Thing'em-bob, and likewise — Oh, Never-mind, And 'Sshs' and What's-his-name, and also You-know-who] but the task of filling up the blanks I rather leave up to you. But it really doesn't matter whom you place upon the list, for none of them be missed, none of them be missed.]

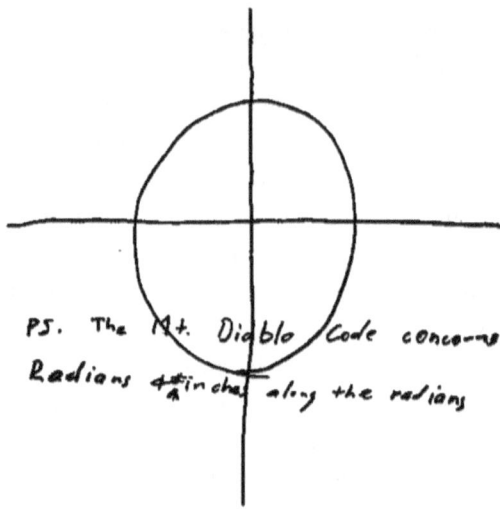

["PS. The Mt. Diablo Code concerns Radians + # inches along the radians"]

It strikes one as ironically amusing. This is some longwinded, sloppily emulated refrain from a 19th century English patter song, and then the coup de grâce is to incongruously end on bomb references with the "Diablo Code." Once again, the implication is obvious—he's a madman close to the edge.

Other than this there were few pursuable clues here, but the mention of radians was and remains intriguing. They represent an obscure mathematic calculation that is a measure of arc. It is such an arcane mathematic equation that it is used mostly by avionic designers and to calculate missile trajectories.

Added to the corpus of his previous letters, the "Little List" dissertation merely underscored ZODIAC's use of things British. "Happy Christmass" (Belli Letter) and "Blue meannie" (April 20, 1970), a term from the Beatles movie *Yellow Submarine*, could also be added to this list of words.

This was about as far as it led except for one other thing: it was obvious that this was a game of cliffhangers and installments. The Phillips map had meant nothing until ZODIAC qualified its use with the "Diablo Code" above.

SFPD wanted to try something. They asked the *Chronicle* to hold back publishing these summer (July 24 and July 26) letters.

The editor agreed. The pompous killer wanted to play a game? Then it was time to start playing.

Months went by and there were no more letters. The snickering misquoter of comic operetta had vanished again. He had vanished for months before, so there was no indication by the end of summer it was in response to not getting published anymore. But by October it must have been a source of frustration for ZODIAC that his letters had not been published by the *Chronicle*. Curiously, ZODIAC didn't go back to another newspaper like the *Examiner*, for instance, or write to the *Vallejo Times Herald* again.

Finally, on October 12, 1970, the *Chronicle* printed the July letters. Paul Avery, their crime reporter, wrote the details.

Delayed satisfaction didn't go far with ZODIAC, if he had any at all. But true to form he capitalized on the new surge in publicity. On October 30, 1970, he sent a Halloween card to Paul Avery himself. As the *Chronicle* crime writer, Avery had covered ZODIAC's sinister exploits since the beginning. It is not surprising that ZODIAC's chose a "secret admirer" card.

In terms of stock, the card came with a skeleton on the front. The stock sentiment was printed in white, quivery "spooky" letters— "FROM YOUR SECRET PAL: I feel it in my bones, You ache to know my name, And so I'll clue you in. . ." Inside the card the sentiment read: ". . .But, then, why spoil the game!" Inside, the card came with the illustration of a dead tree trunk and within the gnarled hole there was a large eye peering out— the secret admirer.

ZODIAC adjusted it with several personal touches. Over the skeleton's pelvis (on the front of the card) he pasted a paper pumpkin, for tongue-in-cheek modesty-sake one should suppose. With commendable imitative skill he drew on the inside of the card 12 more peering eyes on the tree trunk in order to create the unlucky number of 13, which was also his last supposed tally of victims. Then by the skeleton inside he wrote "4-TEEN." He then wrote "You are doomed" around the secret admirer's eye. The inference: Avery was next. He was to be Victim 14. In big letters he also wrote "Boo!"

With the threat there came yet another interesting twist. ZODIAC put a strange symbol on the envelope for the return address. He also signed the card with this strange symbol plus a Z and zodiac cross-hair.

[Halloween card illustration]

From left to right, the symbol from the envelope, the symbol as it appears inside the card, and ZODIAC's new signature.

Naturally, the card merited immediate publishing. ZODIAC's move was a hit. It got him instant publicity. Herb Caen, the *Chronicle* and San Francisco's number one columnist, even wrote a piece. Soon the Halloween card threat to Avery earned worldwide attention. It was the stuff of some old fiction thriller. The reporter who had hounded the trail of a crazed killer had now been targeted.

From the *Chronicle*'s summer silence, ZODIAC must have deduced that threats against the metropolis weren't going to merit quick publication anymore. A threat against an individual who didn't mind the recognition, however, was another matter.

The enormous publicity also inspired some unusual humor.

Employees of the *Chronicle* wore pins reading "I am not Avery." The back of the Halloween card carried a cryptic message:

—Four methods by which ZODIAC was claiming he would kill or had killed. He had already killed by gun and by knife. Who was to be strangled or burnt?— ostensibly the next victims.

The Bay Area was right back to the summer of '69 now. The maniac was still talking about slaves and "paradice." Somehow he seemed so much more real again and potentially capable of coming back and starting all over, perhaps even recycling repeatedly these 4 ways to murder.

The publicity boost was enormous, of course. But although the ZODIAC had set it in motion, he could not have foreseen how it would escalate and merit world news. Nor could he have known that his card would fit into a chain of events that would provoke an adamant and anonymous writer to contact Paul Avery and tell him of a cold case. What would transpire would convince Avery, the *Chronicle*, and SFPD that ZODIAC *had* actually killed long before and truly did have undisclosed victims.

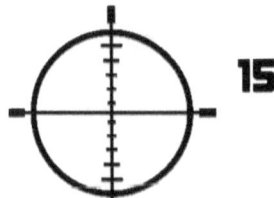# 15

SOUTHERN EXPOSURE

IT WAS A SAVAGE CRIME. IT WAS A PUBLIC CRIME. IT WAS THE TYPE OF crime that was unnerving for a whole community. The victim was a pretty 18 year old college coed at Riverside City College in the San Bernardino Valley town of Riverside. She had been brutally, maniacally stabbed in a vicious frenzy of hate. Disturbing as this was for this quiet college community, it was made worse by the fact she was actually murdered on campus. Moreover, a certain clue sent a chill up the spine. It pointed to heinous premeditation.

The date was October 30, 1966, the day before Halloween. Cheri Jo Bates had been in the campus library that Sunday night. (For students the library remained open late on Sundays.) After she left (perhaps around 6:30 p.m.), she was not seen again until early next morning when the groundsman came across her savaged body. It lay in a dirt driveway between two old wood frame houses next to the library. She lay face down in a dried pool of her own blood.

When detectives arrived the scene shocked them. Cheri had been stabbed several times, her throat deeply cut. It wasn't a sudden death. She had put up a hell of a fight. The ground around her was churned during the struggle. In her struggle she had ripped off her killer's Timex wristwatch. Some of his brown hairs were clutched in her left hand.

Soon the police found Cheri's lime green Volkswagen parked just where she had left it on Terracina Drive by the library. Inspecting it revealed the premeditated nature of the predator. Her car battery was dead. The central coil on her distributor had been removed. As she had turned the car over and over the night before to go home, the battery continued to drain.

The killer must have been waiting in the dark shadows. As the engine hoarsely groaned, he stepped forth and offered her a ride or a phone. They walked down Terracina about 200 feet and then up the dirt driveway between two old wood porch houses. They were abandoned and slated for demolition because the college was taking over the land. Behind them the college was already expanding with a new parking lot. Then, in the seclusion of the area, in the darkness by the ivy laden fences, he ferociously struck. He used a small short-bladed knife no more than 3 and ½ inches long. Her arms, chest and face had been sliced as she defended herself in the ensuing battle. Finally, a cut to her right carotid artery spelled doom for her. She collapsed. In a rage, he still swung at her, plunging the knife into her back. He left her there, her hair frazzled, her delicate pink outfit soiled with dirt and dried leaves.

Aside from the Timex (which fit a 7 inch wrist), there was one other significant clue: a heel print. It would be traced to Leavenworth prison. The inmates made shoes for military personnel. The size of the heel indicated a 7-10 size foot. The only military base nearby was March Air Force Base.

From the evidence, the deduction of Riverside Police detectives was that the killer had intentionally waylaid the coed in order to lead her to the quiet and secluded driveway to murder her.

Such a premeditated and vicious crime plagued Riverside. About 50 students dropped from night classes. Special lights were installed on campus. Parents forbade coeds to go to the college at night.

No leads had panned out by November 29, 1966, when a strange envelope was mailed to the Homicide Division of Riverside PD. The post office pulled it because it didn't have a stamp. Another had gotten through and arrived at the local newspaper, the *Press Enterprise*. The writer was fastidious in a tongue-in-cheek way. It bore the annotation— "Attn: Crime."

Bates' gruesome murder became quite complicated when the police opened the envelope. Therein was a confession letter. Typed all in CAPS, yet the letters were blurred. The writer was quite sophisticated in how he disguised the typewriter he had used. In order to have created the final product he had placed several sheets of carbon paper between a few pieces of regular paper. He typed the letter on the top piece of paper and then sent in the 4th or 5th sheet of paper that had been under the several sheets of carbon paper. The result was that he had effectively concealed the typewriter that had been used. He covered his bases.

BY

SHE WAS YOUNG AND BEAUTIFUL BUT NOW SHE IS BATTERED AND DEAD. SHE IS NOT THE FIRST AND SHE WILL NOT BE THE LAST I LAY AWAKE NIGHTS THINKING ABOUT MY NEXT VICTIM. MAYBE SHE WILL BE THE BEAUTIFUL BLOND THAT BABYSITS NEAR THE LITTLE STORE AND WALKS DOWN THE DARK ALLEY EACH EVENING ABOUT SEVEN. OR MAYBE SHE WILL BE THE SHAPELY BLUE EYED BROWNETT THAT SAID NO WHEN I ASKED HER FOR A DATE IN HIGH SCHOOL. BUT MAYBE IT WILL NOT BE EITHER. BUT I SHALL CUT OFF HER FEMALE PARTS AND DEPOSIT THEM FOR THE WHOLE CITY TO SEE. SO DON'T MAKE IT TO EASY FOR ME. KEEP YOUR SISTERS, DAUGHTERS, AND WIVES OFF THE STREETS AND ALLEYS. MISS BATES WAS STUPID. SHE WENT TO THE SLAUGHTER LIKE A LAMB. SHE DID NOT PUT UP A STRUGGLE. BUT I DID. IT WAS A BALL. I FIRST PULLED THE MIDDLE WIRE FROM THE DISTRIBUTOR. THEN I WAITED FOR HER IN THE LIBRARY AND FOLLOWED HER OUT AFTER ABOUT TWO MINUTS. THE BATTERY MUST HAVE BEEN ABOUT DEAD BY THEN. I THEN OFFERED TO HELP. SHE WAS THEN VERY WILLING TO TALK TO ME. I TOLD HER THAT MY CAR WAS DOWN THE STREET AND THAT I WOULD GIVE HER A LIFT HOME. WHEN WE WERE AWAY FROM THE LIBRARY WALKING, I SAID IT WAS ABOUT TIME. SHE ASKED ME "ABOUT TIME FOR WHAT". I SAID IT WAS ABOUT TIME FOR HER TO DIE. I GRABBED HER AROUND THE NECK WITH MY HAND OVER HER MOUTH AND MY OTHER HAND WITH A SMALL KNIFE AT HER THROAT. SHE WENT VERY WILLINGLY. HER BREAST FELT VERY WARM AND FIRM UNDER MY HANDS, BUT ONLY ONE THING WAS ON MY MIND. MAKING HER PAY FOR THE BRUSH OFFS THAT SHE HAD GIVEN ME DURING THE YEARS PRIOR. SHE DIED HARD. SHE SQUIRMED AND SHOOK AS I CHOAKED HER, AND

HER LIPS TWICHED. SHE LET OUT A SCREAM ONCE AND I KICKED HER HEAD TO SHUT HER UP. I PLUNGED THE KNIFE INTO HER AND IT BROKE. I THEN FINISHED THE JOB BY CUTTING HER THROAT. I AM NOT SICK. I AM INSANE. BUT THAT WILL NOT STOP THE GAME. THIS LETTER SHOULD BE PUBLISHED FOR ALL TO READ IT. IT JUST MIGHT SAVE THAT GIRL IN THE ALLEY. BUT THAT'S UP TO YOU. IT WILL BE ON YOUR CONSCIENCE. NOT MINE. YES, I DID MAKE THAT CALL TO YOU ALSO. IT WAS JUST A WARNING. BEWARE...I AM STALKING YOUR GIRLS NOW.

CC. CHIEF OF POLICE
ENTERPRISE

Because the writer knew the central coil had been removed, information which had not been publically released, the police accepted this sick confession letter as genuine. This is not to say they believed everything in it. Much of the confession strikes one as being a red herring and some is even blatantly wrong. Bates had obviously put up an enormous struggle. Furthermore, it is impossible to hold and strangle someone with one hand and hold a knife with the other. It is equally impossible while doing so to fondle her breasts. On one hand he presents himself as a random homicidal nutcase; on the other he makes it look as if he knew Bates and sought personal revenge for some past slight.

Time would convince the Riverside Police it was the latter. There was no subsequent murder spree of young women. The killer was not a homicidal maniac— QED Riverside Police came to suspect a jilted boyfriend. Two girls had said they heard Cheri say she was going to the library to meet her boyfriend. But police confirmed he was at college in San Francisco at the time. Had she said former boyfriend? Several points came together to finally convince Riverside's detectives that an ex-boyfriend was her killer.

Also, given the circumstances, it seemed absurd to think a stranger could premeditate a crime like this. He would have to be somewhere on campus when Bates arrived in order to associate her with that beetle. Furthermore, pulling the distributor coil presupposes he could foresee only he, and no other student, would be around to render her assistance when her car didn't start.

Witnesses had proven that Bates had parked before the library at 5:40 p.m. and waited 20 minutes for it to open at 6 p.m. She checked out two books, and after 6:30 p.m. no witness could remember seeing her there. The library closed at 9 p.m. Two screams, the second being muted, were heard around 10:30 p.m. by a resident near one of the abandoned houses. The police fixed this roughly as the time of Cheri's murder. This fit with the pathologist's report. At 9:23 a.m. the next morning while examining her body, Dr. Rene Modglin estimated she had been dead 9 to 12 hours; thus no earlier than 9:30 p.m. the night before. Stomach contents indicated she had eaten her dinner some 2 to 4 hours previous.

Friends confirmed she was afraid of the dark. She would never have walked between those dark, abandoned houses with a stranger. Currently in San Francisco her boyfriend confirmed she was fastidious about her beetle. Yet it had been found unlocked, keys in ignition and windows down. It didn't sound as if she thought she would be gone long.

Put together none of the above made sense if a stranger had done this. She obviously went somewhere with someone for hours and then returned after the library was closed. It is now, presumably, she turned over her car and it wouldn't start. Did her date then leave? Did a stranger step forward from the dark? Or did the one who dropped her off seize the opportunity? If the former, why didn't the date come forward and clarify? Yet if it was her date, why would they walk up the driveway now?

As time went by, Riverside PD was hesitant to announce let alone elaborate on the fact they had a prime suspect in the ex-beau. But time and the confusing evidence also brought disagreements. In 1968, the case merited a 6 page article in *Inside Detective* magazine. There was division in the Homicide bureau whether the confession letter was real. Evidence was also presented to the public indicating the killer could have been a stranger.

For instance, in true Agatha Christie fashion, Riverside PD had reenacted the night's events. They had determined that 65 people had used the library during the 3 hours it was open. They had them return, wear the same clothes, park in the same locations. It was determined that a heavyset young man with a beard, probably driving a

1947-1952 Studebaker with faded gray/oxidized paint, hadn't returned. Also, over a hundred servicemen from March Field attended classes at the college. That heel was to a military shoe. It was determined that the Timex had been purchased at a base overseas.

Blood drops had formed a trail back to the street, indicating the killer walked back to the street afterward. A couple of minutes after the screams an older car was heard to start up. It sounds as if her killer had merely baited her up to the houses to offer a phone.

None of the above sounded like an ex-boyfriend, and she would know he didn't dorm on campus.

Still, no stranger could be made to fit. And active duty Air Force men are not allowed to wear beards. The heavyset young man and his old car fade away. Despite the evidence indicating a stranger, detectives still preferred the jilted boyfriend.

Riverside PD had boasted it never had an unsolved murder. By 1969, to their chagrin, they had to admit the murder was still unsolved. They couldn't get the goods on the jilted boyfriend, and it seems the Chief of Police, Thomas Kinkead, was beginning to wonder if they were wrong. He had heard about the Lake Berryessa stabbing committed by ZODIAC. He thought there could be a similarity. It really wasn't the stabbing per se. It was the fact that ZODIAC sent in boasting and taunting confession letters just like the Bates killer had done. Kinkead called and then wrote Napa Co. Sheriff Earl Randol, informing him of the Bates case.

Randol didn't follow through. It just didn't seem quite like ZODIAC. Cranks and killers equally can write similar confession letters, but the circumstances of the crime weren't suggestive at all of ZODIAC's *modus operandi*.

However, the international publicity centered on Paul Avery and the ZODIAC's Halloween card threat motivated a mysterious informant to send a letter to Avery, encouraging him to look into the Bates murder. He noted that the murder had also occurred near Halloween, a significant occult holiday. The anonymous correspondent wrote that he had been brushed-off repeatedly by the Riverside PD, when suggesting a ZODIAC connection.

As a matter of routine follow-up, Avery called Riverside PD and spoke with Captain Irv Cross, the lead detective on the case. Cross agreed to send him an information packet. By November 9, Avery had it. Amongst the information Cross had sent there was a photo of a note on basic lined notebook paper. It had been sent to the police on April 30, 1967, a full 6 months *after* the murder. Written in pencil, the short note was typical of cranks.

BATES HAD TO DiE
THERE WILL Be MORE

The penciled note was written mostly in CAPS, and it seemed as if the writer had held the pencil high up in order to make childlike scribblings. At a contrast to this crude penmanship the note was "signed" by a small little letter at the bottom. This was written elegantly, almost like calligraphy. Avery pondered over it. It looked like a "z." He quickly left for Riverside to pursue a potentially exciting angle in the ZODIAC case.

Depending on how you look at it, Irv Cross either sent too much or didn't send enough information. Although also a licensed PI, Avery was at heart a journalist. He was electrified by the prospects of a story and not a case. He thumbed through Riverside PD's files (he was indeed allowed to) and in there quickly discovered the note for which he had seen a photo. It was, in fact, one of 3 that had been sent. Aside from the PD getting one, the *Press Enterprise* and Cheri's father received one. They were all similar. Two of the notes carried the elegant letter. For a newspaperman like Avery this was a good lead. He opted to believe they represented the letter "z."

Irv Cross cautioned him that these cruel notes had been sent after the *Press Enterprise* had done a big 6 month anniversary story on the Bates killing, which usually opens the door for erratic minds.

Avery read more into it than Cross. The envelope writing looked similar, more so than the writing inside, to ZODIAC's printing, and Avery had seen all of his letters, of course, as they had come into the *Chronicle*. This was looking good, very good to Avery. Then Avery came upon a photo in the file that sealed it for him. It was a photo of writing on one of the college's library desktops. Cross informed him it was classified as the "morbid poem." He then clarified it was written with a blue ballpoint pen. When found in the library sometime in December 1966 the entire desk was removed to the storage room. However, *when* the "poem" had been written no one knew.

> Sick of living/unwilling to die
>
> cut.
> clean,
> if red/
> clean.
> blood spurting,
> dripping,
> spilling;
> all over her new
> dress,
> oh well,
> it was red
> anyway.
> life draining into an
> uncertain death.
> she won't
> die,
> this time
> Someone'll find her.
> Just wait till
> next time.
>
>   rh

R.H.? Were they the "morbid" poet's initials? Was this poem inspired by Cheri Jo's murder? Or was it written before? The morbid poem says she won't die this time. Is this the killer writing this, and Cheri was to be the "next time"?

To Avery, this printing suggested ZODIAC's hand the most; enough so that he got photocopies and headed straight to Sacramento where he had Sherwood Morrill, head of Questioned Documents Section, Criminal Investigations & Identification, standing by.

From the autumn of angst, Morrill had played a very publicized role since all persons of interest's handwriting had been sent to him for his judgment whether they matched ZODIAC's. Yet Morrill hesitated over the Riverside material. It was hard to make a connection between the poem and the content of the 3 letters. He wouldn't be persuaded. However, the writing on the envelopes was more intriguing. For him, this too suggested ZODIAC's writing the most, and this printing he then felt matched the poem found on the desktop. After hours of examining them he became convinced that ZODIAC had indeed written those three nasty notes on April 30, 1967, and the desktop poem at some undisclosed time.

For Paul Avery this was dynamite. The poem was worth more than the 3 nasty notes. It meant more than uncovering a link to Riverside town. It meant he had uncovered a *solid* connection between the anonymous psychopath ZODIAC and Riverside College. This was the clue, he was sure, that would finally out the "Boastful Slayer."

Avery broke the story for the *Chronicle* on November 16, 1970, and then the next day declared the link "definite" in a follow-up article. The response was enormous. Brows raised. Jaws dropped. Riverside PD balked. Irv Cross was certain they knew who the killer was. He conceded that maybe the ZODIAC wrote the nasty notes of April 1967 as some thrill by proxy, but he was *not* the killer.

Maybe so, but there was still enough motivation for Mel Nicolai, also of the California Department of Justice Criminal Investigation & Identification Bureau, Napa's Ken Narlow, and SFPD's Dave Toschi, to head down to Riverside two days later to meet with Irv Cross and detective Dave Bonine to exchange information.

According to Avery, the trio came from the meeting in general agreement that ZODIAC had a connection to Riverside despite Riverside PD's protestations there was no connection to the commission of the murder. Years later Toschi would go so far as to say that Riverside's detectives played everything close to the vest. We can guess why. In his November 19 article, Avery writes: "Now Cross says, he isn't so sure about the youth's guilt." Cross may have given this appearance, but he and Bonine more likely felt that ZODIAC had truly etched that "morbid poem" on the desktop. Therefore even if they didn't believe he was Bates' killer, they believed they had a solid link they could follow to solve the famous case themselves. (Morrill later admitted Irv Cross had given him 6,000 student registration cards to examine in an attempt to find ZODIAC's penmanship.)

However, Irv Cross obviously never made a connection between any student and ZODIAC. And, logistically, it seems none of the northern California investigators could investigate the student body on their own to find someone who matched the ZODIAC stats and sketches. The question of ZODIAC's level of connection to this crime, if any, therefore remains open.

Evidence supports both sides, and for argument's sake it should be noted. To maintain chronicity, we will limit ourselves here to the contemporary arguments. We will have to revisit Riverside later.

On Avery's side was the original typed confession letter. The confession letter structure evoked ZODIAC's contradictory and at times taunting tenor. The tongue-in-cheek sarcasm was obvious in the "By-----" and then the blank line— so essentially "guess." The formal "CC" at the bottom was equally sarcastic. The simple sentence structure and lack of periods at obvious ends of sentences were also similar. There were some unusual misspellings and yet some words like "conscience" spelled correctly; "twiched" was misspelled exactly as ZODIAC had misspelled it. It also took a month for the confession writer to get this mailed, and Z very often took his time.

The similarities between the penmanship of the 3 notes to ZODIAC's overall style remain disturbing. The writer also evolved his style as he wrote, just like the ZODIAC had shown in his first 3 simultaneous confession letters to Bay Area newspapers. First was the note to Bates' father. This note was written with a mixture of capitals and regular letters. In the note he sent to the police, all letters were capitals but 2 letters— the "e" in "Be" and the "i" in Die." The "M" was exactly like ZODIAC. The final note (to the *Press Enterprise*) was written in all capitals. As the writer wrote the notes, the evolution is obvious.

Two of the notes had that strange symbol at the bottom, but not the first to Bates' father. The writer evolved even with his signature. Avery ran with the interpretation they were a "z." In fact, they are not. They almost have the quality of calligraphy, and are closer to the style of a witch's rune, alchemic symbol, or Coptic letter than a letter of the Roman alphabet. While this does not imply Z for the ZODIAC, the 'Zodiac' Killer was capable of very neat calligraphy and unique imitation. He also presented an interest in the occult.

In addition to the above similarities, the envelopes with the nasty notes had double 4¢ postage on them. ZODIAC sometimes sent envelopes with two stamps on them. Postage for a letter was 5¢, so it should be said that doubling postage was commonplace.

Also squarely in Avery's corner was the fact ZODIAC had worn Air Force "Wing Walker" shoes at Lake Berryessa. The heel print by Bates' body was also from a military shoe, in this case a low cut shoe. The closest military base to Riverside was March Field, also an Air Force base. According to *Inside Detective* (January 1968), the Timex watch had been bought at an overseas base.

The biggest thing on Avery's side, of course, is the fact that Sherwood Morrill himself had identified the envelopes of those 3 cruel notes as having been written by ZODIAC and by the same person who had written the "morbid poem" on the desktop.

But to Irv Cross and Riverside PD there was (eventually) no brick and mortar connection to Riverside City College; any connection to Riverside town didn't necessarily go beyond mailing the nasty notes there. This is not a tangible connection to the crime. ZODIAC wore 10.5 Regular at Lake Berryessa, a larger shoe size than Bates' killer. And the details of the crime didn't fit with a stranger.

Cross' theory was that the killer and the confession writer went together. In favor of this theory is the fact that the writer knew the central coil had been removed on the bug's distributor. Double postage on the envelopes of the 3 nasty notes was at a stark contrast to the envelopes of the typed confession letter, which the writer had not stamped. Cross therefore drew a clear circle around the murder and the confession letter, one that excluded the nasty notes of 6 months later.

What it comes down to is this: Riverside PD believed they knew who did it, and it wasn't ZODIAC.

It is not just Riverside PD's stalled investigation that explains why they would fail to bury the controversy. Lo and behold, a few months after Paul Avery's articles included Bates as a ZODIAC victim, the bona fide 'Zodiac' Killer followed his pattern to dovetail on a publicity surge in order to reignite it. On March 13, 1971, he sent a letter to the *Los Angeles Times*. The envelope bore double postage. It also contained the usual "Please Rush to Editor." This time ZODIAC wrote "Air Mail" on front and back in big letters. At a blunt contrast, he had mailed it from Pleasanton, a town south of the Vallejo area in the Contra Costa corridor. In it he declared:

> This is the Zodiac speaking
> Like I have allways said,
> I am crack proof. If the
> Blue Meannies are evere
> going to catch me, they had
> best get off their fat asses
> + do something. Because the
> longer they fiddle + fart
> around, the more slaves
> I will collect for my after
> life. I do have to give them
> credit for stumbling across
> my riverside activity, but
> they are only finding the
> easy ones, there are a hell
> of a lot more down there.
> The reason I'm writing
> to the Times is this, They
> don't bury me on the back pages
> like some of the others.
>
> SFPD—o ⊕ -17+

Seventeen plus— the 17 being those in the Bay Area and the "plus" being an undisclosed number he had killed prior in southern California . . . ostensibly; his inference anyway.

The letter had the effect ZODIAC intended. Now past unsolved murders in southern California became suspect. A whole new ZODIAC publicity glut ensued fostered by the ambiguities in the Bates murder.

Over the past year and a half, with each new letter, ZODIAC had decreased his bragging credibility. Therefore there is no real reason to accept he is the Bates killer merely because he took credit. Taking false credit fit his 1970 pattern to steal publicity. However, there was something about the idea that ZODIAC had killed before that strikes a chord, the resonance remaining constant to this day.

Instinct is very powerful. It sets in motion intuition. Intuition is the product of synthesis— of many facts coming together but not quickly coalescing into a solid deduction. There is something about the Lake Herman Road murders that suggest ZODIAC was not a beginner. He didn't necessarily ever carry off any of his murders without a glitch, but he had remained cool enough to shoot Jensen 5 times in the back, in a "remarkable grouping," after he had coldbloodedly dispatched Faraday pointblank to the head. There should be no doubt that ZODIAC came fully prepared to kill that night. He had even affixed a small pencil flashlight to his deadly .22 small game pistol and already knew how to use it at night when aiming.

Ambiguities were such in the Riverside case that there were reasons to doubt it as an authentic ZODIAC case. Another jurisdiction, however, was far more certain about one of their cases. Santa Barbara County sheriffs had a double murder that had continued to puzzle them. On June 4, 1963, a Lompoc High School couple had been viciously gunned down at a remote spot on the beach at Gaviota, north of Santa Barbara. It was a rural area on the coast, but a place at the bottom of a well-known game trail that led from Highway 101 to the beach. Fishermen and couples often used the spot.

Over time a rough parking area had developed on the highway, in an open area amidst a grove of trees. People would then cross the highway, the railroad tracks, and then head down to the beach along the well-trodden and sometimes steep game trail. It followed the inside edge of the canyon and at last ended at the beach near the mouth of the canyon. Down the center of the canyon a creek trickled into the booming breakers of the Pacific. A large bed of river rocks fanned out at the canyon mouth, made smooth over the years by the caress of the small creek's lazy current to the sea. In the shadow of the limestone cliffs driftwood littered the beach.

Embracing the open beach area was the rugged allure of a desert island. The canyon mouth was wide enough so that a fertile area under sycamores and other deciduous trees could be used as a rustic campsite. An impromptu but sturdy shack had been made here from various parts that had been discarded.

The point is made: it was a rural area. It was commonly known to the locals. The parked cars were easily spotted by anyone passing on the two-lane scenic highway.

The penmanship of the note writer (top) and confession writer (cntr) compared to ZODIAC's penmanship (bottom) on the envelope to the LA Times.

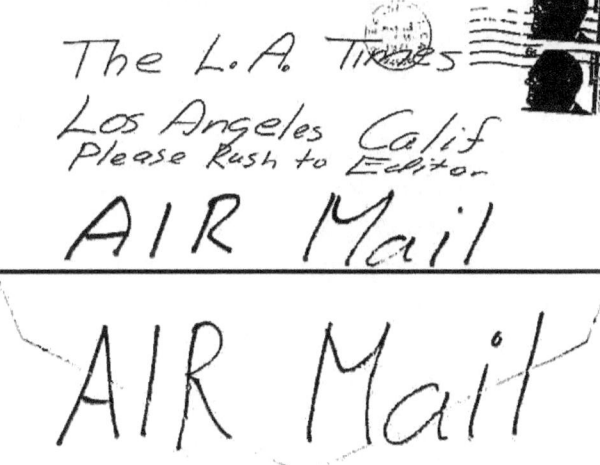

The coincidence to Lake Berryessa, however, does not stop there. The couple, Bobby Domingos and his fiancée Linda Edwards, had relaxed on their beach towel near the sandy mouth of the canyon. At one point, their assailant appeared. By all accounts he had tried to bind them. There had been a struggle in which Bobby had received a fat lip. The bounds had loosened (or never had fully been tied), and the couple then broke and ran. Their assailant gave chase. From the evidence Bobby ran behind Linda, trying to act as a shield. He was shot 11 times. Linda was taken down by a shot to the leg. Then she was pumped with 8 more rounds.

The gun used had been a .22 caliber automatic. Like a J.C. Higgins it must have carried a 10 round clip. The killer had fired 20 rounds in his rage. This means he had to stop to reload quickly. Since Bobby had 11 rounds in him, it is unlikely that the killer shot him 10 times first, stood over and reloaded, fired one shot, and then proceeded to hunt Linda in the jungle island-like underwood of the canyon. Rather it seems he unloaded the first clip into both of them and then reloaded and went back and stood over each one and pumped them full of more holes to make sure they were dead.

Ruthless. Vicious. Sadistic.

Tucking his gun into his belt, the killer then dragged Bobby's body over one of the trodden paths that led to the lean-to and placed him inside. Then he went and dragged Linda's body and placed her on top of Bobby. The assailant then appears to have attempted to set the lean-to on fire. Since there was only one way out of the canyon back to the highway (the long game path back up to the railroad tracks), the assailant must have left quickly before the plume of smoke would rise up and drift over the highway alerting motorists. Instead, it fizzled. He must have been too far up the lip of the canyon to do anything about it. He left in whatever car he had arrived, leaving Bobby's distinctive black and pink 1955 Chevrolet alone in the dirt parking area.

When the couple did not return that night a manhunt was initiated that finally uncovered the car sitting in the darkness off the highway. Lee Gnesa, Bobby's friend, led a highway patrolman down to the canyon. They stood back and waited while the highway patrolman cautiously walked up one of the paths in the underwood. His flashlight beam coasted about and into view came the shack.

The smell of scorched timber filled the air. He looked inside and saw their bodies.

Santa Barbara sheriffs made no headway with this case. Everything stopped at the local suspicion that Bobby's older brother Frank had for some reason followed them there and gunned down his very popular brother and future sister-in-law. Yet that led nowhere either.

Now in 1971, in the wake of ZODIAC's claim, the newly assigned detective to this cold case began to wonder. His name was Bill Baker. He hadn't had the case long, but he had studied it enough to know it came down to this: it had to be someone who knew the spot was frequented by young couples. He had come with rope (or clothesline) ready to bind victims. Baker had a lot of curious clues before him, but only now in comparing the case with the ZODIAC's Bay Area murders did the clues make sense.

For instance, Jensen and Faraday had been murdered with a .22 caliber, and Baker had found that the exact same ammo Super X had been used in both murders. In that case the pistol also carried a 10 round clip. ZODIAC vengefully shot down Jensen as she ran away, scoring 5 hits. At Lake Berryessa he had bound the victims. All crimes, once again, were in rural areas, but main rural areas like the coastline off Highway 101. They were known lovers' lanes and small game hunting and fishing spots.

In addition, Baker also had the copy of the Halloween card that ZODIAC had sent to Paul Avery. On the cross of "Slaves" and "Paradice" the tasteless maniac had declared his 4 methods of murder— By Gun, By Rope, By Knife, By Fire. The Domingos/Edwards case certainly carried three of those elements.

On top of it all there's that gut instinct. When Baker sent a statewide teletype asking for similar cases, both Mel Nicolai and Bill Armstrong responded, giving more particulars and agreeing there appears more than one similarity to their cases.

The one dissimilarity is that Bobby and Linda were murdered on a Monday and during the day and not on the weekend. But 5 years is a long time. ZODIAC's work circumstance could have changed. The general similarities remained— there was even a military base nearby, like in Riverside, and this was Vandenberg Air Force Base.

Another weekday double murder of a young couple along the southern California coast popped up from the cold case files, this having been committed on Wednesday February 5, 1964, only 8 months after the Gaviota murders. This was a strange span. After ZODIAC's first Vallejo strike, he had waited a similar time to strike again—6 months and 15 days.

There is a constant whoosh in your ears from the sizzle of the sea and its breakers. Like all beach sections of San Diego, Ocean Beach is quiet and laidback. Streets cross each other in a grid, crowded with bungalows, apartments, houses, motels, and small shops; all end at the beach. Here there is open space. New buildings are going up. The boardwalk along the beach eventually wends around nearby cliffs. Here the boom and roll of the surf echoes up from the cement seawall, up the ice plant covered ridge to Narragansett Avenue, crowned by silhouettes of apartments and homes beyond a wood railing marking the end of the street.

It is between 8 and 8:30 p.m. The boardwalk has a wide area known as the "patio." Here a loving couple snuggles. The young man is in his Navy jumper, the blonde girl in a leather jacket and plaid capris. By them on the ledge of the cement seawall is a Whitman's candy box— an early Valentine gift for his beloved.

Fifty feet up the ridge behind them stands a man by the wooden railing and traffic sign. It reads "Dead End." Cement stairs lead down to the boardwalk. He takes them a short way down and then stands upon a cement retaining wall. Over his right shoulder in the distance the streetlamps of Ocean Beach are dull pearls in the night's hazy moisture, strung out in crisscrossing lines. He watches the couple cuddle below. He raises a pistol and aims.

The Navy man's head burns. The girl he cuddles collapses

against him, her left upper back burning as well. Then his left thigh went tight and burned. Her left arm stung. Both collapse.

The figure atop the slope strides down the stairs and stands over them. She is lying face down. He fires a round into the back of her head. The Navy man is on his right side, next to the wall. The killer stands over him and puts a bullet into his head near his left ear. He pockets his automatic pistol and walks away.

Minutes later a resident, Ed Nelson, approaches along the boardwalk. The time is about 8:35 p.m. He sees the figures. Shadows in the dark, he thought they had been drinking and passed out. He directs his flashlight beam and sees the pools of blood around them. The man was moaning inarticulacy. Ed Nelson rushed to get the police.

The girl was dead, but the man was rushed to the hospital where he died a few hours later.

The victims were Johnny Ray Swindle and his new wife Joyce. They had been childhood sweethearts in Jasper, Alabama. During furlough he went back and married her on January 18. They drove back out to San Diego and had been living here for only a week in a bungalow 9 blocks away. They were a quiet couple, but they had one habit. Joyce was fascinated by the sea, so each night they went for a stroll along the beach. Each night they passed the same hamburger stand, got coffee, and walked along the boardwalk. (Johnny had bought the Valentine box of candy at a local shop only 30 minutes before they had been shot.)

The San Diego PD detective, O.J. Roed, quickly came to the conclusion that a "psychopathic killer" was responsible, one who knew the area was a popular petting spot.

A thorough police investigation quickly discovered the area had been as busy as Piccadilly between 8 and 8:30 p.m. A couple had been "parking" at the end of Niagara Street, one street over from Narragansett. Another couple had been "parking" in a car lot a street north of this (Newport Street.). A man had been standing on the rocks of the tide pools just south of the "patio." A couple was walking north on the beach. A man was walking on Narragansett. Another man had been running on Del Monte, one street south of Narragansett, at 8:16 p.m.; something in his hand.

The killer was obviously a good shot with good nighttime vision.

He had used a .22 caliber, and from 50 feet up the ridge he went for the head or heart and hit or came close each time. The police had quickly found the 5 shining brass shells where he had stood; and two, of course, had been found by the bodies, where he killer had stood and delivered what the papers called the "coup de grace."

It wasn't long before Santa Barbara Co. sheriff detectives arrived. There was immediate suspicion that the killer of Domingos and Edwards was responsible here. However, ballistics didn't match—it was not the same .22 automatic that had gunned down Bobby and Linda. But it was the same *type* of gun.

There is one thing the Swindle killer realized he could do just by shooting a couple. He could send ripples of panic through a city. San Diego PD Chief Wesley Sharp added many more uniformed officers to patrol Ocean Beach and to perch on rooftops. Warnings went up throughout the district to be prepared for the "sniper slayer." It was a brief but strange foreshadow of what the ZODIAC would intentionally do 5 years later with the entire Bay Area.

In retrospect these two double murders do not stand separate from an earlier murder in Oceanside. It happened on April 11, 1962. Late that night cabbie Ray Davis took a fare to South Pacific Street, the main beachfront road. Whoever the fare was, he shot Davis in the head and back with a .22 caliber and then dumped his body in a POSH neighborhood, the alley behind the then-current mayor of Oceanside and the former mayor. He parked the cab much further up South Pacific in the 400 block before escaping on foot.

This murder was not spontaneous. The killer had wanted to send the entire community into a panic. We know this for certain. Two days before on April 9, he had called the police and said: "I am going to pull something here in Oceanside and you will never be able to figure it out . . ." or words to such an effect. It was dismissed as a crank call. However, a week after the murder the same voice called again. He declared: "Do you remember me calling you last week and telling you that I was going to pull a real baffling crime? I killed the cab driver and I am going to get me a bus driver next."

Oceanside went into an alert. Marines from nearby Camp Pendleton assisted in guarding bus stations and scanning passengers for weapons before they boarded. Two bus drivers were put aboard the buses, just in case. Marshals rode shotgun.

The boast proved to be hollow. No attacks ever occurred against a bus. But by having killed a cab driver, the taunting caller's threat had carried weight.

There should be no doubt the killer used an automatic pistol. A stray bullet hole was in the cab windshield. With the killer seated behind the driver, apparently after the first shot the kick of the gun caused him to squeeze off another round. Since Davis had immediately slumped over the wheel after the first shot, there was nothing to hinder the second bullet from going through the windshield.

The killer got out and put another bullet in Davis's head to make sure he was dead— the "coup de grace" that would soon be seen in the other couples murders.

Chronologically, we thus have a beginner in 1962, two couples' murders thereafter, a dearth for 4 years, and then another couples' murder by .22 caliber on Lake Herman Road in 1968. These southern California murders are essentially the ZODIAC's crime spree inverted, and the Lake Herman Road murders are a strange segue-way into the "Zodiac Murders" of northern California.

More of a connection would be made between ZODIAC and the Gaviota slayings because of events that would soon unfold.

In 1972, Santa Barbara County Sheriff John Carpenter and detective Bill Baker held a TV news conference. Carpenter had issued a formal statement in which he declared that ZODIAC *was* responsible for the 1963 double murder of Domingos and Edwards. In this concisely written statement, Carpenter declared:

*** PRESS RELEASE ***

In response to inquiries that I have received into the recent investigation into the 1963 murders of Linda EDWARDS and Robert DOMINGOS, I would like to make the following announcement:

In June 1963 a young couple was found shot to death near an isolated stretch of beach, north of Santa Barbara. The victims, both Lompoc high school students, had been shot numerous times and their bodies placed in a small lean-to shack a short distance from the beach. An intensive investigation by sheriff detectives failed to reach a successful solution to the killings. Although the case was never closed, no substantial leads were developed. Over a year ago, Sheriff's detectives began a thorough study of the case, examining and re-evaluating all aspects of the crime. A recent development has provided information that appears somewhat promising. Considerable evidence points to the murders of Linda EDWARDS and Robert DOMINGOS as being the work of the infamous ZODIAC. Although the anticipated response to this statement would be one of skepticism, let me say that we do not make this assertion frivolously. Many hundreds of hours, over the past several months, have been spent compiling information concerning the possibility that this man could have been responsible for the killings in 1963. Sheriff's detectives have met with those investigators from those areas where ZODIAC has, admittedly, been responsible for several murders. These agencies have conducted intensive investigations for the last several years in an effort to identify ZODIAC. After conferring with officers in these other jurisdictions, we have found that there appears to be a high degree of probability that this subject is responsible for the double murder in our County. Several significant similarities between our case and the others, as well as other evidence that I am not at liberty to disclose at this time, all tend to connect ZODIAC with this crime. In addition, we have evidence, to be investigated further, which may place him in the Santa Barbara area in 1963.

The last sentence is phenomenal. It could not be said unless Carpenter actually had a suspect. There is no way to place a profile in your jurisdiction in any given year. What John Carpenter was basically saying is that they now have a suspect from one of the *other* jurisdictions. Clues tended to place *him* around Lompoc during this time. This must have convinced Carpenter to take the step he boldly took and link the 'Zodiac' Killer. He promised next:

All possibilities will be investigated to confirm, or disprove, their validity. I would like to emphasize that we are not using the notoriety of ZODIAC to dispose of a difficult case, nor are we closing our minds to the possibility that he may not be responsible. Very simply, this office feels that sufficient evidence exists to warrant further investigation into the feasibility of this assumption. It is hoped that a more factual determination can be gained by combining our efforts with those of other law enforcement agencies already working along these lines.

The press release requests that anybody with information is to contact Bill Baker, though what they are to consider worthy information is hard to say. There is, in fact, no reason to have even made the statement above. The hope must have been that someone would turn in the right suspect completely independent of any guidelines.

The suspect was Vallejo resident Arthur Leigh Allen, a child molester who had come to SFPD's attention the year before. In interviews with several informants, Bill Armstrong had learned there were quirks, shall we say, about Allen's personality that made him a strong suspect. He also wrote "Christmass" sometimes, and used the expression "trigger mech," both used by ZODIAC in his letters.

There were many other reasons why Armstrong heavily favored Leigh Allen, which will be discussed later. But suffice it to say here that when Bill Baker called and told SFPD about Domingos/Edwards, the dormant case of Leigh Allen must have immediately sprung to Armstrong's mind. SFPD knew that in the summer of '63 he had been a lifeguard in Lompoc. This must have been enough to inspire Carpenter to hold his bold press conference in November, perhaps with Armstrong's tacit encouragement, to see if they could dragnet some damning evidence out of Lompoc, the vital evidence against Allen that so clearly did not exist in the Bay Area.

There was also a coincidence that cast suspicion upon Allen. Now in November 1972 there hadn't been a word from ZODIAC since his March 13, 1971, letter boasting of more killings in southern California. Since the summer of 1971 Allen had known he was a serious suspect. It was after this that "coincidently" ZODIAC had stopped writing.

Years would go by before the ZODIAC would write again. When he would, it would be his swan song.

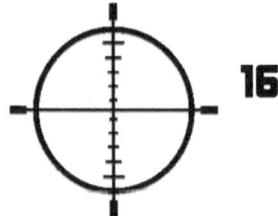

BILLOWY WAVE

He sobbed and he sighed and a gurgle he gave
Then he plunged himself into the billowy wave
And an echo arose from the suicide's grave
"Oh, willow, titwillow, titwillow"

The Mikado

BY THE DAWN OF 1974 IT HAD BEEN CLOSE TO 3 YEARS SINCE THE ZODIAC had written. It had been 4 years and 3 months since he had killed.

Society was firmly within a new decade. The attitudes the counterculture had set in motion were now entering the mainstream, culled a bit, trickled-down and adapted for a middleclass conscious of peer pressure. It was less philosophy and more lifestyle. Hair was growing longer on all young guys. The elaborate coiffures were gone on gals. Long hair, naturally parted in the middle, was vogue. Miniskirts were obsolete. Hip huggers and bell bottoms were "in." Hippies' hybrid Eastern mysticism and the arcane philosophies of the Beat were yielding to the broad brush goals of social consciousness and the free swinging attitude of 1970s' morality.

Something else was quickly fading— the 1960s themselves. From their photos, the victims already looked as dated as they do to us today. Their clean cut looks and bright Kodachrome apparel is not the image of the disheveled 1970s.

Of the 2 victims still living, Mike Mageau had vanished, essentially starting a long drug journey far from the Bay Area.

Traveling along the same path was much of the 1970s' youth.

Drug culture was here. Urban decay was viewed as the harbinger of a new Dark Ages at the door. White Flight was occurring. Jesus Christ was now a superstar. Hari Krishnas chanted along the sidewalks or besieged shoppers coming and going from grocery stores. They were quipped off as the "Hardly Christians." Often they were told to beat their tambourine elsewhere. More than once the beleaguered establishment asked: Where are the mothers of America?

Nostalgia for the past combated with the current social/political turmoil. This struggle found perfect incarnation in one TV show. The theme song of the then-controversial sitcom *All in the Family* spoke for many—"*Those were the days.*"

The investigation into the 'Zodiac' Murders was entirely retrospective now. It searched for some past clue or link, as in the Gaviota or San Diego double murders. There had been the occasional crime articles rehashing the case. "The Arch Killers" in July 1973 showed a picture of 2 detectives working at their desks. The caption: "Old facts and new 'Information' on Zodiac are sifted by Inspectors Dave Toschi and William Armstrong, assigned to the case." But safe to say ZODIAC was essentially buried in the back of the collective public mind.

Far worse crime sprees had eclipsed ZODIAC's self-seeking hype of 1969. Starting in October 1973 San Francisco had been plagued by the bizarre "Zebra" Killings, which were still ongoing and a source of city wide terror. California was stunned by the actions of a militant bunch of chic urban guerillas called The Symbionese Liberation Army. Soon they would commit their most audacious strike, and it would be in the Bay Area.

Part of the dark side of the 1970s was a strange spiritualism. The counterculture had inspired an interest in all things "counter," but when its drug ideology and peace movement collapsed in 1970 the only thing remaining was a searching mindset looking for a new door to open. Satan was written up as representing the ultimate rebel. Despite the whitewash that Satanism was only symbolic of intellectual questioning of the establishment— true devil's advocacy—fear of devil worship and human sacrifice was omnipresent in the mainstream. The darker shades of the 1970s made for an environment in which the movie *The Exorcist*, released in the last few days of 1973, became a powerful supernatural thriller and box office success.

Soon thereafter ZODIAC came out of the past. On January 29, 1974, he mailed his first letter in years to the *Chronicle*. It was his critique of none other than:

> I saw + think "The Exorcist" was the best saterical comidy that I have ever seen.
>
> Signed, yours truley:
>
> He plunged him self into
> the billowy wave
> and an echo arose from
> the sucides grave
>   tit willo   tit willo
>   tit willo
>
> Ps. if I do not see this note in your paper, I will do something nasty, which you know I'm capable of doing
>
> Me - 37
> SFPD - 0

The heavily inked "letters," for lack of a better description, bear a slight resemblance to cuneiform, but considering that a movie about demon possession was the opening line the strange letters were no doubt meant to inspire the belief they represented the script of a secretive cult. Despite ZODIAC's hasty slanted scrawl, he revealed artistic discipline in his drawings yet again.

In lieu of his crosshair there was a significant signature. It isn't just "yours truley." It's a verse from *The Mikado* yet again. Ko-Ko sings of the little tomtit who killed himself over his unrequited love and then warns Katisha that he shall do the same if she spurns his ardor. ZODIAC quotes the verse correctly except for "titwillow" thrice (it's "Oh, willow, titwillow, titwillow")— quoting popular rendition of the lyrics. This is his signature. He couched a serious demonology movie as a satirical comedy and, though he then implied this was his swan song, he dichotomously finishes with a threat of a continued killing spree if his letter is not published. He finally brags he has scored 37 kills.

The ZODIAC was good to his word. This was his end. No piece of mail would ever come again from the 'Zodiac' Killer under that alias or making reference to that alter ego.

But there was no penitence involved. Whoever this killer was he had not awakened and seen the light. The end of his letter makes that clear, as does a subsequent anonymous note. This was mailed on February 14, 1974, two weeks later.

> Dear Mr. Editor,
> Did you know that the initials SLAY (Symbionese Liberation Army) spell "sla," an old Norse word meaning "kill."
> a friend

The alter ego may have been dropped, but ZODIAC was still sticking to his past *M.O.* to dovetail on a major tragic event. The Symbionese Liberation Army had just achieved national attention for the kidnapping of heiress Patty Hearst in Berkeley.

The major urban threats in San Francisco right now were the Zebra Killers and the potential of armed urban guerillas. By comparison ZODIAC's little note was but a burp in the whirlwind of recent true crime escapades. Was it just a little tongue-in-cheek reminder he was still around? It was posted on Valentine's Day— another odd twist to his crimes against couples.

On May 8, 1974, he sent another critique of a movie.

> Sirs— I would like to expression my consternt consternation concerning your poor taste + lack of sympathy for the public, as evidenced by your running of the ads for the movie "Badlands," featuring the blurb: "In 1959 most people were killing time. Kit +

Holly were killing people." In light of recent events, this kind of murder-glorification can only be deplorable at best (not that glorification of violence was ever justifiable) why don't you show some concern for public sensibilities + cut the ad?

                A citizen

Though it was only signed "A citizen," it was unquestionably from the ZODIAC. The letter carried the same printing.

    ZODIAC must have known it would be recognized. He must also have known that it would be recognized as having no spelling errors and as having coherent sentence structure, not his usual simple sentence structure. He was indeed done with being ZODIAC by name. He was therefore equally done of boasting of kills. But the "Badlands Letter," as it is called, suggests he wanted to drop a little bragging, in his tongue-in-cheek way, that he had been hiding his perfect English and spelling all the time.

    He took it further on July 8, 1974. It was a rant on the Count Marco column in the *Chronicle*. He showed he could write with a far more elegant hand than he had been, not surprising for someone who had shown artistic skill in his ciphers and symbols.

> Editor—
> Put Marco back in the hell-hole from whence it came — he has a serious psychological disorder — always needs to feel superior. I suggest you refer him to a shrink. Meanwhile, cancel the Count Marco column. Since the Count can write anonymously, so can I—
>   the Red Phantom
>   (red with rage)

The printing style itself actually links less to the ZODIAC than does the address on the envelope. It is identical to the "SLA" letter.

Red Phantom envelope address, left, compared to the SLAY card envelope address, right.

Is the Red Phantom letter's cursive script the ZODIAC's true handwriting or is it reflective of his artistic ability to imitate? Did he think he would not be recognized? Or is he simply saying you never had a chance of catching me? Not by handwriting. Not by anything.

As history would reveal, this was the last of it. The ZODIAC Killer faded away for good now. For almost 5 years he had proved himself nothing but a sporadic and empty braggart. This was 5 years in which society had undergone a huge change. In that time the ZODIAC's crimes had paled by comparison with what had followed. Worst of all, of course, was the fear that crime sprees like those of the Zebra Killings or the beret wearing Symbionese Liberation Army were only vanguards for more urban guerilla uprisings or cult gang murders. Mindset was fueled by anxiety now, and "What's next?" was the fretful attitude.

Weeds were waist high in public sidewalks now. Winos walked in fashionable business centers. Post Modern skyscrapers were artless glass boxes whose shadows plunged the classic old downtown buildings into cold obsolescence. Fashion seemed a thing of the past. Unkempt was the hairstyle— long and "casual." Hip huggers showed too much. What kind of fashion was "afros"? Morality was in the tank. Disco seemed lewd. The new lingo included 'fuzz,' 'foxy,' and 'far out.'

Society, as a result, had become overwhelmingly nostalgic about "How sweet it was!" before the counterculture movement of the late 1960s and the drug, crime infested culture that now pervaded. Movies may have continued to churn out the "dystopia" genre showing a negative post nuclear holocaust future, but TV with its stricter censorship rules found success in catering to the nostalgia. *Happy Days*, which aired only 2 weeks before ZODIAC'S final "Exorcist Letter," gave us the clean-cut 1950s. It was a tremendous hit, joining the depression era *The Waltons* as the primetime favorites.

Social activist stuff like *Room 222* was already fading from the channels. Light hearted, carefree fare seemed better. *Donny & Marie* came out to great success in 1975; two clean cut Mormon kids from arid Utah dominating the glitz of Hollywood. Times were indeed changing. The mid-1970s was at the equilibrium, where the balance begins to tip the other way; in this case away from the dark aftermath of the late 1960s and toward the more frivolous—corny—late 1970s.

In terms of 'Zodiac' Killer publicity, all jurisdictions but San Francisco had long been out of the limelight by January 1974. ZODIAC's letter writing had kept San Francisco as the center of attention and at the center of his publicity campaign. This made SF's publicity dangerously disproportionate to the meager evidence they had. But since an echo's strength is dependent on the strength of the original sound, it is not surprising San Francisco would always dominate the echo. As echoes also take a while to reverberate, and are only a pale reflection of the original sound, so was the era that was to follow a thin, vain echo of the facts desperately needed to solve the ZODIAC case.

17

TITWILLO

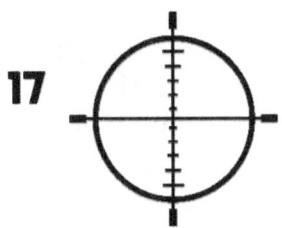

IT WAS AUTUMN 1976— SEVEN YEARS SINCE THE AUTUMN OF TERROR. The case had propelled the flamboyant Dave Toschi and, to a lesser extent, the stable Bill Armstrong into local celebrity status. The duo had been dubbed the "Zodiac Twins." As time went by and the other members of the task force were transferred to other duties, they alone remained "the Zodiac Squad." After Bill Armstrong transferred from Homicide, it came down to Dave Toschi.

The ZODIAC case could not have maintained any real public longevity without a continuing focus, despite the crime spree's once mesmerizing appeal. Now that ZODIAC had left the limelight, Dave Toschi provided that focus. His charm was undeniable. He was showy and unique. He was everything to which the press gravitates.

Before he became a local celebrity thanks to the ZODIAC, he had to cultivate press coverage. He catered to it and he had a network of reporters that he tipped off. His first brush with fame had been a brief one. As a Vice he had chatted with Steve McQueen, who had been directed to him because Toschi was distinctive and always convivial. McQueen was going to star in a San Francisco based cop movie called *Bullitt*, to be released in 1968. Toschi laid out some believable approaches for what it's like on the job.

Good advice, no doubt, but McQueen was taken more by Toschi's appearance than by his counsel. The character of Frank Bullitt would be entirely McQueen's own creation, but he liked Toschi's unique look. Dave Toschi was not a reflection of the late 1960s. Still in place was the old establishment of detectives in their bland suits, pomaded or buzzed hair and *Dragnet* type of manner.

Toschi sometimes wore silk shirts and gaudy bow ties. Instead of pomaded hair he had full, naturally curly hair. Part of this look was the perfect image for McQueen's rogue cop character. The audience would see an example of Toschi in Frank Bullitt's casual loafers, turtleneck, cord pants, and raincoat. And in one other distinctive piece— his custom-made shoulder holster with its quick draw design. Under his left arm was his Cobra .38 special; under the right was a spare ammo clip. McQueen had it copied. This was about as far as fame went for Toschi, and it was more or less a cause for comment only in the police department.

But Toschi's love for publicity continued. Earl Sanders, one of the investigators in the Zebra Killings, recalls (*The Zebra Murders*):

> You couldn't help but like Toschi as a person. He was like a character out of the old Rat Pack, smart, funny, stylish, Italian. But he had a thing about seeing his name in the paper. We all knew it. And no matter how much you might love Dave, if you wanted to play things close to the vest, working with him was a problem. We ended up being teamed a number of times, and on half of the cases it seemed like the press got to the crime scene before we did. I sure as hell didn't call them. But when I looked to Dave, he'd throw up his hands like 'Who, me?' You hate to criticize people unfairly, but unwanted publicity was something that everybody who worked with Dave had to deal with.

When it comes to an accurate historic appraisal of the ZODIAC case, the manipulated press coverage creates a problem. With Toschi's network of reporters in place the result was outsized publicity for him in relation to his work, and far too much literary concentration on San Francisco's involvement and SFPD's compromised suspect sketch.

However much one does not like to criticize a likable man, Toschi's charm is not in view here. The focus on San Francisco is. For the sake of context an assessment cannot be avoided because much of the false echo that has dominated for the past decades springboards from a carefully created impression that Dave Toschi was a "super cop" relentlessly on the trail of the "Boastful Slayer."

On the contrary, Dave Toschi was a rookie on Homicide at the time of the Stine murder. Armstrong helmed the case; the significance of his work must be heard, but first the echo must be stopped.

Throughout 1975 there was little or no reason for news on the case anymore, and Toschi's publicity had dwindled accordingly. In 1976, however, Armistead Maupin wrote a serial ("Tales of the City") for the *Chronicle* that featured a fictional police detective who is working the case of a killer dubbed Tinkerbell. To make the series more believable, Maupin included Dave Toschi in the series as a real police detective with whom the fictional cop, Henry Tandy, consults with. The serial was so popular that Toschi was convinced it was the best publicity he'd ever had. Unfortunately, however, Tandy eventually goes it alone and Toschi is no more in the series.

In an attempt to resurrect himself in the serial, he wrote fan mail to Maupin under aliases. Each alias was that of a woman reader who asked that his character be brought back. The letters declared him to be "a glamour guy," "a real detective," "a very smart and good officer," and "curly-haired and adorable." Unfortunately for Toschi, Maupin recognized these letters as having the same printing. They also matched the personal note in a Christmas card Toschi had sent him. Maupin kept the letters and said nothing.

Things continued as usual in the City. Two years would bring more changes to America. The gritty urban reality of the early 1970s was being cast off for a brighter future in which easier-going social norms were taken for granted. Those late baby boomers who had been kids when the counterculture was in full swing were now 20 years old, and they were far different than their older siblings who had thrown their teachers out of Berkeley. The disheveled look was gone, replaced by hairspray. The popular *Hardy Boys-Nancy Drew* series gave us the era's look and its heartthrobs— the 20 somethings with their new style. For guys it was feathered shags and tight jeans; for gals, Farah Fawcetts, gauchos and tall leather boots.

The Vietnam War was over, and the nation preferred to forget it. Protests now surrounded nuclear power plants, but they were lackluster compared to those of a decade before. One KGO radio host loudly complained that "rent a mob" was responsible. It was truly becoming another 1970s and a new America, and 1977 seemed to be the pivotal year. After *Star Wars* took the nation and then the world by storm, George Lucas, its creator, was asked why he had made the movie. He responded: "I just wanted to make a movie that didn't say how bad everything was." People were indeed ready for a brighter future and better news.

On April 24, 1978, in this very different 1970s, another letter arrives at the *Chronicle* claiming to be from ZODIAC.

> Dear Editor:
> This is the Zodiac speaking I am back with you. Tell herb caen I am here, I have always been here. That city pig toschi is good · but I am ~~bu~~ smarter and better he will get tired then leave me alone. I am waiting for a good movie about me: who will play me. I am now in control of all things.
> Yours truly:
> ⊕ - guess
> SFPD - 0

Dave Toschi picked it up and instead of putting the note through the usual channels he took it to the postal inspector John Shimoda in San Bruno. Shimoda said it was genuine. It became national news, rating even a segment on primetime.

News cameras crowded Toschi's face, lights blinded his eyes—"I have always felt, a gut feeling, that he was not dead and that he was out there somewhere and that he would communicate," declared Toschi. "I was always hoping that he'd communicate and *not* commit an act. A letter I can handle."

The publicity was enormous.

Though the printing on this April 1978 note was similar to the printing on authentic ZODIAC notes, there was something quite curious about it. It mentioned two of the cities celebrities. Herb Caen was the Bay Area's No. 1 columnist. This guaranteed publicity. The egotistical ZODIAC had never given anybody else positive limelight. There had been no news in years, and the case was cold. Yet the letter glorified Toschi as a relentless adversary.

It was this gesture that made Armistead Maupin suspicious. In July, months after the April publicity, he turned the "fan letters" in to SFPD. The context, of course, was that Toschi may also have been writing some of these ZODIAC letters just to angle publicity. He forewarned the bosses he was going national with his story. SFPD approached Toschi. He confessed to the fan letters. SFPD suspended him pending an investigation.

Examining the latest "Zodiac" letter anew revealed it was an obvious forgery. The characters were so rigid that they looked *traced*. The current head of CI&I Questioned Documents, Robert Prouty, said it clearly was not written by the same hand as ZODIAC's. John Shimoda changed his mind and retracted. From his home in retirement Sherwood Morrill had also pronounced the letter genuine, and now this called into question the amount of time he had devoted to examining all the other Z letters.

The publicity was, once again, enormous, but not of the kind Toschi or the SF police department wanted.

The San Francisco *Chronicle*, beneficiary of so much publicity in the 'Zodiac' Killer case due in part to Dave Toschi's phone calls, turned on him. Duffy Jennings reported on July 11, 1978, that Toschi "readily admitted" writing the fan mail to himself, but denied as "absolutely absurd" that he wrote any of the ZODIAC letters. Toschi expressed his shock when he learned SFPD was checking his handwriting. "I wrote no Zodiac letter!" Rather he insisted that the letter "disturbed him and his family very much." He admitted his letters to Maupin were a "silly mistake," but he really didn't know why Maupin had it in for him.

Jennings was a careful artist. He then writes: "In the serial, Tandy's motive for the murders was his jealousy of Toschi's publicity." He quotes the character Tandy: "'It hit me that here I could make it as a super-Cop once and for all,' said the fictional inspector at the end of the tale. 'Christ! Toschi with his goddamn Zodiac!'"

Maupin had spoken with Jennings. He told him he had been "embarrassed" for Toschi but had said nothing in 1976. However, he said he did try to subtly tip him off. He left a clue in the ending of his series. Jennings clarifies: "The character Michael Tolliver, talking to Mary Ann Singleton after Tandy's arrest, said: 'You have to give him credit for being thorough. He even wrote notes to himself from Tinkerbell that showed up periodically at the police department. Toschi said that most of the guys down there think Tandy's days are numbered.'"

Obviously, Maupin was sending a rather harsh insult to Toschi through those lines. It also showed that Maupin had already in 1976 suspected Toschi of writing ZODIAC letters. Now life was imitating art, thanks to Maupin. The article closes with Toschi excepting his new demotion to Pawn Shop Detail.

Jennings was a brutal but not unjust artist. His article clearly showed Toschi as someone whose fame rested only on the ZODIAC case, and someone who was so vainglorious it blindsided him.

Three days later, however, the hatchet truly came out in an article by Michael Weiss. "Exclusive interview. New Zodiac disclosures." It dovetails on Maupin's claim he had already suspected Toschi in 1976 of having written some ZODIAC notes. A picture of the "Exorcist Letter" from 1974 primes the reader. "Police officials are investigating the possibility that inspector David Toschi forged a Zodiac letter to the Chronicle in 1974 as well as a similar letter the newspaper received earlier this year."

The controversy had, in fact, escalated. Now Weiss portrayed Toschi's as nearly incoherent and rambling for over two hours.

> As Toschi talked rapidly and nervously, skipping from subject to subject like a man who has too much feeling to control or regulate, he never mentioned any of the 100 other homicide investigations in which he participated. Only Zodiac. . .And at every juncture he turned the conversation back to his accuser, Maupin, expressing only hurt and bewilderment. . .He tilted back in his brown naugahyde recliner and nervously pulled at his nail bitten fingers. His mobile, expressive face was remarkably boyish.

The article made it evident there was a lot of animosity within the department against Toschi due to his kink and now it had been released by his stupid mistake of sending himself fan mail.

The news footage of the press release was damning. His letters were posted on a bulletin board for the press to photograph. "Fan Mail from a Cop." There was little sympathy for Toschi. By his drive for publicity he had put himself in this situation.

Deputy Chief Clem D'Amicis had used the term "ego conflicts" within the department to explain Toschi's demotion. It's not hard to imagine the contention. Within the bureau he was viewed as a lazy detective whose record was no better than others. Yet Toschi had frequently pandered for publicity and received it.

One glaring example was within the Gay community, recently empowered by Supervisor Harvey Milk. Over the 1970s, there were about 60 unsolved murders of Gay men. Despite this number, only a few ever achieved a modicum of publicity; essentially only 5 victims over the period of 1974-1975. These were credited as victims of a catchy moniker "The Doodler." He was supposedly a young black man who sketched caricatures of his intended victims in Gay bars as a means of ingratiating himself. Then he left with them and knifed them, either at some trysting location or in their apartment.

The victims come down to us as Gerald Cavanaugh, Claus Christmann, Fred Capin, Jae Stevens, and Harold Gullberg. In addition to these 5 names there was said to be 3 survivors, two at the POSH Fox Plaza (a "diplomat" and "prominent citizen") and one "nationally known entertainer" elsewhere. It is usually said, for unexplainable reasons, there may be as many as 14 more.

Curiously, however, The Doodler didn't even achieve contemporary news. It took a couple of years to even get a passing note in SF newspapers. The Doodler comes down to us today thanks largely to Dave Toschi. In 1977, in the wake of his fame in "Tales of the City," which had as its object the serial killer "Tinkerbell," he visits Gay bars and ingratiates himself.

Writing in the popular Gay newspaper *The Bay Area Reporter* (July 1978), George Mendenhall establishes: "Dave Toschi is well known among Gay journalists, who have considered him a friend. He sought attention and received it, but he was also considered competent in his assignment in attempting to crack the many Gay murders of 1975-1977. He attempted to develop a pattern of crime and widely circulated a sketch of a suspect known as 'The Doodler' ... Toschi was tenacious in his work and spent many hours in Gay bars attempting to find leads."

The leads went nowhere because, in my opinion, it was an exercise in publicity. I don't even think The Doodler existed as a serial killer. In my investigation of the Gay murders, the SF Coroner's Office confirmed for me the existence of dozens of reports. There was little reason to see why the 5 "Doodler victims" were linked or merited more attention than the others. As for the 66 year old Gullberg, the coroner wasn't even sure if it was homicide or an accidental death. In Toschi's hand, The Doodler became a catchy handle to apply to a few unrelated cases. In essence, he was the creation of a real-life "Tinkerbell" per Maupin's popular "Tales of the City."

After his downfall, the rumors of his laziness crept out. In the same issue of the *B.A.R.* Paul-Francis Hartmann takes off the gloves. He reminds his readers that 18 months prior the *B.A.R.* had complained about Toschi's lack of results. For this, it had received scathing criticism. "What was a more serious transgression was that the B.A.R. blunderbuss," recalls Hartmann, "maligned one of the 'best friends' the Gay community had in the Halls of Justice: Homicide Inspector Dave Toschi. The cooperation, the hard work, the dedication of this man were legendary. . .His integrity had been insulted, and when apprised of the B.A.R. indiscretion, Toschi said his feelings were hurt. . ." Nevertheless, "The Gay murders continued and Toschi's batting average didn't change. . . Toschi's excuse of being unable to solve the Gay murders was that nobody in the Gay community would cooperate with homicide [sic]. No one would come forth as a witness (to solve the crime for the bureau). No one would come forth as the killer (which would also solve the case for the bureau)." Hartmann continues: "Gay murders were Toschi's private preserve – he was working hard – he was above criticism – what more could anyone ask? No one was around to press the victims' cause."

Excuses as he gave in the bogus Doodler case also pollinate the ZODIAC case. It was only a cab killing. They don't leave much evidence. If the perp isn't identified within 48 hours, the murder will likely go unsolved. Riverside PD played it close to the vest and didn't help. A *new* Browning 9mm could not be traced.

The news fallout of 1978, both general and niche, was it for the charming Dave Toschi. He faded from the news. Some months later he was quietly restored to his Homicide post. His love for his name in print, however, would remain, though it would remain largely unfulfilled until 1986. Of the documents released by SFPD, Armstrong's work forms the bulk of it. In fact, Toschi's contributions come to us only through a single author in that year.

It was his penchant for his name in print that no doubt caused Toschi to forsake his lesson-learned and befriend a former cartoonist at the *Chronicle* named Robert Graysmith. Ironically, the motivation *again* may have been to play the real-life part Maupin had made his character play in "Tales of the City." Though Graysmith was no longer working at the *Chronicle*, he made no secret of the fact he was writing a book. When Graysmith would finally achieve publication in 1986, his book *Zodiac* would largely be like Maupin's series. Dave Toschi would play his mentor and be billed as a "super-cop."

Graysmith's *Zodiac* is a wonderful tale that makes rustic Vallejo the center of the drama and Darlene Ferrin's unconventional lifestyle crucial to uncovering the identity of the ZODIAC. Vallejo gossip always said there was a connection between the two. This alone was Graysmith's compass. The book becomes a biography of the obscure bon vivant of the blue collar and the pent up, bald child molester Arthur Leigh Allen. He becomes Graysmith's sinister nemesis. His story culminates with his personal encounter with Leigh Allen at the hardware store where Allen then worked. He finally saw the evil arch killer for himself, the man he had sought for years. The result was that Graysmith created the obscure Leigh Allen into the second most famous serial killer in history.

Zodiac is a watershed in the public perception of the case. It was not just because it was one of the first books on the mesmerizing case that makes it significant. It was the only book for decades. Thus the author's assertion he had solved the case remained unchallenged and the "facts" he offered in support constituted the narrative recycled by the press.

The folklore had arrived.

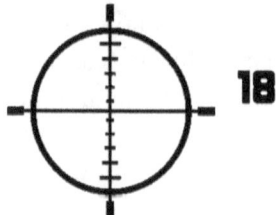

FIDDLE AND FAR...OUT

PERSON OF INTEREST IS NOT THE SAME THING AS A SUSPECT IN THE argot of lawmen. Suspect is a much more solid class of potential criminal whereas a person of interest is merely that: someone who is of interest but upon further investigation may be easily ruled out. Thus interest in them usually doesn't last long in a very quick process of elimination.

In the case of the 'Zodiac' Killer there were about 2,500 persons of interest, but only a few graduated to the next level of "suspect." Over the course of his inquiries, Robert Graysmith came across a couple of these names. Unfortunately, he was limited to Persons of Interest being turned in only after 1976, the year he began his own sleuthing. This being the case, a San Francisco movie projectionist named Rick Marshall, who had come to law enforcement's attention that year, would influence the early chapters of his book. Then in 1977 Graysmith was in place to catch the excitement over the discovery of Bill Grant, a local gin guzzler in Vallejo. Soon, thanks to Vallejo PD's Jim Husted, he would be revealed as having been Dee Ferrin's stalker back in 1969. Lastly, in 1980 he heard in *retrospect* about Arthur Leigh Allen. He discovered Allen had been suspected in 1971, long before the other two on his list. Then he discovered that Allen had first come to the attention of Vallejo PD in October 1969, making him the only one of the three whose name was raised contemporarily with the murders.

Despite Graysmith's initial zeal for Rick Marshall, he would come to play only an ephemeral role in *Zodiac*. The book would concentrate on "Bob Hall Starr." In direct contrast to Graysmith's later claim, it must be stated here by this present writer that "Starr" is not an alias for Leigh Allen; it is an alias for Graysmith's suspect. Any textual analysis of *Zodiac* reveals that more than half was written by the time Graysmith heard of Leigh Allen in 1980. It is evident that for the first half of *Zodiac* the description of "Bob" fits Bill Grant. Only later in the book is Starr described similar to Allen. Thus "Bob Starr" is an alias for a confused composite of two men. In the end, Graysmith would opt to declare Starr to be the 'Zodiac' Killer. But Graysmith's ZODIAC is not an individual. He combined the lives of both men to create a totally false single villain.

For example, on page 17 (hardcover 1st ed.) Dee Ferrin's sister Linda Del Buono describes Bob at the painting party: "The dark-rimmed glasses, the hair curly, wavy, an older type man, he did have the dark rimmed glasses like Superman wears. Overweight, he was about five feet eight inches tall or so." This description is echoed by Pam Suennen, Dee Ferrin's younger sister. She describes the mysterious guy in a white car leaving a parcel at the door. She said he was wearing horned-rimmed glasses and that he was the same older man she would later see at the painting party.

This is indeed Bill Grant, who in 1969 was 49 years old, stocky, had thick, wavy hair, and wore dark-rimmed glasses. And initially Graysmith believed Grant was ZODIAC. Thus in such episodes involving Grant he is referred to as "Bob."

However, on page 292 (hardcover 1st ed.) the mysterious man bearing gifts is still Bob Hall Starr, but Graysmith's description of him now matches Allen. "Also, according to Linda and some of her friends, there was a man bringing Darlene presents from Mexico. All they knew was that he was called Bob. She described him with close-cropped hair, paunch, muscular. It sounds a lot like Starr. Evidently she got the connection across because the police were looking into people named Bob."

What caused Graysmith to shift away from descriptions of Grant to descriptions of Allen and yet retain the same alias name of Bob Hall Starr? We come to the answer shortly. But suffice it to say here he shifted not so deftly. This can be said despite the fact he created an entire chapter to dispose of Bill Grant as ZODIAC. This chapter "Andy Todd Walker" created the pointless character of said Andy Todd Walker (over pages 185-194) as the alias for Bill Grant. In this excising chapter he described Walker identically to "Bob" at the painting party, and on page 189 even writes that Walker *is* the one that Del Buono identified as the man at the painting party. Graysmith quotes the detectives confirming that Walker had a 1968 white Biscayne, and this of course ties him to the strange man bearing gifts to Dee from Mexico. On the anticlimactic (and paradoxical) last page of the chapter, Graysmith declares: "I now believe that Walker is not the Zodiac killer," though he admits he was the best suspect anyone had so far come up with. In spite of this, Graysmith didn't go back and edit out the early episodes that were inspired by Grant. At the very least, he should have switched out the name "Bob" at these places in his MS and replaced it with "Andy" in order to be accurate and consistent. Doing so, however, would make all that material (more than half his book) and thus those crucial vignettes in the "Graysmith legend" now pointless.

The fact that "Andy Todd Walker" culminates everything Graysmith had so far presented as representing "Bob" (up to page 194) makes it certain that Grant was Graysmith's ZODIAC prior to the point he took up the trail of Leigh Allen.

Ardor for the Graysmith legend is the motive for fans to turn a blind eye to the inconsistencies or prefer to speculate that Allen wore wigs or toupees in order to be "Bob" at the painting party. The other camp rejects Allen altogether and accepts that Grant was indeed the ZODIAC Killer.

The reason so many fans of the legend haver between Grant and Allen turns on the strength of Vallejo PD's investigation showing there was a connection between Dee Ferrin and her killer. Grant most certainly had the connection, and Allen could be curry combed with toupees to fit.

Vallejo PD's initial theory was perfectly legitimate. Those phone calls to Dee's family soon after she was shot remained a provocative coincidence indicating the caller had been the shooter. Her lifestyle had roped in a lot of strange people, and the reason that Mike Mageau and she went to the park that night, supposedly spur of the moment, seemed like a cover for something else. Theoretically, ZODIAC could have been a drug connection who also had a thing for her like so many other pent-up males the investigation had uncovered and eliminated. So when he saw her with the snotnose Mageau, the theory goes, he shot them both in a fit of maniacal jealousy.

Contemporarily, Vallejo PD had established that she had a stalker in her life, but he continued to remain unidentified. They couldn't get George Waters to stick for the role, nor a couple of other denizens of Section 8 who were sweet on her. Then in 1977 the information finally came in. It began with Dee's old babysitter, Karen. She finally had something to tell.

While babysitting alone on the night of February 26, 1969, Karen looked out the Wallace Avenue apartment window and saw this man sitting at the wheel of a parked white sedan. She saw his features only for a moment when he lit a cigarette. The next day she approached Dee about it. Dee casually asked what he looked like. After hearing the description, she told Karen: "I guess he's checking up on me again. I heard he was back from out of state. He doesn't want anyone to know what I saw him do. I saw him murder someone." Dee told Karen the man's name.

When Karen finally came to Vallejo PD, she could no longer remember his name, but she recalled that it was a short, common name. Detective Jim Husted was now in charge of the case. He put her through a session of hypnosis, but it was to no avail.

However, Husted soon received a windfall of information. On June 5, 1977, a confidential tip from a "reliable informant" said Bill Grant was the ZODIAC. Back checking Grant also proved he was a stalker. There was no doubt this was the man Karen had remembered. He was now about 58 years old. It would seem easy to dismiss Grant as the 'Zodiac' Killer on age alone, but Husted's subsequent investigation turned up some disquieting information.

Between 1942 and 1945, while serving in WWII, Grant had had 7 months of cryptography and eventually became an instructor. Needless to say, this connection was intriguing. He was a pervert, associated with soliciting around the Hunter Hill station, a rest and weighing area on Highway 80, coming down into Vallejo from Sacramento. He had been an alcoholic and was unemployed at the time of the ZODIAC crimes, giving him lots of free time.

Husted's report draws an ugly but not inaccurate picture of how Bill Grant stalked a young woman in Fairfield. He would sit outside her apartment in his car for hours each night. He even talked to the building manager in an attempt to garner information about her. He once followed her some 200 miles when she visited family. It was the same *M.O.*, perhaps even more extreme, as what he had used on Ferrin in 1969.

Grant appeared to be the most viable suspect Vallejo PD ever had. Moreover, Husted made a mistake and believed a white car had been associated with ZODIAC. His belief they had found their man is palpable from his report. In it he stated with dogma:

<u>Point #3</u> He [Grant] apparently knew the family of the victim's as a mysterious caller. Placed three separate calls within 1 ½ hours after Darlene Ferrin's death to each of the family members. These calls were made before media announcement of the murder and made certain reference indicating the caller knew Darlene.

Again, these phone calls were a damning coincidence to Vallejo PD, and Husted reveals here in 1977 that he now believed Grant had made the calls. Despite his age, Grant fit as the ZODIAC. He fit in appearance. He had that thick mop of hair of the Napa composite, thick-rimmed glasses of the SFPD composite, height, weight, cryptography background, and the circumstances.

From the first 200 pages of *Zodiac*, one can easily see that Robert Graysmith had fed off the crumbs that fell from the table of actual police investigators. Vallejo PD had truly believed that Dee Ferrin and ZODIAC had known each other, and Bill Grant and Dee most certainly did know each other. Until Allen appeared in Graysmith's scope, Grant was indeed a tempting prospect. He fit the theory.

On the other hand, Leigh Allen didn't fit the theory. There was no evidence he had ever known Dee Ferrin. So we come back to the question— what could possibly have attracted Graysmith to Allen? The answer is Dave Toschi.

By Graysmith's own admittance he first heard of Allen in 1980. He was now being mentored by Dave Toschi, who could fill him in about his own investigation. Toschi told him that Allen wore a Zodiac brand wristwatch. He could also confirm how Allen had admitted he had liked *The Most Dangerous Game*. He was closer to the right age (30) than Grant. Toschi told him about the interview with Allen at the refinery, the search of his trailer in Sonoma, and even Toschi's trip to Riverside to explore the connection with the Bates murder (Allen used to go to the races in Riverside).

Graysmith could now enlarge his book considerably and include the SFPD investigation into Allen, which included Toschi's role as central in what has become, thanks to Graysmith, more key moments in the legend. Here and there Graysmith would be on the phone informing Toschi of his own discoveries as he tried to get the elusive goods on this, the most evil villain in history. Toschi would inspire him to look further and to keep him posted.

In *Zodiac*, Dave Toschi is clearly repeating his fictional role from "Tales of the City," the mentor counseling the fledgling sleuth. Graysmith even bills Toschi as a "super-cop," the same term Armistead Maupin used for him in the serial. The grand connotation for his mentor compensated for Graysmith's own lack of authority. But considering his presentation of himself as the relentless amateur sleuth risking life and limb to get the goods on the man Toschi himself could not, Tandy is ultimately the hero in *Zodiac* and not the "super-cop."

Perhaps Graysmith was being his most accurate when he portrayed Toschi as unenthusiastic about Leigh Allen. Already by 1978 Toschi had reaffirmed to a reporter that the fingerprints they had were solid evidence that would identify any suspect as the 'Zodiac' Killer. This attitude was reaffirmed after *Zodiac*'s release when in 1989 Bill Armstrong also said the same thing. Effectively, this negated Arthur Leigh Allen.

Enough evidence exists to suggest Toschi had no idea Graysmith was going to claim to have solved the crime; that his book was to be anything more than an accurate account of the crimes and investigation. He certainly distanced himself from its promotion.

SFPD had cleared Allen by the same methods they would clear any suspect— handwriting and fingerprints— but Graysmith didn't know the difference between investigating and processing. Most of any investigation goes into finding a viable suspect. When this is achieved, the rest is processing him through the evidence. Graysmith rather continued to search for coincidences and inferences with a man who had been cleared. Coincidence and inference can lead to a suspect, but afterward they cannot convict one. SFPD had long lost interest in Leigh Allen by the time Graysmith even heard about him in 1980, four years after he had begun his book.

In 2000, Graysmith's sequel *Zodiac Unmasked* was released, filling in more legendary information and this time naming ("unmasking") Leigh Allen openly rather than using Bob Hall Starr as his alias. Allen had died in 1992 and did not have to be protected by an alias anymore. This precipitated the events that would begin to unravel the Graysmith legend, and the internet provided the conduit.

As more documents were released and gathered, and more people who had actually been involved spoke out, it was clear that Graysmith's *Zodiac* was almost fictionalized. He even invented a fake back street that led from one crime scene to Allen's Fresno Street home. At a contrast to his image as a relentless, obsessed pursuer, his book reveals he also did very little legwork. This is reflected by the fact he misidentified the crime scenes, despite asserting that the local law enforcement led him to the locations. He has the wrong peninsula at Lake Berryessa, causing him to ludicrously reenact the crime in total error. His map of the Washington-Cherry crime scene is also wrong. He fatuously misidentifies where Fouke saw ZODIAC. His book shows no pictures of Blue Rock Springs Park parking lot, and it was not necessary that Vallejo PD guide him there.

The last instance became especially frustrating for me. It took lots of time and effort at the Vallejo Historical Museum and the help of Dr. Jim Kern and Mike Turrini to find old pictures of the park in order for me to visualize what Columbus Parkway and the parking lot looked like back then. As one might imagine, no one goes to a park to take pictures of the parking lot. Yet it was necessary that I have it laid out again in front of me in order to recreate the sequence of events of the crime.

There is, indeed, little indication that Graysmith did any real investigation. Even when he relates the dialogue of some so-called personal interviews, the language is verbatim from police reports that are now released and visible to all. He spoke to a few friends of Dee Ferrin in Vallejo and, as time would prove, took the accurate descriptions of Grant to incongruously lead us to Leigh Allen. ZODIAC enthusiasts giggled *Zodiac* off as the "yellow book," though it was hardly sensationalized. Graysmith merely tailored everything, none so well in my opinion, to add himself and Allen late in the game. Allen remains as "the prime suspect" in the folklore today only because there is the false impression that his candidacy is the result of extensive investigation on Graysmith's part rather than the hasty improvisation it appears to be.

Poor Leigh Allen languished in the limelight over the years he was suspected. When he died in 1992 it even merited national news, billed as the passing of the man suspected of having been "The infamous Zodiac."

To wind this down to a close, it is necessary to highlight a great irony. It was necessary, of course, to create some association with any ZODIAC suspect and Dee Ferrin, since that was the pervading view in Vallejo. However, it was an effort in futility. Years later (2003) it would be discovered that Leo Suennen, Darlene's brother, had made those phone calls. Dee was to have gotten him some marijuana that night and he was calling the family homes to see if she would pick up so he could figure out where she was. There finally went the only link that *inferred* Dee Ferrin could have personally known the ZODIAC.

Although Graysmith created an exciting legend out of Vallejo folklore, he was not the one who created the franchise. Clickbait, long before that word was even coined, was responsible. Paul Avery was the first. To churn out more stories, he promoted ZODIAC as being capable of a wide variety of *M.O.*'s. "I shall no longer announce to anyone when I comitt my murders," ZODIAC had once somewhat unconvincingly baited his readers. "They shall look like routine robberies, killings of anger, + a few fake accidents, etc." Those like Avery promoted this improbability, and the legend bought into it. In the hands of others the case could wildly expand and wander to include dozens of other unsolved murders, muddling and meddling their evidence with ZODIAC's known crimes.

Amateur and professional detectives alike have examined ZODIAC's undeciphered cryptograms and poison pen pal letters with a metaphoric zeal usually devoted only to Biblical exegesis; each sure that the fateful clue to his goading, infamous identity lay therein. Mathematics has been done to try and find a code or sequence in the ciphers that would finger the culprit.

The legend of the ZODIAC Killer became a vast universe and captivating franchise; not necessarily to be condemned but something of which one must be cautious. I prefer the advice of Gerd Gigarenzer. When head of the Max Planck Institute for Health, he said that the intuitional component of intelligence is not found in knowing what is important but in knowing what is *not important* so that it can be discarded from the equation. Excising truth from irrelevance in The Zodiac Case is not an easy task, especially when considering that the franchise was ultimately created by ZODIAC's paper persona, which eventually did nothing but broadcast irrelevance. Even minus the legend, one is dealing with the most incompatible and motiveless crime spree since Jack the Ripper.

At this point I had done enough research to put in place the entire crime spree and its aftermath, summarize the legend and avoid the hype and hyperbole. The next step was clear. I had to analyze the data and synthesize the most important clues into a chain that would reveal the most probable pathway to the real 'Zodiac' Killer.

19 "CLEWS"

IN CONTRAST TO THE FOLKLORE, THE ZODIAC KILLER DREW HIS OWN image. He drew this image for himself in the pattern of his crimes and in the clues that he wrote. These were not the clues written in nasty blue felt ink. Those were only boasts. I speak of mistakes. He, in fact, made many mistakes. A crucial mistake is found when ZODIAC explains in print to the *Examiner* on August 4, 1969, how the police knew his car color was brown. Yet it had not come from a "shabbly negro." It had come from Mike Mageau. Due to the darkness and Mageau's state of mind, Ed Rust had to take his assessment of the killer's car color with reservation. Thanks to ZODIAC's mistake he essentially confirmed he had a brown car.

Such a mistake is tantalizing because it is not one of the false clues ZODIAC intentionally laid to set the hounds to a drag. This was a mistake he had not realized he had made. Not knowing that Mageau saw him drive off is also significant because it tells us ZODIAC was not in a position to have read the Vallejo *Times-Herald*. On July 8, the paper had published: "He [Mageau] described the killer as short and heavyset, and said he was driving a brown car similar to Mrs. Ferrin's brown 1963 Corvair."

Over the span of his crime spree, the ZODIAC had shown zeal, to say the least, in following news reports of his evil exploits. He followed the *Los Angeles Times*, and even knew when the *Modesto Bee* mentioned him. Yet he seems not to have been able to regularly follow the Vallejo *Times-Herald*. This would heavily suggest ZODIAC was *not* local to the Bay Area.

There is also a more tenuous clue in support of the above; that

ZODIAC did not mind mentioning his car color could indicate he didn't use his own vehicles or that he came from such a distance he didn't believe he would ever be suspected.

For all the sensationalism given to ZODIAC's unnerving ceremonial hood, it is nevertheless a clue that leads to nothing tangible. It merely gives us insight into his character.

ZODIAC's mistakes can be divided between the two types above: those that lead to a tangible clue (1) and those that give us insight into his true character (2). Following the first type of clue places us on the true path to the 'Zodiac' Killer.

The collective evidence regarding ZODIAC's features introduce disturbing possibilities. Mageau tells us he is young, short and stocky, with light brown, almost blonde curly hair. The three coeds give us a sketch of a young man, tall, heavy, styled black or dark hair. But this image is not of a man in perpetration; he just hangs about, intent unknown. Its potential accuracy is augmented by Bryan Hartnell. "Victim stated he could also see hair through the mask's eyelets and observed the hair to be dark brown." Thus ZODIAC had hair long enough to be styled. The coeds' image is further augmented by footprint impressions at the crime scene indicating a villain 210-225 pounds. The SFPD sketch gives the perpetrator light hair as Mageau described, now cut into a crew. The exact features, however, are unreliable, influenced by the false assumption a skinny, young serial cab robber was responsible. The kids across the street declared the perpetrator to be in his early 40s. When Don Fouke's input was sought, he too placed early 40s as the average age for the man he saw. The amended sketch, inspired by Fouke, is merely the compromised original made to look middle-age.

The most discouraging interpretation of the above is that there are two men involved in the crime spree. Mageau's stature estimate isn't too significant since a shooter would have to hunker somewhat to hit the driver's side, but there remains no easy explanation for the other differences. Napa's investigation could have helped clarify things, but instead it creates a loophole. Ken Narlow didn't pay sufficient attention to Dr. Rayfield and his son David to understand that they had been down by the lake for a while when the unknown subject was seen to wander down. Because there was no follow-up we don't even have a face, hair color, or age for the man David Rayfield saw. He is wearing a distinctly different shirt than the one the three coeds described on the young, heavyset man.

The two major sketches— Napa's left, SFPD's right.

The Napa and San Francisco suspect sketches project the conundrum. The sketches aside, the one consistency in descriptions is that ZODIAC was heavyset, 6 foot or a couple of inches under.

The possibility there were two men perpetrating the ZODIAC crimes is to be discussed later. The preponderance of evidence, however, favors a young man, especially at Lake Berryessa, and equally favors the sketch done by the three coeds. Regardless of the evidence for a second man, this is the one most clearly in view here.

While ZODIAC's confession calls were not accidental mistakes, they are with hindsight significant mistakes that allow us to confirm one element of the Lake Berryessa profile above. Dave Slaight took the call and declared the voice was young. That was also Bryan Hartnell's impression.

The confession phone calls also give us insight into his character. In each call he believed he had killed both sets of victims. Obviously, ZODIAC didn't spend a second longer than necessary at the crime scenes, not even to assure himself that his victims were dead.

But the most important clue here is not the clue to his character. The most important clue is his haste at the crime scenes. The reason is obvious: his killing locations were not remote in the true sense of the word. Backroads though they were, they were main roads in rural areas. With this there came a high degree of risk of being seen if he tarried too long. The result: the ZODIAC's thrill always had to be short lived, very short lived, as his need to escape was immediate. Therefore it is impossible not to view these locations as significant clues. In short, why did he limit himself to these risky areas?

Astrological theories are fun to play with, but they don't fit. Astrology could not tell a prospective killer that the two Vallejo "backroads" also had petting spots where couples could be quickly shot and the perpetrator could swiftly escape to his choice of three highways. It would be an astronomical coincidence indeed if there was some celestial significance to these areas and, lo and behold, they were also the most convenient places to find local teens petting.

Nor could astrology tell any killer that Lake Berryessa was the *only* remote lake where he could find a suitable (young) couple for his needs. Students came from nearby Angwin. How many can we place there that day?— Brian-Celia, Wayne-Denise, John-Helen, the three coeds, among others. Aside from being the only remote lake to find young couples, it was also best for an extended attack away from a main road. It is not astrology that brought him to the lake. His actions argue that he wanted or *needed* to knife a young couple and sufficient time and cover to do it.

Actually, when removing astrology as a factor motivating ZODIAC his attack at Lake Berryessa becomes especially revealing. The young, heavyset man had protracted knowledge of the area. He knew on a given day during Fall semester he would be assured of coming across a *young* couple here. This knowledge could only have come from experience and *not* from star gazing.

ZODIAC's connection to rural areas unintentionally creeps out in his boasts. For example, when his authorship of the Lake Herman Road murders was challenged by Jack Stiltz, he quickly responded. "Bullshit that area is srounded by high hills + trees. . ." before bragging how he had cleverly affixed a pencil flashlight to his pistol and by this method just sprayed down Jensen like using "a hose."

This little bit of gratuitous bragging subtly betrays ZODIAC's previous connection to rural areas. It is one thing to stream a circle of light across one's ceiling and walls and see the dark dot that represents the gunsight. It is an entirely different matter to think this is going to work in real life. It requires putting it into action. ZODIAC would need rural land somewhere, accessible by night, where he could test and fine-tune his gunsight.

Accepting that it is not astrology that led ZODIAC to these locations, one must propose that it was his lack of knowing other locations that *limited* him to these spots. The uniquely accessible nature of these locations also tells us that the 'Zodiac' Killer did not have to be a local to know them.

Columbus Parkway was a significant northeast Bay Area road, even if your average metropolitan didn't know it. It was the first exit off Highway 80 coming from the east. It was just before Vallejo. It skirted the town by wending along the grassy foothills where it continued on to Highway 780 or, midway, connected with Lake Herman Road, which was also not a dead-end country road but the main rural road to Highway 680.

While locals more than metros knew how these roads connected, thousands who used the lake or visited the park would have learned over time how they were a major convenience to the highways. Anybody who had come to hunt the foothills could easily come to learn where the lovers' lanes were; likewise anybody who had been involved in building the new Humble Oil refinery.

In fact, to get more surgical here the combined clues suggest ZODIAC didn't know Vallejo at all. His confession call directions to the park reveal he merely came from Highway 80 (the park is 1 mile east from the off ramp). It's a famous park. He could merely have said its name and not waste time with directions. Considering how fast he struck, he may not have even noticed the park's signboard.

It is unavoidable to conclude that ZODIAC's connection with the area is from driving these backroads and not with Vallejo at all.

Presidio Heights also suggests convenience. ZODIAC's choice supports Marty Lee's surmise that he knew the location from some past connection. He could have ordered a cab to any location. A gunshot in a cab would have been a relatively quiet affair in many parts of town. Again, the motive could not have been astrology. It is convenience. Presidio's streets were largely quiet at night, and it was also on the edge of a huge wooded area. The chance of witnesses was remote. It was also POSH. A cab killing in Potrero Hill isn't going to rate much news or upset the powers-that-be.

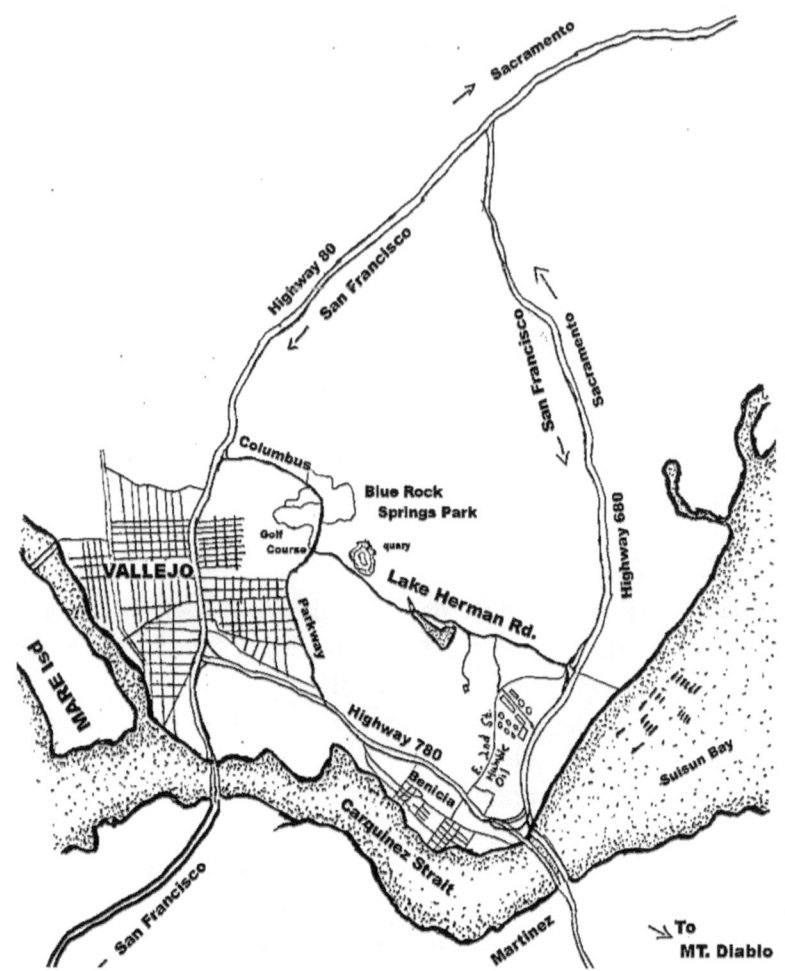

A short little country jaunt along Columbus Parkway/Lake Herman Road connected the motorist with all three highways.

ZODIAC's attack locations were spread over the Bay Area. Obviously he drove long distances to commit his crimes. Why should we not assume that he drove long distances in the very beginning to attack along the two major backroads between Benicia and Vallejo? Nothing, in fact, indicates ZODIAC was a Bay Area resident.

Another pattern indicates that ZODIAC commuted to San Francisco to mail his letters. Three times he mails sets of letters close together. This naturally makes it look like he is a local, which is a false impression a killer based far away would like to give.

Except for his hasty reply to the *Examiner*, his paper was Monarch, Eaton brand. His quick response to the *Examiner* was on Woolworth Fifth Avenue brand. Again, this suggests his regular lair, where he wrote his letters and formulated his ciphers, was at a distance and perhaps he only visited the Bay Area for short periods.

Each time the ZODIAC struck, the chunky braggart made a calculated risk that his car might be seen. Three times a car was associated with him. The first time was by James Owen, who saw a dark, midsized car with "low chrome" sitting next to David Faraday's Rambler just minutes, if not less, before the young couple were brutally gunned down. Mike Mageau saw the shooter's car during the act, and hence this makes it the best sighting. Coupled with Jim Owen's description, Mageau's description of a brown car similar to Dee Ferrin's car sounds very much like it was a sedan version of the Corvair. At Lake Berryessa the description of the car by the coeds easily identifies it as a 1966 or later Chevy Impala, a family car and not one, as the coeds noted, to be driven by such a young man. (The coeds noted that its taillights were no longer round but rectangular. The last year the Impala had round taillights was 1965. They were then switched out to long, rectangular lights.) Two Chevrolets thus are likely associated with the 'Zodiac' Killer, one relatively new.

Minus the poison pen letters this is the nefarious ZODIAC. He was a heavyset man about 30 years of age who limited himself to convenient killing at locations he knew. This reality is truly a stark contrast to his paper alter ego.

Yet the letter-writing publicity campaign does help us to reveal this plain truth. With it we are allowed to see a bland killer evolve before us into a malevolent comic strip villain. He went from taking no credit for killing teens. Then he used letters signed with a symbol. Then he proclaimed his name at the beginning of each letter like the introduction of an old radio broadcast. He labored on a theatrical appearance suitable to his controlling astrological name; then at Lake Berryessa overlaid this on the appearance of an obsolete bum. He spent hours, perhaps days, making up cryptograms to manipulate the press, tease the public, and aggravate the police. He was indeed like some nemesis out of *Batman*, worthy of being his own scourge in Gotham like Riddler or The Penguin . . . but he drove Chevys. He confined himself to convenient places, but gave himself

Above, a 1964 Corvair sedan. Below, a 1966 Impala.

the moniker of the Universe. He promoted himself as a malevolent oracle, but he used the syntax of a cheap punk.

Ultimately, ZODIAC believed his boast: "The police shall never catch me, because I have been too clever for them." He believed nothing he had written could lead to him; and however clumsy he might have been in the execution of his murders he believed he had left no evidence that could be traced to him. Even after he had been seen, he didn't believe he would ever be within the ensuing dragnet.

For me this underscored my conclusion: the 'Zodiac' Killer came from afar to commit his murders. Uncovering this from the collective clues I believed created the biggest chink in his armor, for coming from afar appeared to be the one factor in his *M.O.* that he relied on the most to maintain his anonymity. He never thought he would naturally be suspected.

I had spent an enormous amount of time and effort merely to put back in place all the facts and analyze them to recreate exactly what had happened in order to come to the most valuable clues. It was time now to start my own hunt for the "Boastful Slayer."

20
EAST BY NORTHEAST

COMING "FROM AFAR" IS A BROAD TARGET. WHAT DOES IT COME down to? The zodiac symbol can truly be taken as the symbol for the search for ZODIAC, for it can equally represent a compass. The truth is ZODIAC could have come from north, south, east, or west. North means Marin County. However, a Marin based killer is close enough to return to his lair to use his own paper. He doesn't need to buy Woolworth Fifth Avenue in order to compose a quick reply letter. South?— depends how far south. Otherwise the same rationale applies. He didn't come from the Pacific Ocean to the west. As far as I could see, the best direction to begin was east of the Bay Area. Ultimately, I believed it was quite a distance from his killing fields. This meant his lair would have to be further east than Fairfield and probably a lot closer to Sacramento than Vallejo.

The ZODIAC's varying *M.O.* supports this conclusion. His December 20 and July 4 attacks were essentially drive-by-shootings. His September 27 and October 11 attacks required extensive setup and prowl. His first 2 strikes are on Friday night; his second 2 attacks on Saturday. Inferences: ZODIAC had a job and could cruise the East Bay on Friday night but needed a day off for the involved attacks; the East Bay was closer for cruising than San Francisco.

There are clues in the investigation that also guide us, a discussion of which may not always be pleasant. This long after the crime spree acrimony is counterproductive, and it was distasteful but unavoidable that I had to touch upon the creation of the legend of super-cops and motiveless rummies and child molesters. Suffice it to say, however, that there is some acrimony that is relevant to acknowledge at this stage. Detectives in some jurisdictions did not trust the evidence in other jurisdictions. Although this differs with each detective, all seem to share the same caution over Sherwood Morrill's vetting bravado, namely, that he could instantly spot ZODIAC's handwriting merely from a bank deposit slip. This was essentially the cornerstone of the process of elimination, especially before the bloody latents were lifted from the cab in San Francisco.

A real possibility exists that ZODIAC was on the early POI list and slipped through because Morrill simply glanced at a handwriting sample and said "No." The other way of slipping through the system is the detective didn't feel a POI fit the suspect sketches. Dave Toschi felt that John Lynch wrote Arthur Leigh Allen off the POI list because Allen was bald. His vetting had been so poorly done that a case could be built against Allen almost two decades later and sustained in the popular forum to this day.

Because I believed ZODIAC most likely had some past connection to the areas of the murders, I reasoned that someone from his past had turned him in not knowing he had moved away. This would have got him on the POI list and thereafter he slipped through the process of elimination because he didn't fit the criterion of being a kooky dreg based nearby.

Thus it was worth a shot to begin with original POIs. Guided by my analysis it wouldn't be as arduous as it sounds. Practically speaking, there was only a narrow window in which a viable person of interest could have been turned in to the police. This was after the first televising of the Napa sketch of the heavyset, young man with the obsolete fashion. (Despite insinuations, interpretations, and gut flutters there was more than one ZODIAC, the one who attacked Hartnell was definitely a big guy with dark brown bangs long enough to have gone with styled hair.) My backtracking would have to look through this window again— early October 1969.

Unlike with other cold cases, the fame of the 'Zodiac' Killer crimes inspired the release of several official documents. Fortunately, Vallejo PD's case log was one. This is a boon because after the October 3 broadcast it is to this jurisdiction or Napa that a concerned citizen would have turned.

Browsing this log turned up familiar names. George Waters, the denizen of late night bars, was there. John Lynch's one time encounter with Leigh Allen was recorded. Some very unusual persons of interest were followed through, including one oddball who sometimes slept in his car at Blue Rock Springs Park. The extent to which VPD relied on Mageau's description was also evident. Many young local blonde men had been pursued. None of them fit my profile...until. Until a curious entry which seemed tailor-fit.

In response to the first broadcast of the Napa sketch, Dave ---- contacted the security guard, Hal, where he was employed at Sear's in Concord. On October 7, Hal called Vallejo Police. The police annotation reads in part: "He [Hal] states that one of the employees at Sears saw the composite of the murderer at Lake Berryessa on TV. This composite strongly resembles a person that he went to school with in San Francisco." They both graduated San Francisco's George Washington High in 1959, and this schoolmate, Steve, had written him a fairly lengthy note in their graduating yearbook. John Lynch was assigned to go pick up the yearbook in Concord. And that is basically it.

The entire official investigation is reflected by only a terse annotation in the police log, and it was never followed through. There are only a few reports from Sherwood Morrill concerning hand printing analysis of persons of interest. There is never mention that the yearbook was returned and Dave's old "friend" was eliminated on printing analysis. There, in fact, wouldn't be a report. Lynch would later convey somewhat critically Morrill's method of approach. Innumerable times, Lynch recalled, Morrill would simply glance at samples and say "No good." This left Lynch with nothing else to do but the basics. The log records he checked for a rap sheet. From the fact this person of interest wasn't pursued, I could deduce he had no rap sheet and had never been personally contacted.

It wasn't difficult to obtain a copy of the GWH 1959 yearbook and browse the senior pictures for Dave's old schoolmate. I came across Dave's photo and eventually pages later there was a plump Stephen Haeberle. He did, in fact, *strongly* suggest the Napa sketch. He was also 28 years old in 1969, the exact age the coeds estimated the heavyset young man to be.

In addition, the location of GWH was intriguing. It is in the heart of the Richmond District, taking up almost an entire hill. From it one can easily see Presidio Heights. This may not have meant anything by October 7, but in a few days it should with Stine's murder.

Why then did Lynch not follow such a tantalizing tip? Aside from Morrill's implacable attitude, there was another factor here. Graysmith somewhat critically conveyed Lynch's methodology. Confronted with Lynch's superficial criterion for assessing Leigh Allen on appearances alone, he wrote: "Lynch's replacements over the years did not go back and check the early suspects cleared by Lynch." In essence, I was doing that now. In this case, some quick digging revealed Steve lived in Sacramento at the time, about 45 minutes inland from Vallejo. This would have made him of little interest to Lynch.

Paradoxically, for me this made him of greater interest. My profile, of course, required ZODIAC had come from afar, preferably from the east, and Sacramento fit perfectly. It was a straight drive along Highway 80 to Columbus Parkway.

What had become of this man with the "strong resemblance" to the ZODIAC in the decades thereafter? Alas, Steve H. had died. Death records revealed he had died on October 1, 2010, almost 41 years to the day of the Napa sketch's broadcast. He was 69 years old. He had been suffering from diabetes, and his weight complicated things with arterial stenosis. He died of pneumonia, with the complication of sepsis. He had lived uneventfully all these years.

The obit was rather anodyne. But it held three intriguing references. He liked snorkeling. He had been a Folsom Prison guard. And he had been in the Air Force. At the time of the crimes, I discovered he had been a glorified paperhanger with the State Department of Human Resource and Development down the hall, somewhat figuratively, from Sherwood Morrill.

There is no substance harder to dig through than time. I would have to fill in the span between two brief moments. The moment in front of me was a quick snapshot of a serious looking young man in 1959. The other brief moment was in 1969 when one of his old mates thought him capable of murder, and not just murder but also of boasting about it.

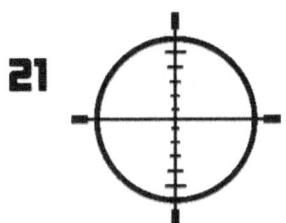

21

Steve H.

Steve Haeberle lay in his bed in Wilford Hall Hospital at Lackland Air Force Base, San Antonio, Texas. He had just been discharged. He hadn't even finished his 4 years yet. He joined in September 1963 and then in March 1964 he made officer. Two years later, as was customary in the Air Force, he had been promoted from the lowest officer rank of Lieutenant Second Class to Lieutenant First Class. He held this rank for a year and not even four months. Now in July 1967 he was out— "separated" at the hospital.

Wounds from the bamboo fields of 'Nam had not sent him to the hospital in Texas. Four months of observations at the hospital had upheld the original diagnosis that had him sent here: "NOT qualified for AF commission."

Steve hadn't been a war hero. His career hadn't even been dynamic let alone stellar. In fact, he hadn't even had an average career. Like all Air Force cadets he had basic training at Lackland AFB. Then after being promoted to officer he had been transferred to Amarillo AFB. And this is basically where he had remained as a glorified paperhanger for his whole career. He was the Personnel Officer; always the Personnel Officer. In all this time he had only one post abroad. Not to 'Nam. This was to a spit of land in the Pacific south of Hawaii called Johnston Atoll. That hadn't lasted long. He was assigned there on 27 November 1966. This is where he fell ill and had to be sent back to Lackland's Wilford Hall Hospital by April 1, 1967. Only 4 months abroad; and he had only been the Personnel Officer for the 10th Aerospace Defense Squadron and then the 24th Support Squadron— another paperhanger job. No medals. No commendations.

In all his time in the Air Force he had one award, one distinction; in all his career only one. It was well-earned in his short time in the Service. He had the Expert ribbon in small arms. This meant he was a deadeye.

There are three ranks of marksmanship— Marksman, which is most every serviceman, then Sharpshooter, then the best, the Expert. This required that he hit the target at least "41 times out of 45 rounds fired, and land 25 hits within a 10 inch circle on the torso of the target and 6 hits within a 6 inch circle on the head of the target." Steve passed easily.

Aside from nearly 4 months in the hospital, paperhanging and being a deadeye were the sum total of almost 4 years in the Service. Now it was time to pack up and go. Cure or recovery still precluded him from remaining in the Service. Despite Vietnam, the Air Force could do without him. They had never really used him beyond paperhanging purposes anyway.

Photo used for induction into the Air Force.

The Air Force liked small guys as pilots, but Haeberle was too heavy and better suited to the ground. He was 5 foot 11 inches tall, but he was a chunky guy—215 pounds. This stability made him a steady deadweight for handling a gun, but it gave him little other advantage in the Air Force.

Now in the summer of 1967, as he packed up at Wilford Hall, his Air Force career quashed by 4 months in the hospital, Steve H. had few options before him. He had no intention of staying in Texas. And he sure wasn't going back to Kansas where he had grown up and where his mother had made an embarrassment out of herself.

Steve liked California. He had liked it ever since his mother uprooted him in 1958 and brought him with her to San Francisco for his senior year in high school. But there was little reason for him to want to return to San Francisco. His mother and her latest husband had already moved south to Salinas, and he and his mother weren't really the best fit. He preferred his grandmother, who lived in Sacramento. There he had moved in 1959 in order to attend Sacramento State University. After graduating with a BA in Psychology in 1963, he surprisingly chose the Air Force. He would list his grandmother as "next of kin."

Steve had spent less than a year in San Francisco, and there was a huge difference between the San Francisco of 1959 and now July 1967. The Summer of Love was in full swing, and from the hospital TV Steve could watch it unfold since June 14 when it was first broadcast. Having lived on 25th Avenue, just north of Golden Gate Park, he knew this area well. It looked licentious now, and this may have reminded him of his mother strobing with various husbands.

To date, at 27 years of age, Steve Haeberle's biography wouldn't make for interesting reading. He had been raised in Kansas, born in Wichita to Helen Noeller, a 17 year old single mother on January 12, 1941. At 16 she was already a beautician, pregnant, and obviously more than casually interested in boys. Steve's father was a doctor's son, Paul Wilcox. "Single" mother is a state of mind perhaps more than a legality. The newspaper announced the birth to "Mr. and Mrs. Wilcox." But basically the marriage was a mistake, whenever it occurred and whatever its motive. The father did not remain in the picture, but Steve's stepfather would . . . for a while anyway.

John Haeberle was 4 years older than Helen, born in 1919 from old Kansas homesteader stock. Drafted into the Army Air Corps in World War II, he became a B-25 pilot based out of North Africa. On January 12, 1944, while flying over Italy he had been shot down, captured and taken to Stalag Luft 1 where he remained until June 4, 1945— a year and a half suffering at Nazi hands. After the war he had married Helen.

Shy and retiring, John was a student at college, getting his education on the GI Bill. Helen was an outgoing beautician in her early 20s. With a young son, she needed security. John provided that security. He adopted young Steve and gave him his surname. It must have been a curious irony that he would marry a young woman with a small son who had also been born on January 12, a day which held little joyous meaning for him.

It was and perhaps was not an unexpected match. They seem to have had certain things in common, though perhaps for different reasons. For some strange reason they never celebrated holidays—no Christmas trees, no firecrackers on the 4th of July, no egg basket at the door on Easter. Were they simply not too festive in character or was it to justify not celebrating young Steve's birthday on the day John had been shot down and then dragged off to a prison camp? It seems hard to imagine there wasn't some celebration of Helen's birthday. It was on Christmas.

Nevertheless, John's influence on Steve was significant. He was coming of age when his stepfather was still studying to be an aircraft engineer. Young Steve, at that very crucial, impressionable age learned much of aircraft and mathematics from John, even something as seemingly useless as radians; a measurement of arc, avionics is one of the rare professions that require knowledge of computing radians. Moreover, after John graduated he became a mechanical engineer at Boeing and later at Beechcraft, and sometimes he would take Steve to the factories. Each day after his stepfather returned from work, he overheard the talk of test flights and of the successes and failures at new developments. He had many model aircraft, which he had put together with care.

The unlikely marriage didn't change Helen. At age 17 she had already been a beauty operator who wanted to live a more exciting life when Steve came along quite unintended. Helen didn't want any more kids. . .and she grew discontent quickly. With John, life was stable; but she was stuck in the boring Wichita suburb of Derby. She wanted more excitement.

Income was not a problem for the family anymore, but John and Helen's relationship completely soured anyway. It may have been Helen's desire to be a manager at a beauty shop in Wichita. It may have been John's desire to take over his father's farm. His father was aging and wanted to retire. But it may just have come down to desire itself in the person of Charles H. La Grange. He was an electronics tech at Boeing, and you can well imagine through whom Helen had met him. Charles and his wife Irene knew John and Helen through work, of course. Helen, the eager beautician who had flung virtue to the wind at age 16, wasn't going to be a farmer's wife. She eloped with Chuck and they married secretly in Missouri in July 1957. With equal haste Chuck died, died so quickly that he had failed to divorce his wife Irene. She is already listed as his widow in 1957. There is

Presidio Heights as seen from George Washington High.

no mention of Helen. But then there would be little reason to mention a secret, bigamous marriage. So far as the fractured world of Derby society knew, the two had run off together.

Understandably, Helen's new desire was not to go back to Derby. Well, not for long. She had thrown John out of their house and moved Charles in. He is listed in the census with her and Steve. It was soon thereafter that Charles H. put the phonograph needle in the air and was laid to rest.

In the summer of 1958 she took Steve with her to San Francisco to make it as a beautician in the big city. It must have been quite a move for Steve. He had been a junior at Derby High School and on the honor roll, to boot. Now for his senior year he would attend and graduate from the huge George Washington High School in San Francisco's Richmond District. The campus sat on its own hill and from it the hazy skyline of every district between the Pacific Ocean, Mount Sutro, and Pacific Heights, was in view. Nearby Presidio Heights cringed like a miniature doll playset before the looming curtain of the forested Presidio, San Francisco's old army fort.

But as to what had attracted Helen to the blue collar district we do not know, other than it was sure far from Kansas. We can suspect, however, it was because her mother was forgiving of her foibles. Agnes had divorced her husband in the late 1940s and moved her furrier business to San Francisco, soon buying out Fred Beetz Furriers. She remarried to a Maltese wholesale food buyer and lived in the district, having relocated the Tenderloin furrier shop to nearby Clement Street. Actually, Steve would live with his grandmother, but Helen would not. She lived in an apartment on Post Street.

Here she soon met another Charles H., this one with the last name of Osborne. Although she preferred to use La Grange for professional purposes, legally there was obviously a problem since her marriage had been bigamous. When she and Charles Osborne popped up in Carson City, Nevada, in April 1959, for both to tie the knot, she had to use John's surname Haeberle, not La Grange, on the wedding certificate, though she appears to be the same beauty operator in San Francisco that year known as Helen LaGrange— from a professional standpoint a decidedly upmarket surname. (GW high school also knew her as Helen LaGrange.)

Like John, this Chuck H. would also have influence on young Steve. He was a draftsman for Soulé Steel Company in San Francisco, drawing up the plans for pipelines and bridges. Steel and forging companies peppered the East Bay Area, with the new Humble Oil refinery in Benicia being slated for Lake Herman Road, a backroad hunting spot in the foothills. Small game hunting was a main past time for any Kansas boy. (He wasn't an Expert in small arms in the Air Force for no reason).

When he returned to California in 1967, he had to make a choice. The first civilian job of choice for military men is usually security guard. But Steve had been an officer and had a BA in Psychology. Sacramento was thus a good option— maybe law enforcement or even a government job. He was soon a "determinations officer" with the State Department of Human Resource and Development— a paperhanger. He held his paperhanger job with the State without much distinction until he retired in 1986.

Not so surprisingly, his mother's life did not remain stable. She was true to form and ditched this Charles H., who unlike the previous one survived her, and she later married a man by the name of Rogachefsky. He had the privilege of having survived her too. She died relatively young in 1987, and her son buried her under a headstone with no sentiment.

The above information was intriguing, to say the least. Much might be called the dull snippets in the records of a seemingly uneventful life. However, it isn't hard to see how some of the incidentals fit ZODIAC's profile.

I had to dig deeper. I've already expressed frustration that there must be more to the ZODIAC case than the single simple motive of some sex killer. With such a narrow motive there's no need for letters threatening kill rampages, invoking occult rewards, and wiping out school busses. Societal terror as the ultimate motive could make sense; kids at petting spots simply become easy victims, a résumé so that ZODIAC's paper saber rattling is taken seriously. But Lake Berryessa wasn't easy, and confession phone calls are irrelevant to societal terror. Live Action Role Playing the paper character with that ceremonial hood is also pointless. None of what ZODIAC did and claimed adds up unless he really was nuts.

I indeed had to dig deeper. Following parallel paths was turning up more than other potential suspects. Through a couple of repeating hobbies, a strange connectivity between them all was emerging, and this included potential (so far) contact with Steve H. as well. Altogether the collective clues introduced two annoying problems.

As I awaited my search for vintage samples of Steve's penmanship to bear fruit, I had to tackle the first problem— Riverside. Here like with ZODIAC the confession letter, the nasty notes, the supposed confession call to the police, were all incongruous with the brutal murder of a single coed. Their purpose was societal terror. The murder either gave a demented crank the opportunity to indulge his letter writing thrills, or the killer did both murder and letter writing because he needed more than murder to sate his lust for thrill.

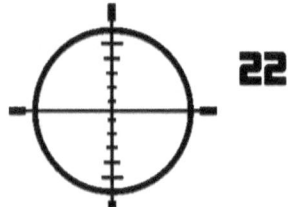

RIVERSIDE RUSE OR PROTO-ZODIAC?

IN ORDER TO MAINTAIN A SEMBLANCE OF CHRONICITY IN "SOUTHERN Exposure," I limited myself to the evidence and arguments current to 1970/71 when Paul Avery broke the Riverside Connection story. But much has come about in the decades since which does bear on whether to accept or reject a ZODIAC connection to anything Riverside. When the Riverside PD tried to bury the connection yet again in a 1982 press release, they stated something undeniably true. "The showing of very old composites and the review of previously examined cryptic writings by some of the media, have resulted in considerable interest by the rest of the media whose knowledge is based on out-dated information linking this investigation with those referred to as 'Zodiac' cases." Just switch out "media" for "internet" and the danger of not addressing the accumulative evidence which updates the "outdated" is apparent.

Those who continue to promote a definite ZODIAC link to Riverside and those who continue to deny it rely on the same material: Riverside PD's investigation. Its strengths and at times its weaknesses opened loopholes that were never closed.

Its strengths were seen in how carefully they reenacted that night's events. This revealed that a 1947-1952 Studebaker and a heavyset young man with a beard did not return to help. They triaged many Air Force men from March Field because of the heel print and the Timex wristwatch. Finding no obvious connection (active duty Air Force men cannot have beards) they began to concentrate on Bates' past.

Circumstances, especially the missing time, indicated she had gone somewhere with her killer. They came to believe this killer was a former jilted boyfriend, and the certainty of their 1982 press release is contingent on this. The heavyset man, a *stranger*, who failed to return for the reenactment didn't favor their jilted lover scenario. Alas, in 2000 the jilted lover was finally ruled out by mitochondrial DNA (samples from the hair Bates had clutched). This allows the heavyset man with a beard to remain in a loophole.

As regards the confession letter and 3 nasty notes, their status in theories somewhat parallels the jilted lover theory. Detectives, at least some of them, could accept the typed confession letter of November 1966 as being from the actual killer. It was because of the statement therein: "I first pulled the middle wire from the distributor." Other detectives, however, could doubt. The very day after Bates was murdered newspapers, including the local *Press Enterprise*, had reported that her car had been disabled. "The distributor coil and the condenser to her car's engine had been torn out. . ." Any car savvy punk/crank would know this meant the central coil. Everything else in the confession letter is bogus. Nothing suggests the writer had firsthand knowledge of the crime.

Excluding the killer from having written the confession letter, of course, does not rule out ZODIAC as the writer. He may just have been a crank writing letters at this time to get his jollies.

In any case, it is natural to suspect a Riverside College student was the writer. The lengths to which the writer disguised the exact typewriter suggests he needed to hide the identity of the actual machine, for identifying a college typewriter could identify those who had access to it. The 3 nasty notes of April 1967 now come into play. Handwriting analysis of the envelopes appears to give us a link to the one who wrote the "morbid poem" on the college's library desktop. Again, this indicates a student at the college.

The importance of having identified the "morbid poet" in 1966 is therefore quite obvious. He could have been eliminated as the killer and confirmed as the crank writer. This would have removed the confession letter, the poem, and perhaps even the April notes as those of a demented college crank. With his identity known, this would have eliminated him as ZODIAC in 1970. Or, even better, it would have made it possible with minimal investigation to tag the college crank of 1966/1967 as the ZODIAC.

Instead 3 decades of squabbling over penmanship had ensued until the jilted lover was eliminated. Squabbling over penmanship resumed and has continued unto the present. Nobody is sure if ZODIAC is killer or crank or either in the case.

What we do know is the writer of the confession letter and nasty notes went to inordinate lengths to conceal his identity.

For the confession letter it was disguising the typewriter. For the notes, the penmanship inside was heavily disguised. Intrinsically, it is evident that the 3 nasty notes were written in a very different mechanical way to normal writing. The letters ap-

pear to have been formed slowly, awkwardly, without great pressure, and some basic strokes (like crossing a "t" or making an "h" in the accompanying example) take more than a single stroke. This can be explained by the note writer holding the pencil high up in order to disguise his printing. Similarly, the envelope addressed to Joseph Bates appears written in the same style, but the next two envelopes indicate the writer got tired (or found it hard to write this way on a small envelope) and held the pencil in a more normal mechanical way. And, as we know, it is *this* printing on *these 2 envelopes* which then suggested a connection to the morbid poem and the address on the confession letter envelope. For Sherwood Morrill, this printing on the envelopes also suggested ZODIAC's penmanship.

Disagreements over the nasty envelopes of April 1967 escalated to such a degree that in April 1974 the FBI experts were asked to examine them and the envelopes to the typed confession letters to determine whether any of it had been written by the "writer of the Zodiac letters." On May 2, the answer came back inconclusive because there weren't enough similar words to make a valid comparison. It was perhaps the worst reply. But it was an honest reply, and one has to ask: why hadn't this been Sherwood Morrill's reply? The answer is preserved in the very first news report.

On November 16, 1970, Paul Avery penned: "The CII handwriting expert, Sherwood Morrill, after preliminary examination of the Riverside evidence, said it is quite possible the Zodiac killer authored the notes and poem." Actually, Morrill was only certain the *same person* had written the poem *and* April notes. The ZODIAC was "possible" not because of evidence; he was possible because Morrill engaged in psychology, something far outside his purview. "There are minor differences, but, says Morrill, this could be due to Zodiac's ever-worsening mental condition— a murderer growing more and more confident he can kill at will and never be caught."

Eager to take credit, Paul Avery continued to strip away any caution until dogma took its place. The very next day, he declared: "Sherwood Morrill, the State Crime Bureau's handwriting expert, said printing specimens on letters discovered by The Chronicle in Riverside Police files are 'unquestionably the work of Zodiac.'"

Grave misgivings exist to this day over why Sherwood Morrill engaged in psychology to divine a link rather than limiting himself to the tangible evidence in front of him. At first he immediately rejected the printing on the inside of the notes, but then after hours of deliberation (with Avery at his heels) he basically convinced himself there was a connection on the envelopes. (He notably flubbed in proclaiming the 1978 fake Z letter as genuine.) Free of psychological rationalizations (and Avery fidgeting about), the FBI conclusion is far more trustworthy.

SFPD accepted that Morrill's examination was compromised. In a letter to the FBI on May 16, 1978, requesting yet another examination of the letters, Chief Charles Gain noted that the Riverside material was disputed. The department had recently gone to John Shimoda, Director of Western Postal Crime Laboratory in San Bruno. "On May 11, 1978, Mr. Shimoda examined, for the first time, these Riverside, California letters and formed the opinion that they were not authored by 'Zodiac.'"

Part of the problem here is that Shimoda had declared the fake Z letter of the month before as genuine. If he was using that letter as the standard to interpret the Riverside material, it doesn't eliminate ZODIAC as the writer in Riverside. Thus we are really left with only Morrill's divining in 1970, and this isn't saying much anymore.

And thanks to Paul Avery's assertive articles, Morrill's tea leaf reading was not publically disputed for years. This gave Avery an open field to milk Riverside for all it was worth. This more than Morrill's genuflecting over the material has entrenched Riverside into the ZODIAC narrative. Yet Avery's narrative should have been challenged vociferously by more than Riverside PD. For it was born from nothing else but his hasty desire to accommodate a connection between ZODIAC and Riverside. When facts consistently mitigated any connection between Bates' murder and ZODIAC's *M.O.*, Avery reported them; yet he did so in the vein that ZODIAC was capable of a slew of different *M.O.*s.

Proffering this Procrustean attitude, Avery also became the unintended father of the ZODIAC franchise that brought us the concept of a super villain killing countrywide via a dozen different *M.O.*'s.

For example, immediate with Avery's breakthrough story clues emerged indicating Bates was murdered by a stranger who stalked campus towns. The story in a nutshell: sometime in 1968 a Good Samaritan came along and saw a man helping a young coed push a VW along Telegraph Avenue (it heads straight to the campus of UC Berkeley). At the wheel there was another coed steering. The Good Samarian offered help. The man already helping, aged 25-40, became upset and left. The Samaritan now helped the coed push the car. Yet it still wouldn't start. He had them pop the hood. The central coil on the distributor had been removed. The girls then told him that the guy had approached them earlier and asked them if he could give them a lift. They said no. They had their own car. He left. They went to a snack bar. Under an hour later they came out and their beetle wouldn't start. Strangely, the same man was at hand. He offered them help. The Good Samaritan now told this story to the *Chronicle*. The Berkeley Police, we were led to believe, were seeking the ID of the two girls in order to pursue the link. Obviously, the police were interested whether this strange man could have been Bates' killer.

Nevertheless, Avery writes: "Meanwhile, Berkeley police also are considering the possibility that *Zodiac* may have tried about two years ago to attack two young girls whose car was mysteriously sabotaged in the same manner as was Miss Bates." [7]

Independent ZODIAC investigators have uncovered clues far better than Avery. Ricardo Gomez dug up a newspaper account of a nonfatal stabbing which took place near the Riverside campus on April 13, 1965. It had been committed against a young coed by a

---

[7] Italics mine.

student, Rolland Lin Taft, and the circumstances aptly fit the sentiment of the "morbid poem." Gomez suggests it could have been written by Taft himself or, more likely, by someone who had been inspired by the much publicized stabbing. This is suggested by the first line of the poem—"Cut, clean." The newspaper headline had read "Clean-cut youth sought in stabbing. . ."

Thus over a year before Bates is murdered we could have a morbid student who dovetails on the reports of major crimes near the campus. Is he also the confession letter writer and then writer of the nasty notes? From the handwriting comparisons, it would seem so. But is this ZODIAC?

If ZODIAC is sitting at desks in Riverside for over a year occasionally venting his morbid tendencies, he sure doesn't sound like the .22 caliber killer who already ruthlessly dispatched the Swindles and vengefully eliminated Domingos/Edwards. Yet these cases, *not* Bates' murder, do match ZODIAC's *M.O.*

To feel that ZODIAC had murdered before Lake Herman Road and that savage December 20, 1968, is not an easy feeling to shake. There is a certain coherent progression in the couples' murders in California which suggests the same perpetrator was responsible. And it is incongruous to fit Riverside into this progression.

But it is not incongruous to pursue a link between ZODIAC and the ruthless southern California "Shadow Zodiac." We can ignore Riverside, with some reservations, and proceed on the premise that the southern Cal murderer and ZODIAC are either the same person or two men somehow conjoined.

Fleshing this out became more of a priority for me at this point than proving more or less suspicion about a ZODIAC and Bates connection. It was becoming obsessively important because of the prospects two persons had been involved at Lake Berryessa.

The tire tracks, you see, behind Brian Hartnell's Karmann Ghia were most certainly not those of a late model Chevy Impala. Axle span was 63 inches, not 52 inches. Stock tires were 7½ inches, and they would have been relatively new. The very narrow tires that Harald Snook describes belong to an older car. The narrow line down the middle suggested an older car as well. The line meant the tire was a retread.

I simply cannot dismiss the young heavyset man in the blue Impala as a coincidence and opt for a faceless ZODIAC who drove in later in another car. I must then accept as coincidence that he was also heavyset and had similarly out-of-fashion hair. Once again, Bryan Hartnell had said "he could also see hair through the mask's eyelets and observed the hair to be dark brown." We should take the ZODIAC's bangs to be long enough to be styled.

In the art of sleuthing, no matter what the subject of discovery might be— whether in the sciences or mystery theater— inductive logic is prized above all. Deductive logic is basic. Deductive logic distills what is known. Inductive logic reveals what is hidden. Inductive logic ponders definite facts, and these facts induce the next step the seeker takes.

Inductive logic is closely akin to the Rules of Circumstantial Evidence in court. One may make a single inference from a set of circumstances that can be established as fact. Your traffic light turns green at an intersection and you prepare to hit the gas—but suddenly a car zooms across. What is the inference? Obviously, from the circumstances the other car ran a red light. You did not see his traffic light was red. You infer it from the facts. That is not speculation. There were a series of facts in place that make it a legitimate inference to assert the other car ran a red light.

Speculation is just something off the top of the head, anchored to no progressive series of facts.

In the Zodiac Case there are a series of facts that do create the legitimate inference there were two persons somehow involved, and the facts begin at Blue Rock Springs Park. Mageau tells us the killer is short, stocky and almost blonde here. Nancy Slover tells us: "Subject's voice was mature." This requires some interpretation. It usually means early- to mid-30s or later. On the other hand, interpretation is not needed for Lake Berryessa's confession call. Dave Slaight tells us: "A male voice, young sounding, possibly early 20s . . ." At Lake Berryessa, the coeds describe a young man driving a blue Impala: "Suspect desc. approx. 28 yrs 6'0 6'-2" 200-225, black [or dark] hair possibly styled with part on left, rounded eyes, thin lips, med. nose, straight eyebrows, small ears, well built, nice looking, wearing black short sleeve sweatshirt bunched in front + t-shirt hanging out in back, dark trousers." Once again, Hartnell describes the killer's hair as being dark brown and long enough to hang forward into the eyelets. He "thought suspect was 20 to 30 years of age by voice concept." In San Francisco the killer has light, short hair again, similar to what Mageau reported, and fitting Slover's "mature" voice estimate he is described on average of 40 years.

Thus it seems two men are involved. Yet the syntax of the confession calls is identical. However, Slover tells us: "Subject seemed to be reading or had rehearsed what he was saying." Both could have been reading from prepared statements.

It would be pure speculation to merely dismiss the young man in the blue Impala because the tire tracks behind Hartnell's Karmann Ghia belong to an old jalopy with a retread tire. It would be the purest speculation to likewise dismiss the tire tracks behind Hartnell's car as coincidence.

There is no easy resolution because the damning mistakes involved in Napa and San Francisco's original investigations hinder the next inductive step.

Neither Rangers nor Sheriffs ever went to the location where the coeds and David Rayfield respectively reported their subjects in an attempt to confirm the presence of the Wing Walkers. Finding them would confirm that these sightings were of the same man who would attack Hartnell and Shepard. Narlow didn't even go back and have Rayfield do a subject sketch. Thus the man Rayfield saw has no face, age or hair. He's only heavyset, 5'10", and wearing a long sleeve shirt— a visible contrast to the young man in the Impala.

It is pure speculation to say that the young man in the Impala simply changed shirts, especially in light of tire tracks behind the victims' car that cannot possibly be those of a Chevy Impala.

The conundrum is further aggravated by SFPD's investigation. In light of the witnesses' descriptions, there was no logical reason to assume Stine's murder was the act of a young serial cab robber. The original handbill declared the killer to be 150 to 175 pounds and between 25-30 years old. This is not inspired by the witnesses in the Stine murder but by the cabbie in the previous robbery. The kids specifically said the Stine killer was in his early 40s and this was the average estimation by Don Fouke as well.

How to reconcile this older light haired man with the coed's description? It might be possible to reconcile this with the man Rayfield had seen, but Narlow never returned to even get a better verbal description of the man. Thus he remains ageless, faceless, hairless. And we have the "coincidence" of a set of tire tracks behind the victim's car that cannot be from a Chevy Impala.

The very concept of an accomplice in the Zodiac Murders is the most annoying problem of all. It is harder to develop than establishing ZODIAC was just a crank letter writer in Riverside before developing his own murder spree in northern Cal.

It must remain speculative that the "Shadow Zodiac" and ZODIAC are two different killers yet somehow connected, for there is only one fact to induce the theory. The Z murders begin with the southern Cal *M.O.* There could be one killer and Riverside has nothing to do with it. Or there could be two killers, north and south, somehow conjoined, and one of them was also the crank writing letters in Riverside. If this sounds convoluted, it is. The ZODIAC is himself at this stage in dark shadows with questionable sketches preserving different features. Now to posit there is someone further in the dark behind him, whose features have never been captured by witnesses, who never wrote a word or left DNA, makes him a phantom that cannot be pursued except by outing the ZODIAC first and finding the link.

I hate the concept of the "Shadow Zodiac" the most, but I am disposed to be objective about it because by this time in my long investigation I had uncovered enough clues to believe in a conspiracy of silence, that is to say, more than one person strongly suspected who the ZODIAC was and yet for reasons unknown (yet) kept silent.

The first clue to such a conspiracy was encountered in, not-so-ironically, the actions of a suspect. I did not uncover the clue. I encountered it. This clue pointed to the existence of a suspect harder to follow than one who had fallen through the system. He was the hardest kind actually. He had no name. The suspect had been *inferred* to exist. But he had not been pursued or even substantiated to exist. I had to look *for* him.

23

THE OMICRON SUSPECT

CONSIDERING ALL THE PUBLICITY THAT SURROUNDED THE ZODIAC Killer crimes, I found it hard to believe that there hadn't been one viable clue sent in to the police (*any jurisdiction*). At least one citizen must have sent a tip that led to the real ZODIAC. It just had not been recognized for what it was. This intuition drove me to pursue Dave's lead for Steve H. It also urged me to study every bit of official documentation released on the case.

As I waited for penmanship samples in Steve's case, I had to face a great irony, one that should give pause to any investigator faced with coincidences. There were many more coincidences in the life of No. 1 ZODIAC suspect Arthur Leigh Allen than in Steve's case and yet Allen had been exonerated by the applicable evidentiary tests—handwriting, fingerprints, and eventually posthumously even by DNA lifted from a stamp on one of ZODIAC's envelopes.

Exoneration, of course, doesn't require the detectives to explain how so many coincidences could possibly exist. They move on to the next POI, and in Allen's case there was no closure regarding these coincidences.

Bent on nothing but the process of elimination, the 1971 investigators didn't consider the one logical compromise— that Allen was a *link* to the real 'Zodiac' Killer. In fact, the coincidences they uncovered not only suggest this, a very curious clue could even rate as evidence. For a brief moment a window was opened in Allen's past and a man emerged so nebulous that I had to give him the name

The Omicron Suspect, a name inspired by the Greek symbol for the void of space.

It is necessary now to look into the 1971 investigation into Arthur Leigh Allen to pursue the circumstances that reveal the existence of The Omicron Suspect. Fortunately, Bill Armstrong was in charge of this facet of the Zodiac Twins' investigation. He did a lot of follow-up, and there is much information as a result.

I have already touched on the October 1969 "triage" of Leigh Allen. It was essentially John Lynch coming to look at him and ask him a few questions. Renewed interest in Allen, however, began in 1971 in the unlikely place of Manhattan Beach, a coastal suburb of Los Angeles. A nearby Torrance businessman named Don Cheney had been struggling with the idea that his old Vallejo friend had been the 'Zodiac' Killer. He consulted with his friend, Sandy Panzarella, who also knew Leigh, though not as well. (Both knew Leigh through Leigh's brother, Ron Allen, while they attended Cal Poly Pomona together in the early 1960s.) Cheney was disturbed about a recent murder in Grass Valley, California. The suspect was described in a manner that matched his recollection of Leigh. Panzarella agreed they best move forward. On July 15, 1971, they spoke with two detectives from Manhattan Beach police department.

Chief Charles Crumly was impressed with their account. He wrote to Dave "Doschi" [sic] on July 19 instead of Vallejo PD (probably due to the high level of publicity that surrounded San Francisco's investigation). Chief Crumly wrote:

> Mr. Cheney (who apparently spent more time with Allen) related that on different occasions Cheney and Arthur Allen would go hunting together and engage in conversations. On one occasion, Mr. Cheney and Arthur Allen were talking more or less in a science-fiction type story with Arthur Allen stating to Cheney "Have you ever thought of hunting people?" Allen talked on, using the terminology "If I did this or that," relating how he (Allen) could go to lovers' lanes areas and use a revolver or pistol with a flashlight attached to same for illumination and an aiming device, would walk up and shoot people. Allen went on relating that it would be without motive and how difficult it would be for the police to investigate. Allen stated how he would send notes to police or authorities to harass and lead

them astray, and Allen then signing the notes "Zodiac."

Cheney replied "Zodiac, why that, why not something else?" Arthur Allen at this point became very emotional and stated. "I like the name Zodiac and that's the name I'm going to use." Mr. Cheney also related that Arthur Allen also talked about shooting the tires of a school bus and picking off the "little darlings" as they come bouncing off the bus.

Cheney recalled that the conversation had occurred in January 1968— therefore before the ZODIAC crimes.

Cheney and Panzarella had forewarned that Allen was a child molester. They also told an exaggeration. They said Allen went everywhere armed. (Apparently Allen was fired once from a school job when it was discovered that he had a gun in his car.) He had also been discharged from Valley Springs School while working on his college credentials. Again, it seemed he was too friendly with children. They also said that Allen hated his mother. She indulged him but complained about his increasing weight. He had once been athletic, even taught kids trampoline and swimming, but now he was fat and balding.

Instinctively this must have sounded too good to Bill Armstrong to be true. He was sure that Cheney was a reliable source. He started investigating right away.

Since Leigh Allen wasn't in their jurisdiction, SFPD's Lt. Ellis contacted Vallejo Chief of Police William Garlington on July 27, 1971, and informed him of the lead they had from Crumly. He sent it down to Sgt. Jack Mulanax who was now in charge of the Ferrin murder case.

Mulanax got on it right away. He first did the routine check of the records at CI&I and anything they had on Allen locally. Allen had been a witness and/or victim of a couple crimes, but he had only one arrest and that was while in the Navy. The charge had been dismissed. Mulanax contacted DMV and got his photograph. He then cruised by Allen's house on Fresno Street, and noted a parked Ford sedan. He checked and it too belonged to Allen.

From Mulanax's subsequent actions, it is clear how seriously he took Allen as a suspect. Without raising suspicions, he carefully spoke with neighbors to get an idea of how Allen behaved. He then took it beyond that and quietly got handwriting samples from various sources.

Dave Toschi and Bill Armstrong weren't due in Vallejo until the afternoon, so Mulanax had time to visit one of Allen's former employers. Here at Harry Wogan's grimy corner gas station Mulanax could appreciate Leigh Allen's decline from promising teacher to fired one-too-many-times child molester. Allen had worked for him for several months in 1969 and thereafter quit to attend Sonoma State College. Wogan praised Allen as efficient and honest, but "he showed too much interest in small children." Wogan soon became worried about his own three children, for they frequently came around the station. Even after Allen had quit working for him, he came by his house and took his 13 year old girl fishing. She reported to her parents that Allen had made "improper advances."

At 2 p.m. the "Zodiac Twins" arrived. Soon Mel Nicolai from CI&I in Sacramento was also there. They had their meeting. Armstrong declared he was certain that Cheney was reliable. In fact, he was "strongly" in favor of Cheney being a solid source. Over the last weekend he had gone to Los Angeles to interview him personally. Armstrong's confidence rubbed off on the others. It was decided between them that Jack Mulanax would probe further into Allen's background before they would make contact. Both of the "Twins" wanted in on it, and Mulanax promised them he'd inform them so they could return and join in the meeting. Armstrong left his background report there, and Mulanax got to work.

Over the next week Mulanax stealthily snuffled about. Most of Allen's Fresno Street neighbors were older and had a high opinion of him, since he had grown up in that house and all had known him since he was a boy. His father had died just 6 months before, and had been a highly decorated commander in the United States Navy. (According to Crumly, Cheney had said Allen's own tour in the Navy had been cut short; supposedly there was a dishonorable discharge.) Although he continued to live at home, he did not live in his room upstairs. He lived in the basement. Mulanax also learned that Leigh, as he liked to be called, presently worked at Union Oil & Gas in Pinole (which is across the Carquinez Bridge). It was only a summer job. (As mentioned earlier, he was returning to Sonoma State this fall to get a degree in biology).

Having this amalgam of information before him, Mulanax thought it best to follow the lead at Union Oil. He confirmed that Leigh Allen would be available for interview. This, of course, is what led to the much storied interview between Leigh, Mulanax, Toschi and Armstrong, thanks to Robert Graysmith featuring it in his book *Zodiac*. Mulanax had worked out the interview with Allen's supervisor, Mike McNamara, and Allen was not to be informed of the purpose of their visit until it had commenced. At 10:30 a.m. August 4, 1971, he was led from the lab (where he worked as a junior chemist) into McNamara's office. There the three introduced themselves. From Mulanax's report:

> After identifying ourselves as police officers, Allen was notified by Armstrong that we were investigating the Zodiac murders. He was further advised that it had been brought to our attention by an unnamed informant that Allen was alleged to have made certain statements approximately 11 months prior to the first Zodiac murder, which, if true, were of an incriminating nature.

Without identifying who this informant was, Armstrong then read aloud the notes, in which Allen was alleged to have said he'd hunt people and would send letters to the police to taunt them using 'Zodiac' as his crime moniker. "Allen was asked if he had any recollection of having had such a conversation with anyone and replied that he did not recall such a conversation."

Then Allen was asked whether he had followed the ZODIAC case at all. He admitted that he did early on. He lost interest, he said, because it was "too morbid."

To the surprise of the investigative trio, Allen then admitted he had been questioned earlier by a Vallejo sergeant. It was after the Lake Berryessa murder. He now told them what he had told the sergeant (Lynch), and it was basically the same story Lynch had recorded in the daily log. Allen said he had gone to Salt Point Ranch and met a serviceman and his wife. He had their names written down at home somewhere and injected that he could find it for them if they wanted. He added that he had returned home that day around 4 p.m. He had forgotten to tell the Vallejo sergeant that his neighbor, Bill White, saw him arrive. Since White died a week later,

Allen didn't bother to update the police. Without prompting yet again, he told them "The two knives I had in my car with blood on them, the blood came from a chicken I had killed." (Mulanax later writes: "He evidently of the opinion we had some information regarding a knife we did not possess.")

This was not the only time Allen offered information needlessly. He also freely offered that he had been in Riverside at the time Cheri Jo Bates had been murdered. Offering this was naturally quite intriguing. He also admitted being interested in guns, but he only owned a .22 caliber. Allen also freely offered he had read a book in high school that had left a very lasting impression on him. This book was *The Most Dangerous Game*, a story the investigative trio knew had a plot that centered around shipwrecked survivors being hunted like animals on a remote island by a mad Count Zarhoff. Each of the detectives, of course, already knew that Cheney had told Armstrong that Leigh had brought that story up to him in conversation. Each also knew that a veiled reference to it was found in ZODIAC's first cryptogram: killing people "is more fun than killing wild game because man is the most dangeroue anamal of all."

On top of all this gratuitous information, there was Allen's distinctive watch. It caught their collective eye. Examining it revealed it to be a Swiss "Zodiac" brand watch, with the crosshair emblem on its dial. When asked, he said his mother had given it to him as a gift approximately two years ago.

Allen was then asked if he could remember anybody he might have had a conversation with regarding the ZODIAC crimes. In response he mentioned a Mr. Kidder and a Phil Tucker with the Greater Vallejo Recreation Department.

Allen also expressed his willingness to help the investigation any way he could, and he even admitted that he hoped there'd come a day when police are no longer referred to as "pigs."

Ignited by their encounter with Allen, especially the discovery of the Zodiac watch, the trio left to continue investigating. Toschi and Mulanax went back to Vallejo and talked with Ted Kidder. He told them Allen had worked there for about 5 years and in this time he had never had a conversation with him about the ZODIAC. He then called in Phil Tucker, and with this we come to a significant clue.

Tucker admitted he did have a conversation about ZODIAC, but it was with Kidder only a few weeks before. He then dropped the bomb. The purpose was to express his concern that *Leigh Allen* could indeed be ZODIAC. Not only had Allen told him once that he had been a suspect, but he recalled Allen having mentioned that he had an idea about taping a flashlight to the barrel of a gun for accurate night shooting. In conversation with Tucker, Allen's context wasn't about killing people. It was for night hunting.

With Phil Tucker the investigators had come across a gem of a discovery. Unfortunately, Jack Mulanax's summary of their conversation in his report didn't do it justice.

> On another occasion he and his wife had visited Allen at his home. Allen had made the remark that he had something he would like to show them. Stated he only showed this thing to 'very certain people' or something to this effect. He took from a grey metal box, located in his bedroom, a piece of paper. This paper was hand printed and pertained to a person who had been committed to Atascadero State Hospital for molesting a child. It rambled on and on about this person having been betrayed by his attorney, using language of a legal nature or terminology. Also in this script were several symbols similar to those used by Zodiac in his coded messages. Symbols and code very neatly done. Tucker expressed a polite interest in the paper but his wife showed genuine interest. She asked Allen if she might borrow the paper to study it but Allen refused to allow her to take the paper. He did promise to have a copy made to give her. This he never did.

Pursuing this lead, Mulanax later interviewed Joan Tucker:

> She related substantially the story as her husband had given. At the time she was shown the writings she was preparing for an examination in college in psychology and admitted that she was very interested in the contents of letters. Allen had explained that he had received these papers from a patient at Atascadero and Mrs. Tucker's interest was primarily directed towards the working of this person's mind. The exactness and neatness of the printing and of the symbols used made an impression on her. She was shown photostatic copies of some of the codes sent by Zodiac. She identified numerous symbols used in Zodi-

ac codes as being the same as she saw in the papers shown her by Allen. It was her recollection these papers were drawn with a felt-point pen.

Thus it seems enters the ZODIAC. This was it. The one download of information, but an iota, into a large omicron of space that is the pursuit for the 'Zodiac' Killer's identity. This alone gives us The Omicron Suspect. In a reading of all the documentation that has been released on the investigation hereafter there is not one followup. There is not one "t" that was crossed, not one "i" that was dotted regarding this lead.

Amazingly, Mulanax never pursued it. Along with Toschi and Armstrong he was bent on proving or disproving Leigh Allen as the ZODIAC and that was it.

The hardest part of any investigation is uncovering a viable suspect. After that it is matching the evidence; in this case, the priority being fingerprints and handwriting. But when Allen was cleared, this did not excuse them from following through with the logical alternative: that Allen may, in fact, have known the man, even *inspired* the man, who became ZODIAC.

On the face of it, Leigh Allen seemed compliant, even helpful in his interview at the oil company. But offering information the way he did was quite curious. What to make of his gratuitous attitude?

The answer in part— Jack Mulanax had probably not been as discreet as he had thought. Despite thinking he was being very stealthy on Fresno Street, it is more than likely that a neighbor had told Allen the police were asking about him. Allen's entire attitude indicates he was, if anything, anticipating being questioned.

Nothing Allen said, when it came to things he *offered*, was false or incriminating. Yet his denial of having talked about a hypothetical murder spree does seem false. Allen must have remembered his conversation with Cheney. If not, why offer his impression of *The Most Dangerous Game*? He must have assumed the "informant" was Cheney or somebody else with whom he had the same compromising conversation.

Cheney had forewarned them that Allen was "antiestablishment." Did this attitude inspire him to play games with the police rather than admit he had hatched elements of the ZODIAC's *M.O.* in idle chat with others? But there seems to be more here than that. He seems to be laying the foundation of an alibi should he be accused of being an accomplice before-the-act. I surmise here that Allen heavily suspected he had inspired the 'Zodiac' Killer, but for reasons (so far) unknown he wasn't going to name him. However, come what may, Allen had these interviews as proof he spoke freely about some things that became aspects of the 'Zodiac' Killer's *M.O.* He basically was making the police his alibi that he never *intentionally* inspired any perpetrator. With hindsight, however, the investigators chose to have viewed Allen's actions as having been goading and nothing more.

Their narrow goal must explain why they didn't ask for even basic clarifications. The investigators did not even confirm with Allen's mother when she had given him the watch. According to Allen it was Christmas of 1969, which is after the ZODIAC murders were over. According to his brother Ron, it was Christmas 1968. Establishing that he had it before the murders doesn't incriminate him as ZODIAC, but it could mean he was in a position to have influenced *somebody* else.

Years later Don Cheney would consider this alternative. In an interview with Tom Voigt on December 30, 2000, Cheney was asked if he still believed the late Leigh Allen was ZODIAC. He replied "I've thought about that from time to time and I don't see any way that it could not be Arthur Leigh Allen. If it was not him, it had to be somebody that looked like him and was a close friend of his. Somebody that, maybe they conspired together, or . . . or that he talked to the way he talked to me." Is Cheney's intuition right?

From the documentation it does seem that Allen talked to a few people about aspects that became part of the ZODIAC's *M.O.*, at least about the gunsight, mention of *The Most Dangerous Game*, and a hypothetical murder spree. Is it possible that he discussed this with a nutter at the Atascadero State Hospital?

In the early 1960s Allen was working on his teaching credentials at Cal Poly San Luis Obispo, about 20 minutes away from Atascadero. He liked the area and remained in the vicinity after graduating, getting a job in Lompoc as a lifeguard. The summer of 1962 becomes crucial here. During this summer, and this summer alone, he worked in some teaching capacity at Atascadero State Hospital. It is likely at this time that Allen formed some kind of bond, whether intentionally or not, with the inmate who wrote the letter that intrigued him so much he showed it to a psychology student.

Leigh Allen was the kind to have befriended such a patient. He found forgivable humor, even generic pity, in the plight of those at the hospital. Ironically, due to his own problems with child molesting, Allen would be committed to Atascadero in the mid-1970s. We get a glimpse into his attitude about inmates from a letter he wrote to his old Lompoc friend while an inmate there himself.

> Drawer A
> Atascadero
> 93422

Dear Mike

Sorry to take so long to write, but I've always had a habit of putting things off. Actually, I'd probably have put it off even longer, but I just thought of a great improvement for your car for the show next year. It can be done one of 2 ways, actually. The first would be to enlarge the rear trunk to, say, about 2 feet wide, 4 feet high and as long as you can make it. Then, if you can get it to hinge at the bottom. A lock can be fastened onto the top to fool anyone who wants to peek inside. Then, when I crawl under your car to take a look at the underpinnings, I just won't come out. then [sic] you can secure the bottom of the trunk so it won't fall open as we putt on out of the gate— that _would_ be embarrassing. Nobody'll miss me until 9:30 bed count, and we can be long gone _way_ before then. Hell— I'll even treat you to a beer (keg) or 2.

Damn hard to write with the lites out (its 8:45), but as long as I can see the lines on the paper I'll write.

You were asking what types of people there are down here, and I only got as far as us sex fiends.

[second page]

Now it's tomorrow, and I considered going to church. But only briefly. I haven't gone for 30 years, and I can't see spoiling a record like that.

Anyhow, the other two categories are Mentally Ill and Criminally

Insane. There are various mixtures of the categories, depending on what the patient did. We have a nice old black fellow on the ward—really a gentle, great old guy, who doesn't even remember killing his wife. He wouldn't even believe it, except that he's seen the court records. He was a professional boxer (and a good one) at one time, and she must have done something that enraged him + he clipped her one. Then, when he realized what he had done, he couldn't handle it and blacked that action from his mind for good. Then we have a UCSB football player who tried **LSD**— once. Now he hears voices all the time. Sometimes they're in control and sometimes he is. The poor guy is intelligent enough to see exactly what happened, which may be the worst torture of all. Then there's the engineer here, a specialist in explosives, who'd like to blow up the hospital and everything in it, including himself (his one <u>good</u> idea). Of course, all those facists in Sacramento would be next, etc. Then . . . but I'll save some for later. Write me when you get time. It sure makes the time pass a lot quicker. Till then, don't do anything I wouldn't drink.

Hang Loose,
Leigh Allen

Again, considering Leigh Allen's perceptive, even lighthearted interest in other inmates, he seems like the right person to have gained the trust of a bitter inmate during his summer of 1962. His letter also reveals something else. Allen's elaborate and jesting plot to break out with Mike's help shows to what extent he could spontaneously hatch wild scenarios, not unlike the farfetched ZODIAC crime spree which Cheney claims Allen presented to him in hypothetical terms in January 1968.

In his sequel *Zodiac Unmasked*, Robert Graysmith attempted to capitalize on the existence of this mysterious piece of paper. However, his rendition focused on Karen Allen as the one who saw the strange symbols. Then she redrew them under a police supervised hypnosis session (in 1978). Graysmith was allowed to see her work and then, as an artist, copy the symbols as best he could for presentation in his book. This vignette was used to imply Leigh had actually written the letter and therewith support his claim he had solved the case by naming Leigh Allen as the ZODIAC.

More applicable to our own quest, Graysmith claims Karen saw this letter first in November 1969. He has Phil Tucker remembering that he and Joan were first shown the letter 18 months prior to Toschi and Mulanax's interview with them (August 1971), so this would place it as February 1970 (though Graysmith later writes June 1970). Yet there is no qualification when the letter was written.

I had to identify this Omicron Suspect by name. I had two scenarios to use as a template. He came from the Bay Area and Allen had already known him. Or, he had been an inmate at the State madhouse during the summer of 1962 and formed a bond with Allen.

This might finally be the lead I desperately wanted to connect both north and south California couples' murders. I didn't like the idea of complicating the ZODIAC crimes by trying to add cases and perhaps even an accomplice, but I couldn't deny Leigh Allen represented a genuine conspiracy of silence. For some reason he wouldn't talk and it would seem more than antiestablishment was keeping him silent.

It would be equally difficult to say it was direct complicity that kept him silent. Every tick and twitch from him underscores he only had suspicions about that former Atascadero inmate; at least at the time he showed Joan Tucker the letter. I don't know what his ultimate purpose was— to ask a psychology student to tell him whether this writer was killer material or not— but it is not a leap in logic to suggest that Allen suspected he had unintentionally inspired the actual 'Zodiac' Killer in some roundabout way. How and when he suspected he had is not important to work out yet. What is important to understand is Allen's quandary.

Allen was deep in mire. For whatever reason, he kept lots of ex-cons in his coterie of friends, and I suspect the Atascadero nutter was one of them and somewhere indirectly down the pipeline from his foothills fantasies. Examples of Allen's extracurricular activities give us an idea of the types within the U-joint of his life. In 1981, a search warrant was served on him. The result was surprising. Evidence clearly points to Allen being involved in professional bomb making, perhaps for over 10 years. The following was found in his basement— 4 pipe bombs, one can of black powder, a primer cord, 7 "Railway Torpedoes" (impact devices), 2 green safety fuses (@98.5 feet long), 2 rolls orange safety fuses, 9 nonelectric blasting caps, 2 one-inch galvanized pipes, each with an end cap, 5 pipe threads, 6 pipe vices. This is only a partial accounting. There were other types of powder and an arsenal of weapons.

When faced with the pipe bombs Allen said he was storing them (9 years!) for a dead ex-con/friend. Roy Conway lied to Allen to catch him off guard. He said they found his fingerprints on them. Allen had a lame excuse about having moved them once to clean. The truth is Allen probably was storing them for others and had never touched them. From an engraved lighter, Vallejo P.D. got a name and traced it to a living convict. He denied leaving bombs with Allen, naturally. But how many living (and dead) ex-cons were not traceable because they hadn't left behind a clue?

Allen was a vainglorious babbler. He was the kind to enjoy the murky prestige (within a certain crowd) of being suspected as the most cerebral killer in history. But he was also dumb like a fox— dumb enough to get caught in the first place but smart enough to elude the hounds— as the old saying goes. It is a fact that he cultivated suspicion for a crime for which he could not be prosecuted. Why? Was it to draw attention away from worse crimes for which he *could* be convicted if the evidence was put in the right context?

All that was found in Allen's basement was far more sophisticated than ZODIAC's trite BS bomb. It heavily suggests the bomb igniting New Left. The Waller Street bombing specifically comes to mind in which officer McDonnell was killed. The Weathermen were suspected, and it is a fact they reached over the country, from San Francisco to D.C., and at that time Leigh Allen was proficient as a pilot. Even if he was only storing equipment and transshipping terrorist cell members, he still has the dreck of the bombings on his shirttails as an accessory before or after the act.

Until becoming a convicted child molester, Allen's murky notoriety didn't seem a problem. Afterward is another matter. He now had more than one strike against him. He was so identified in Vallejo with being a ZODIAC suspect that he needed to forge a letter purporting to be from an official declaring he had passed a polygraph and was not the ZODIAC. Its forging could be traced to the time he was an inmate in Atascadero working in the print shop. The letter no doubt had various uses when seeking employment. Recidivism, or employers' fear of repeat offenders, was a problem Atascadero prepared inmates for.

Thereafter Allen didn't revel in the notion he was a suspect, but he cautiously implied he knew the ZODIAC's identity. Yet when it came to anything smacking of conspiracy, he firmly kept his mouth shut. His antiestablishment attitude would not have extended to protecting a killer of necking teens . . . unless he suspected that killer of being in his extended coterie of antiestablishment kooks.

Allen had so many ne'er-do-well friends he might not have been able to work out the intricacy of the connections. But I don't think it's vain to second-guess that he spun quite a bit in his mind. Whether the gears meshed is another matter. By 1970, when we know he first began showing that letter, we were in the post Manson Family reality, in the midst of the Weathermen and other Boomer conspiracies. Like the other groups, ZODIAC's motive on paper was to cause terror and impeach the establishment. Allen would have been justified to ponder how the former Atascadero inmate overheard his story and how involved the ZODIAC crimes might be. It might have been the better part of wisdom to fear more than one person if he talked.

I had to find Omicron and see how deep his connection went. My search began at Atascadero. I discovered that records may exist, but it is impossible for me to get any. The inmate would need to approve of the request, if not him then his lawyer. If the former inmate was dead, it was even worse. The next of kin and a lawyer would be needed to even start a search for records. How to do that on only a nameless inmate *possibly* from the summer of '62?

There was one other way. I knew it would come down to the hard way. The hard and *long* way.

During this arduous pursuit, I was thrown a curve.

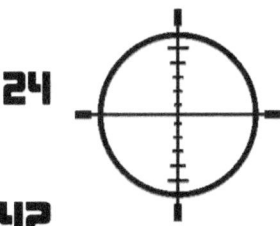

24

SIGNED, YOURS TRULEY?

Knowing that vintage handwriting samples were the first and most accessible step to identifying ZODIAC, I had set myself to vigorously study the villain's letters. I disagreed with Sherwood Morrill's bravado that ZODIAC could be identified from a mere bank deposit slip. Taken collectively, his corpus shows he had been *disguising* his printing to some extent. Fortunately, he had sent such a volume of letters that it was probable he had slipped enough times to reveal his daily penmanship. It would therefore be possible to pick out samples and put in place what was likely to be closest to his casual penmanship.

The exceptions in the braggart's writing became provocative.

The M from the Badlands envelope ("Mission") is radically different from his usual M (samples from 3 different Z letters).

Mission Mail Map My

"Badlands" proved very significant for two other letters.

B B   p P

The first B above is from "Badlands." This is the *only* time ZODIAC made such a one-stroke cursive B. The second B is from his *Examiner* response. It is his commonplace style throughout his many letters. The first p is one-stroke and also from "Badlands" and representative of all p's in the letter. The second p is his common 2-stroke p found throughout his other letters.

"Badlands" suggested ZODIAC normally made his letters with single strokes like everybody else. The 3-stroke k, 2-stroke y, p, were all attempts at disguise. This supposition is reaffirmed by examining ZODIAC's letters carefully. The first p he would make in any letter would naturally be in the word "speaking," as "This is the Zodiac speaking" was his obligatory preamble. If his 2-stroke letters were attempts to hide his common writing style, it is here where he'd likely make a slip. This he did in his "Little List" letter (July 26, 1970.)

This is the Zodiac speaking
This is the Zodiac speaking I

The 1-stroke p exception (top); his usual 2-stroke p (bottom).

Unless he wrote slowly, as in the Belli Letter or in a couple of first lines where he proclaimed himself (as just presented), ZODIAC naturally slanted.

Mechanical analysis proved discouraging, however. In some letters the pressure points, where the pen was first applied to begin the letter, were at the bottom of the letter rather than at the top where expected. This can be done by writing upside down, backward or holding the pen at the end, indicating very careful printing. In letters such as the Stine Confession Letter, the printing was normal, with the pressure point at the top of the letter. Sometimes it was in strange places, often at the apex of a letter for some reason. This topsy-turvy displacement of the pressure point is quite curious and most certainly indicates intentional disguise.

"again" from Belli Letter, with pressure point at bottom and unusual spacing indicating some of it was written upside down. "And" from Little List showing pressure point at bottom. "own"— pressure point at end.

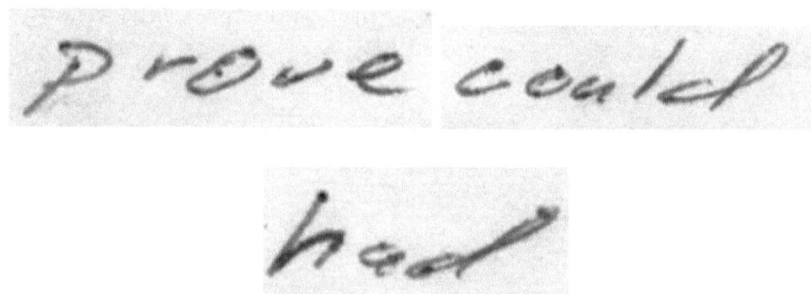

"prove," "could," and "had" from Stine letter. Pressure points at beginning of letters or nonexistent due to speed of writing.

From just these few samples, I had to accept I was not going to find a string of sentences from any suspect's daily notes that would match ZODIAC's writing. I had to look for broad variations in a person's writing that matched those in Z's penmanship.

Finally, I was able to obtain samples of Steve H.'s printing from his Air Force records. I felt a military notation would be the best because it would date to the mid-1960s, and would therefore be closest to his writing style in 1969. Steve's documents were particularly relevant because he *was* the Personnel Officer. Therefore official annotations could be compared to his personal annotations and reveal more samples of his hand. I had short bursts of penmanship from a man who wrote with an unusual slant to his hand.

Below, ZODIAC on left, Steve H. on right.

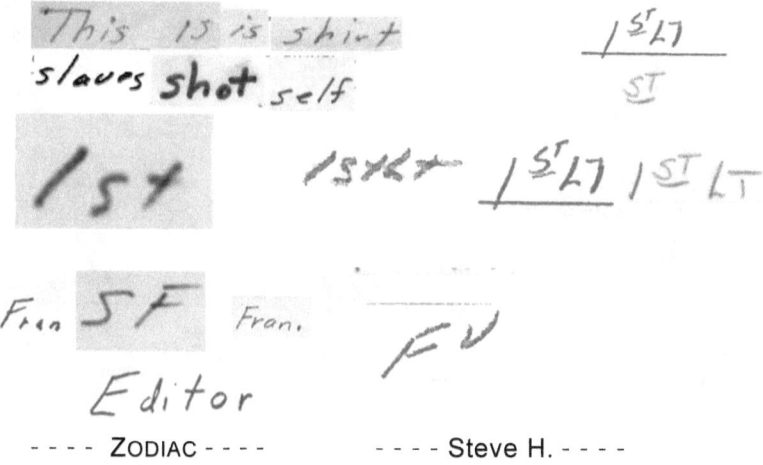

The comparison below between "July" shows how ZODIAC's "July" is just a more slanted example of Steve's.

Steve, top; ZODIAC, bottom.

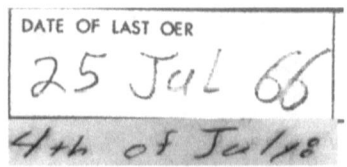

Steve's "6" undergoes unusual variation, exactly like the ZODIAC's, and on occasion he makes the same type of rare "9" that looks like a reversed 2-stroke "P." The "69" taken from the car door of the Karmann Ghia compared to Steve's notation:

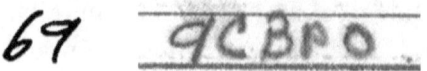

As the "25 Jul 66" notation shows, Steve's numbers at first appear radically different from ZODIAC's utilitarian numerals. But Steve varies constantly and radically. Steve's hand at work:

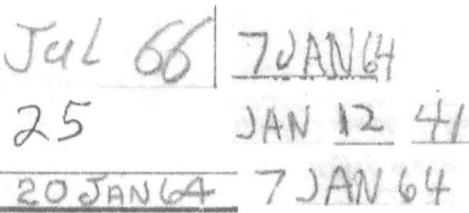

The numerals are very close to those printed by ZODIAC, below:

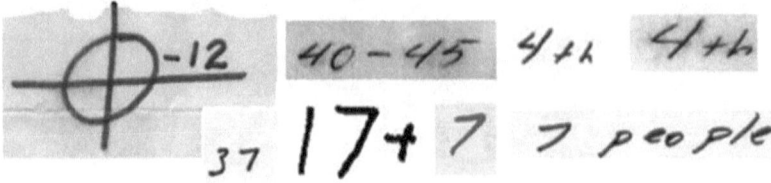

Steve's capital "P" undergoes the same variation as ZODIAC's. Below, Steve's 1-stroke and 2-stroke "P".

Although I had finally obtained vintage penmanship, technically what I had were the annotations of the Personnel Officer of Steve's old squadron records. This was, of course, Steve himself. Some of the above were from dental documents, which had clearly been filled out by the patient. But there was no overt statement as to who owned this hand that had the same remarkable variation as ZODIAC.

I was also able to obtain photo quality copies of a couple of Steve's pictures. One picture showed Steve older than any picture I had, dated in November 1966. With his military haircut, coupled with the way he parted his hair, from the front he would look like he had a crewcut. The picture shows the eyes and crewcut of the SFPD sketch, and the big face and high cheekbones of the Napa sketch.

The samples of vintage penmanship do not stand alone. Hunting and pecking had uncovered clues which placed the penmanship in a disturbing context.

The most important were clues to Steve's medical problems while in the Air Force. To put it frankly, he had gone mental on them. The exact diagnosis was "anxiety reaction with manifestations, not qualified to return to isolated duty." The problems began in 1964 when he started experiencing infrequent chest pains and a "tight feeling." This had been evaluated, and the doctor believed it to be "secondary to nerves." However, with his new posting to Johnston Atoll it must have gotten severe enough to fly him to Hickam Field, Hawaii, in February 1967. "The problem sleeping, excessive worry, and nervous trouble all refer to recent anxiety reaction with manifestations. . . Examinee denies all else."

This wasn't just a case of nerves. He was thought to be a danger to the Air Force and to himself. Although he was then officially declared "not qualified for AF commission," more specialist evaluation was recommended. By April 1, 1967, he was shipped off to Wilford Hall Hospital, Lackland AFB, Texas, where he'd remain in observation until separated in July. This is an interesting timeline. Instead of being released, he is 4 months in some kind of observation.

"Examinee denies all else" is a provocative line to leave one dangling with 50 years later. Denies what? Denies assertions made by other officers or commanders as to his behavior? Or does the answer lie in psychiatry's outlook (in the 1960s) on "Anxiety Reaction."

I had to study the period's professional view on this particular mental disorder. According to Drs. Jane M. Murphy and Alexander H. Leighton (*Anxiety: Its Role in the History of Psychiatric Epidemiology,* Psychol Med., July 2009): "The first American Psychiatric Association's Diagnostic and Statistical Manual (DSM-I) (1952) was formulated largely on the basis of psychoanalytic thinking. DSM-I's introduction to the major category called 'Psychoneurotic Disorders' indicated that 'the chief characteristic of these disorders is anxiety.' The sub-categories were called 'Reactions' with Anxiety heading the list followed by Dissociative, Conversion, Phobic, Obsessive-Compulsive, and Depressive Reactions."

I discovered that, surprisingly, depression was considered a manifestation of psychosis back then and not neurosis. Steve had a BA in Psychology. He would have known enough to deny any such "manifestation" of his anxiety problem in order not to be diagnosed as "psychotic." This seems the basis for the statement "examinee denies all else"— he was denying any other symptoms. But considering that 4 months of hospitalization ensued, the doctors may not have believed him.

At the earlier examination in 1964, Steve had already admitted to chest tightness and insomnia. These were only 2 physical symptoms that were part of the gamut known as "Manifestations." They are: "nervousness, palpitations, dizziness, shortness of breath, cold sweats, fainting spells, nightmares, pressure in the head, hands trembling, sick headaches, hands sweating, upset stomach, health troubles, fingernail biting, and sleep difficulties." How many did he have by the time they committed him for 4 months? However many "manifestations" he may have had, they didn't want him immediately discharged from the Air Force despite already having diagnosed him as unfit to remain.

Was it the guinea pig mentality of the time? They had a subject they might study for free for a while. Four months of forced psychiatric treatment at an Air Force hospital might have turned Steve into something quite antiestablishment.

The above samples of Steve's writing were all very interesting, but I held none in as much esteem as his many, many examples of signatures. These linked him to a specific ZODIAC letter—"Badlands." It is not surprising considering the B in Badlands was so suggestive of handwriting. I had no capital B from Steve, but he made other looped letters similarly.

The B from Badlands compared to Steve's handwritten ph.

Given the evidence that ZODIAC wrote some words/letters upside down, it is interesting to note that in the *Examiner* response, the one letter we know was the product of haste, Z's writing is closer to the cursive of the Badlands "B," and the "d" is merely the upside down version of Steve's "p," the same "p" in Z's "Badlands" letter.

Examiner:

Badlands:

At this stage, I had to remind myself of the FBI summation of their examination of the Riverside material. "It was not determined whether the questioned hand printing . . . was prepared by the writer of the Zodiac letters...because of variation in the material. Nothing of particular handwriting significant to. . ." make a valid comparison. The above material was obviously not enough. But ultimately that is not the reason to pause with caution.

By the time I had attained this information on Steve H., Omicron was firmly in my vision. Omicron was a definite link to Leigh Allen. Steve, on the other hand, represented only a tenuous link. Like Allen he was an enthusiastic snorkeler/skin diver. Unlike southern California, it's a small crowd in northern California. Each somehow comes to know of the other, even if only on a first name basis or by description. Thus Steve could have been downwind of Allen's tall tales. But he certainly wasn't Omicron. I wanted to dismiss him. Now I couldn't. How could he possibly fit in with Allen's reject crowd?

The answer lay beyond a fork in the road, one before which straddles Leigh Allen. Along one path is Leigh's old Atascadero inmate. Steve H. represented the path that curved out of sight. The joins may be there between all three, but unless I found Omicron I knew I couldn't work a lead.

Much has transpired in 50 years since Sherwood Morrill boasted he could identify the ZODIAC's printing merely from a bank deposit slip. Some accept and some reject the bloody fingerprints in Stine's cab. Some accept and some reject that ZODIAC is also the gunman in southern California. Some don't trust the DNA lifted from stamps. Others do. Some accept Riverside. Some don't. The most destructive arguments surround the viability of using penmanship as evidence. Just what is being used to triage suspects? Clearly, it depends on the jurisdiction's or individual detective's standards.

The ramifications for any thesis are obvious. I had to refine my quest even more and protect it by the sheer volume of argument. I also had to gaze through the looking glass to contemplate the world into which I was walking.

25
THROUGH THE TRIAGE GLASS

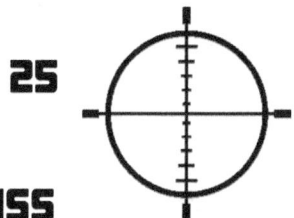

THOSE WHO CREATE AN ELABORATE CONTROVERSY OVER WHAT constitutes evidence mimic the contradictory methodology contained in Robert Graysmith's second book *Zodiac Unmasked*. Numerous comments are made, intentional or not, which muddy everything but maintain Leigh Allen, who matched none of the evidence, as a viable suspect. For example, he quotes Dave Toschi as pessimistic over the bloody latents in Stine's cab. "Toschi knew that less than twelve points of similarity would be subject to an expert's 'opinion' and that fragmentary prints, such as they had, most often could not be positively matched." Yet independent of Graysmith both Toschi and Bill Armstrong had declared their certainty (1978; 1989) that latents were *the* source via which to identify ZODIAC.

Which rendition to believe? Perhaps the answer is not beyond the looking glass but down the rabbit hole.

Arguments over hand printing go beyond the possibility of intentional disguise, at least thanks to Graysmith's rendition. One expert (Terry Pascoe) told him not to discount Allen on hand printing because of altered psychological states. Then, amazingly, Graysmith writes that Sherwood Morrill disagreed. He didn't believe altered states of mind would affect printing. Yet an evolving mental state had been Morrill's excuse in order to support Avery's claim that the Riverside material could have been written by ZODIAC.

Sherwood Morrill didn't compromise with Paul Avery alone, if Graysmith is to be believed. He attributes an absurd quote to Morrill. Concerning Allen's printing, Morrill tells Toschi: "Sorry Dave.

There's just no match. I'm sure you have the right suspect and I'm sure you're on the right track." So much for handwriting analysis. Yet Graysmith turned to Morrill for a second opinion on Leigh Allen's official handwriting sample. "I do now note that the printing that Allen is doing is contrived and not natural to his own."

Accepting any of the above only creates one thing: an atmosphere of doubt, precisely what one would want if they don't want their special suspect to be triaged out of the game.

Having a copy of Allen's official handwriting sample, I made a comparison with his letter I had to his old Lompoc friend. It is indeed obvious Allen was disguising his printing during the test. It was not the product of an altered state.

> In answer to your asking for more details about the good times I had in Vallejo, I shall be very happy to supply even more material.

> All people who are shaking hands shake hands like that.

> In answer to your asking for more details about the good times I had in Vallejo. I shall be very happy to supply even more more material.

> All people who are shaking hands shake hands like that.

Above, Leigh Allen wrote this while Toschi and Armstrong stood over. Below, Allen's natural style taken from his letter to an old Lompoc friend.

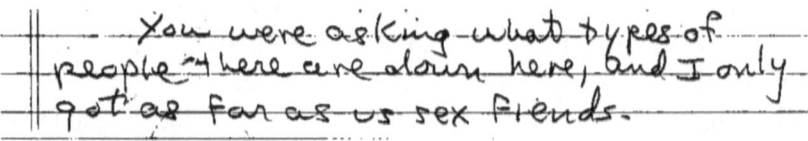

Sherwood Morrill was right about Leigh Allen's handwriting sample. But how many times did it take him to examine samples and in what context before he could render a consistent conclusion? Graysmith quotes John Lynch: "[E]very time I'd take a handwriting sample to Morrill, he'd just sit at his desk and I'd hand it to him and 'No good.' He did that I don't know how many times."

The world of triaging was fraught with pitfalls, and John Lynch's quote reveals Morrill's weakness. It is apparently via this method he triaged out all persons of interest. There was also no champion for a specific suspect standing over him, coming back with excuses and mitigating reasons to question each sample. There was, in fact, no one pushing such points with him over any of the samples from any person of interest except Paul Avery (the "morbid poem") and Graysmith (Leigh Allen) and on those two occasions Morrill did brodies back and forth.

Official investigators can't help but be cynically affected as well by a claim of "matching" hand printing. But it isn't because of the art of handwriting analysis. It is because too much finagling has been done to support popular suspects that it desensitizes one to the claims of matching hand printing.

I perhaps have not helped in the previous chapter. I do not take the extreme view that penmanship is an easy path to the solution. Nor the other extreme that it was so disguised it is utterly fruitless to follow that path with any suspect. Enough of ZODIAC's actual penmanship comes through along with the bogus so that penmanship can heavily suggest a suspect and guide us onward.

Context is also key to hand writing analysis. Armistead Maupin, for instance, not only recognized the "fan mail" handwriting matched the Xmas card's personal note from Toschi, but the "fans" with matching printing were the only ones writing in to resurrect Toschi's character in the series "Tales of the City." Maupin was qualified enough to draw the right conclusions because he had context. Nothing shown to Morrill except the Riverside material was really in context to anything derived from an investigation.

All the rage today, DNA would seem to be the sure-proof way to identify ZODIAC. There are problems here too. DNA exists in only one place: stamps on letters sent to the *Chronicle*. Yet this is also called into question. Someone else may have licked the stamps, or the DNA could be from a postal employee handling it when selling it. For quite some time these were the excuses to keep Leigh Allen viable, since his DNA also didn't match that taken from stamps. Yet more DNA was again isolated in 2018 and declared to be viable. However, nothing has come of a much anticipated genealogical database matching, the method via which J.J. DeAngelo was identified as the East Area Rapist that very year.

As for the bloody latents, there is another loose string. Were those bloody prints in Stine's cab checked to see if they were Stine's? Clutching his dead hand, ZODIAC could have placed them on the handlebar. Stine's body was hanging out the passenger side door, arms over head. Why? ZODIAC could have pulled his body by the arm, partially closed the door, and still have reached the outside handle with Stine's bloody dead hand.

Because Don Cheney modified some statements (*e.g.* when he first heard Allen's tale) there have been attempts to discredit him. While he sometimes suffered from memory contamination in later life due to repeat exposure to zealous enthusiasts, his original statement to the police is the sole source here. His later modification was only minor, stating it was some time before January 1969 that he heard Allen's foothill's crime fiction scenario.

An event has occurred recently which underscores the complexity of ZODIAC's game. His hitherto undeciphered 340 Cipher has been cracked by an advanced specially designed computer program.

Decipherment occurred on December 11, 2020. Generating thousands of potential sequences for the code symbols to represent the English alphabet, finally the program sent back a largely gibberish rendition of Roman letters. But within it words could be made out: **I HOPE** and specifically **GAS CHAMBER**. Using this as the key the amateur codebreakers, Jarl Van Eycke, David Oranchak, and Sam Blake, discovered the cipher was broken into 3 parts.

The first two parts were of 9 lines and the code message was encrypted diagonally. The last two lines were the third part. They ran horizontally left to right and right to left. It was a complex and convoluted way to encrypt a code, but the message that came forth fit ZODIAC's vocabulary and the circumstances of early November 1969. This was obvious by the reference to the *AM San Francisco* TV episode and "caller Sam" which had generated so much national news. Sam had expressed his fear of going to the gas chamber. When cracked, the 340 Cipher read:

(First 9 lines read diagonally)
I HOPE YOU ARE HAVING LOTS OF FAN IN TRYING TO CATCH ME. THAT WASNT ME ON THE TV SHOW WHICH BRINGO UP A POINT ABOUT ME. I AM NOT AFRAID OF THE GAS CHAMBER BECAASE IT WILL SEND ME TO PARADCE ALL THE

(Second 9 lines read diagonally)
SOOHER BECAUSE E NOW HAVE ENOUGH SLAVES TO WORV FOR ME WHERE EVERYONE ETSE HAS NOTHING WHEN THEY REACH PARADICE SO TREY ARE AFRAID OF DEATH. I AM NOT AFRAID BECAUSE I VNOW THAT MY NEW

(Final two lines read horizontally)

LIFE WILL BE AN EASY ONE IN PARADICE.
(All misspellings and miscodings are ZODIAC's)

On the first line of the second part, LIFE IS was encoded in normal left to right order rather than diagonal. I did not include it in the reading above. But when added to the misplaced DEATH ending the cryptogram, it reads:

LIFE IS DEATH

A large number of errors exist which can be explained now briefly. I manually backworked the codebreakers' results and discovered that 1 symbol went unused in the first part (probably because ZODIAC misspelled WAS NOT to WASNT) and on the 6th line of the second part of 9 lines he had misplaced the correct symbol one space to the left, causing all the words associated with that line to be misspelled by one letter— *e.g.* worv for work.

Decipherment proved ZODIAC was no expert, but its complexity shows to what extent he indulged in his game of terror. That he did not expect it to be cracked easily is reflected in his Belli Letter of December 20. Therein he mimics the demented attitude of Caller Sam, but in the cipher he had already admitted he was not Sam.

This is not a villain who simply dashed off his letters in his normal everyday hand. Nor is it likely he licked his own stamps.

The cracking of the 340 Cipher reveals a disturbing and significant clue. "I now have enough slaves to work for me. . ." We know this to be a true statement. Time has proven it so. After ZODIAC achieved the sensation of metropolitan terror he did something undeniable. He quit. This clue should have loudly reverberated. ZODIAC had already decided to quit after Stine, and he hid this fact in a complex cipher that took 50 years to crack. He did so in order to continue his terror campaign via bogusly claiming more victims.

Why did someone who committed the ultimate crime, in the hazardous circumstances in which ZODIAC committed his murders, just as easily stop after metropolitan terror was achieved? There was something far more complex here than just the acts of a sex killer and momma hater. Was ZODIAC within Allen's crankcase crowd of rejects? Was there another involved and this truly was a conspiracy?

The potential of The Omicron Suspect grew with each turn of the calendar page. He, a mere idea, haunted me and influenced every caution I had. He had become a black dog on my back. And every syllable from Leigh Allen reinforces the concept of Omicron's existence and his implicit refusal to cooperate. Even in this chapter we encounter Allen engaging in deception. Why, if totally innocent, contrive his hand printing sample? I don't like the idea of conspiracy, but I couldn't shake Leigh's behavior at the oil refinery interview and the clues that he suspected someone around him had purloined his inventive crime scenario. He was dirty or he feared something or someone.

. . .I was finally to discover. . .

26
THE IOTA OF OMICRON

GOING THROUGH NEWS REPORTS AND LEGAL EXTEMPORANEA OF court sentencings, I uncovered a surprising number of perpetrators committed to Atascadero State Hospital who fit my criteria—sex psychopath who had spent the Summer of 1962 as an inmate or someone who had come from the East Bay Area and who might have already known Leigh Allen before or after being committed.

To appreciate how large this corral was, the reader must understand how the system worked. After a judge felt the guilty was a candidate for lunacy, he was stashed into the State bedlam for 90 days observation. If they agreed he was mental but treatable, he'd be sentenced to serve time there. Thus I had to look at sentencings from 1959 through 1967, the latter part of the range made necessary since Omicron, as mentioned, could have already known or come to have known Leigh Allen in those years and had no connection to the Summer of 1962.

This was a broad target indeed made wider by the fact I was not limiting myself to child molesters. It was never qualified if that was merely Leigh Allen's excuse to the Tuckers or whether they saw a reference in the letter. Phil, who showed little interest, relays Allen's claim, but Joan does not. From her we only know it was a letter from someone who felt he had been railroaded into Atascadero.

The hard way had been tedious and time-consuming. I had to determine how long each inmate had been committed, where they had come from, and determine if any had a military stint in his background. Though a daunting task, this hard way had proved the better way. It was unlikely I could have missed the Omicron. From the above criteria, I had uncovered 3 candidates.

Not to get ahead of the narrative, but I got photos and— well, it complicated things immensely— two looked like the Napa sketch! In terms of suggesting a link between ZODIAC and Leigh Allen, this was impressive "coincidence." But it was not so much intriguing as what I next uncovered. Both knew the East Bay hunting and fishing scene, the only avenue that fit a *continuing* connection to Allen.

Even before I had pursued Omicron's identity, the outdoorsman angle had come to mean much to me. It was not because ZODIAC knew rural areas. It was not just because Don Cheney had heard Allen's fanciful hatchworks about a "Zodiac" crime spree during one such excursion. It was ZODIAC's pants. They were peg-leg, cuffed, pleated, roomy, baggy if you must, something out of the 1940/50s. He wore a dark pair at Lake Berryessa and then a rust brown pair in San Francisco. There is a third color: olive drab. I knew this because I had the olive drab in the early 1980s. These three colors and old pleated style continued to be manufactured even until then. They were sold to gardeners and fishermen, etc., through sportsman's stores and catalogs because they were roomy and comfortable. Before the old-style fashion was popularly reborn in the mid-1980s the said same obsolete style of pants continued to be made in a limited variety and for a limited use. And these are the pants ZODIAC wore. He chose something he most likely already had.

Those pants and color schemes, because I could identify their origin and use, had nagged as being a significant clue, and here a search for Omicron raised more than one ZODIAC look-alike who was a sportsman and Atascadero reject for sex psychopath.

On his hunting and scuba diving excursions, Leigh Allen babbled on and anybody within the general sphere could have picked up on his stories. If I was right that Allen suspected he had inspired the 'Zodiac' Killer he might have wanted a psychological student like Joan Tucker to go over the letter and tell him if the writer was killer material. For some reason, however, he got cold feet, leaving The Omicron Suspect an inference I had to prove.

Without Leigh Allen's inadvertent clue it would have been impossible to infiltrate the nuances of the East Bay outdoorsman culture. This was a freewheeling crowd that wouldn't necessarily cooperate. This is underscored by a factor in the Lake Herman Road murders. This bothered the original investigators back then. Old Frank Gasser and young Bob Connelly lied. There is no other way to put it. "He [Connelly] states that approximately 5 minutes later [after the Yours] they drove in his truck, a '59 Chevrolet, red in color, with white wood sideboards, cattle guards on the sides. They drove this truck back to the Gasser ranch heading towards Benicia and they passed the car [David's Rambler]." When Lundblad and Butterbach asked them where the Rambler was parked in the turnout, they gave a totally fatuous reply—"They described the light colored 1960 Rambler S/W that was parked at the gate. It was parked Southwest of where we finally found the car. This discrepancy wasn't noted at first." The detectives went back and asked Connelly. "[He] insists that the Rambler was parked on the bank. That would be on the South side. He did not see any person in the car."

For inclusion in the report, the detectives drew a map. The map reflects the impossible. It requires one to believe that as soon as the Yours passed around 11:07 p.m. David Faraday moved his Rambler to the bank area. Then after Connelly and Gasser passed about 5 minutes later, he parked back where they had been before and where the crime was then committed.

The easiest thing to believe is that Connelly and Gasser lied. They didn't head toward Benicia and pass the turnout. They went to Vallejo in the other direction.

I suspect that around 10 p.m. while traipsing through the field to get to the pumping station (where they admit to treeing and shooting a raccoon) they likely saw the Rambler parked on the bank. David moved it later and they simply didn't know that. Or they saw the white car Bingo Wesner had described parked there at 10 p.m. They associated that car with being the Rambler. Either way they lied. For whatever reason, they didn't want to admit to their whereabouts after encountering the Yours.

I'm not incriminating them. I am pointing out that their story has irreconcilable contradictions. The reasons can be debated. But the poignant example contained in the above is this. These are two very different men, age 69 and 27, who came from as far afield as Napa and the outskirts of Benicia. They are representative of many bands and braces of men hunting the East Bay corridor. Many are now dead, those remaining can't remember, some have reasons to

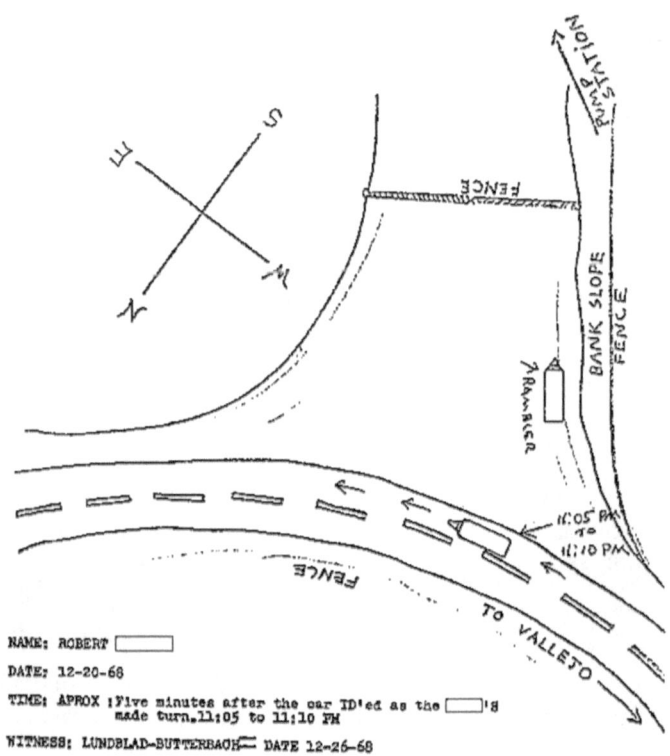

NAME: ROBERT [ ]
DATE: 12-20-68
TIME: APROX :Five minutes after the car ID'ed as the [ ]'s made turn. 11:05 to 11:10 PM
WITNESS: LUNDBLAD-BUTTERBACH DATE 12-26-68

lie. The most important point is context: each and every one could have been downwind of Leigh Allen's tall tales. Now multiply this by 100 outdoorsmen. To search all these leads would be throwing darts without a board.

The importance of The Omicron Suspect is thus evident. Without that void of space given us by Leigh Allen, I could not have focused on Atascadero and a time frame. And thus it would have been impossible to have discovered the disturbing iotas of information that now lead us onward.

It is not necessary to go through the steps of elimination I took. It is best to cut to the chase. Of the two who matched the sketch, let's go to the Summer of 1962 and ZODIAC's dead ringer.

The case of Gary Warren was but a minor one insofar as the legal news was concerned. In 1960, he proposed to his girlfriend and she said no. The result: he tried to strangle her with his hands and then snuff her with the pillow. This was more than enough to get him bounced into Atascadero.

Gary Lee Warren was born in Glendale on May 22, 1939. By the time he was 10 years old, his father Leon was a credit manager at a loan company in Los Angeles. During his high school days his father and mother were separated. He had been a mediocre student at John Burroughs High, Burbank, involved in Basic Aeronautics and the California Cadet Corps. He was also working part time at an auto dealership. This got him photographed with his employer, Art Hartgraves, in the *Valley Times* on April 6, 1957. But he didn't go into the auto business. He graduated with the intent to become a draftsman. He also entered the Air Force Reserve.

Gary was just 1 year out of high school when his father Leon suddenly died at the age of 42 in 1958. His mother Barbara Hope remarried 3 months later to Chester Partis, a man also in the financial business who now ran his own collection agency in Santa Barbara. I learned that "financial business" meant car repossession.

It is during this time that he met Pauline Kupker, a waitress at the *Blue Onion* café in Santa Barbara. His stepfather and mother lived on De La Vina Street, but as a part of their properties his mother owned a trailer near Ventura. It is here that young Gary proposed to Pauline in June of 1960. It is here she said no and it is here where he tried to choke her in response.

According to the July 5, 1963, *Ventura County Star Free Press* Warren had been in Atascadero since 1960 and he was now being returned to Ventura county jail from Atascadero State Hospital because "Hospital officials say Garry [sic] Warren, 24, is still a sexual psychopath, but is not amendable to hospital treatment." A hearing was scheduled for July 17. "If the court finds him to be a sexual psychopath he probably would be sent to State Department of Mental Hygiene [Chino Institute for Men] for prison placement. If not, he would stand trial for a charge of assault."

This was a big statement. Placement at Atascadero was usually for about 2 years. At that time the inmate would have improved and been returned for sentencing or further deposition, such as to serve his time at the hospital. In Warren's case, he had been there for close to 3 years and was now rejected.

A plea bargain instigated by his attorney had dispensed with a trial. "In 1960, Warren pleaded guilty to the assault charge and a charge of assault with attempt to commit murder was dropped." So the plea bargain allowed him to exculpate himself of the intent to kill his girlfriend. He had simply gone nuts. Now on July 17, 1963, his attorney, Lawrence Chapman, stood by and his client spoke. "Warren said he blacked out and could not remember the alleged attack. He was in the U.S. Air Force at the time." If the new claim of blacking out didn't work, he faced being sent to Chino.

And this was indeed his fate. On July 19, the newspaper reported that Judge Jerome H. Berenson "found that Garry [sic] Warren, 24, is a sexual psychopath." He was committed to Chino.

Next we hear in the Oxnard *Press Courier* for February 2, 1966, that Warren has applied for probation.

From what I had, I could imagine how bitter he was. Not only was there a plea bargain that got him committed to the State madhouse, but it had come from his girlfriend's charge. He had spent 5 years in Atascadero/Chino. It had not been prudent to admit to guilt. But what was the alternative?— a trial for intent to murder. Yet I was uncovering snippets that he was an intelligent man who took up his schooling again in Santa Barbara and continued his sportsman routine *over* California.

I had a dead ringer in Gary Warren, an unamenable sex psychopath at Atascadero in the summer of 1962 who was also a dedicated outdoorsman. From what I was continuing to turn up, I had no doubt Warren was indeed The Omicron Suspect. I had found him.

The trail had indeed led south where I wanted it to lead. What really had gone down in his case and in his life thereafter? I didn't have to walk a long and ambiguous path to find out. Ventura County Superior Court came through. I got all the dirt.

27

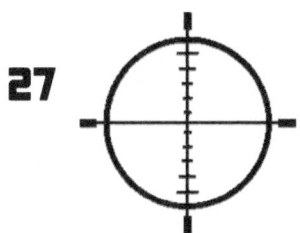

DEAD RINGER

"He is one of the most dangerous people I have seen. He is likely to choke you. I wouldn't be his girlfriend for anything in the world. I wouldn't be at all happy with him on probation. I would be uneasy." — Philip R.A. May M.D., Court appointed psychiatrist.

ABOUT 3 O'CLOCK IN THE AFTERNOON ON AN AVERAGE DAY IN MAY 1960, 21 year old Gary Warren came into the *Blue Onion* restaurant in Santa Barbara. Dutch immigrant Pauline Kupker was one of the carhops. "He asked me if I would like to go to the movies that evening with him. . . . I got off work about 6 p.m. and waited for him and he came by around 7 p.m." They went to the Airport Drive-in in Goleta. "There was no kissing. He was very polite." After the show he drove her back to the *Blue Onion* and dropped her off by her car around midnight.

This is how Pauline's friendship began with Gary. He was a husky guy, about 5 foot 10 and a beefy 185 pounds.

A week later Gary pops up at the *Blue Onion* again. It is 7 p.m. "We didn't have a date. He just came and said 'Let's go to the Drive-in.'" To her surprise: "That night he asked me to marry him and I said no. It was kind of a surprise to me. He didn't try to kiss me. Well, maybe later he kissed me once."

> He seemed like a nice guy, quiet, doesn't talk much. I didn't notice anything unusual about him. He took me back to the car to the restaurant where my car was parked about 11:30 or 12.

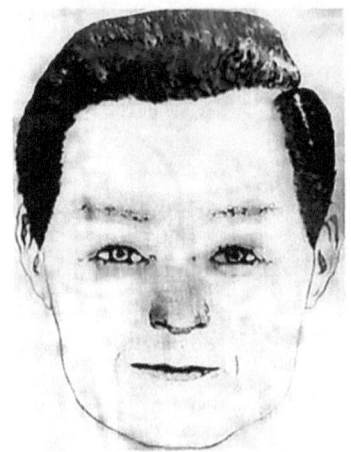 

The Napa sketch, left, compared to the photo used for high school graduation of Gary Lee Warren, 1957.

On the night of June 17, 1960, Gary's younger sister was to be married in Las Vegas. Gary should have been there preparing for the festivities. Pauline didn't know this, so she wasn't surprised at what next transpired. She got off work about 6 p.m. and took some of the other girls home. She returned to the *Blue Onion*. The other carhops told her that Gary had been there looking for her. She got in her car and drove downtown. She saw him in his 55 Mercury driving the other way. She pulled over and he did a U-turn. She got in and they got gas and drove out of town down Highway 101.

Pauline wanted to get something off her mind. Another one of the carhops, Betty Nunez, had said Gary tried to kill her. "He said he didn't and I believed him. He didn't talk all the way to the trailer and he seemed nervous."

They arrived at his mother's house trailer on the beach by the Knickerbocker Motel and Café (Breakers Way today).

> We stopped near the trailer. He opened the door and let me in. He told me he had to pick up his jacket. I was wearing my Blue Onion uniform. When we got in the trailer, he asked me if I liked the trailer and I said yes. He asked me if I would like to see the back of it. Then he said 'Betty wasn't kidding. I tried to kill her and I'm going to kill you tonight.' He pushed me on the bed and put his hands around my neck. I started screaming and he put a pillow over my

head. Then I kicked him someplace, then he told me I had to turn around. I did, and he let up a little. Then he tried to choke me again. I kept trying to scream but couldn't very well.

I was unconscious almost. I didn't scream anymore and didn't breathe. I think that's why he took his hands away, I guess. Then I stood up and he asked me if I would marry him. I said yes that time. I just wanted to get out of the trailer.

Gary told her that he would take her back to her car and she could pick it up and they would head later to Las Vegas ". . . but on the way back he didn't talk about it. He drove me back to Santa Barbara and dropped me off." She went into the *Blue Onion* and talked with Mr. Longmire, the manager. After she told her story, he called the police. The bruise marks on her neck were obvious. "I had bruise marks on my neck for a couple of weeks."

The Santa Barbara responding officer naturally started an investigation. It began with Betty Nunez.

She recalled that her incident with Warren occurred on the 4th or 5th of June. She was walking home when Warren drove up "nearby" and asked her if she wanted a ride. She said no. He drove 'round the block and pulled right up to her. He "got out of the car and placed a knife next to her stomach and said, 'Come on.'" Of course, she got in the car.

However, as soon as she got in the car Gary told her he was kidding. He just wanted her to ride around with him. He then drove her to his house trailer behind the Knickerbocker Motel and Café. After a few minutes, Gary said:

"What would happen if I really meant that I was going to kill you?"

She replied that she didn't know.

"The defendant then stuck a knife next to her stomach and said: 'I'm going to kill you.'"

According to the police report:

> Miss Nunez states that she pleaded with him for a few moments, then he seemed to snap out of it and asked her what had happened. She advised him that he had placed a knife next to her stomach and had told her that he was going to kill her. At this

point, she reports, the defendant acted as though this were funny and that he could hardly believe it. He did tell her though that this happened to him a couple of times before and that she could turn him over to the police if she wanted.

Betty told Gary he should see a doctor and he said he was going to do so. He then drove her back to Santa Barbara. "He attempted to date her once or twice following this incident but she refused. Upon her refusal, the defendant reportedly said: 'Why won't you date me? Is it because I pulled a knife on you?'"

Investigation was going backwards now to November 1959. Gary dated a girl named Sherrie Maco or Macko. "They went to a Drive-In and afterwards parked on the way home. She reported that the defendant spoke to her of killing himself because of the difficulties in his personal life. [His fiancée and he were having trouble; his late father's business partner had married his mother and was no good.] She stated that her back ached and the defendant started massaging it. He reportedly said: 'This won't hurt,' and began choking her. She reports she tried to break loose and tried to claw his arm with her fingernails but her nails were not long enough. She states that he choked her for at least 3 minutes and that she began to get dizzy. When she found she could not get free she acted as though she had died and the defendant released his hold on her throat. Afterward the defendant apologized, adding, 'I lose my temper easily.' As he was taking her home, he stated 'I don't suppose you want to see me anymore after this?' Red marks on the girl's throat subsequently turned black and blue and remained for approximately three days."

Going back further, the police investigation seemed to be getting to the root of the problem. He had broken up with his girlfriend and couldn't get over it. From some point in 1958, a year after he had graduated high school, he had been going steady with Kathie Rull, another John Burroughs student, three years younger than he. This relationship got rocky in Autumn 1959 and ended in February 1960 when she was in her senior year. She reported that during December 1959 Gary had choked her over some "small argument" they had had. Then in February she was sick at home and he came by to visit. She refused to let him in. He was leaving when her mother pulled up. He returned with her and she let him in. "He conversed for a few moments, then the defendant left." Shortly afterward, the mother went to the store. Soon after Kathie was alone, Gary had quietly returned and let himself in the back door with a key he had stealthily taken from the mantel while speaking earlier with mom. "The defendant then reportedly told Kathie that he was going to choke her and proceeded to do so until she became unconscious."

When the girl regained consciousness the defendant was sitting in the living room acting nonchalant. It is reported that during the incident the defendant used such force that a necklace the girl was wearing became imbedded in her flesh and caused bleeding. The marks on the girl's neck lasted some three weeks.

Kathie had to think quick. She told Gary that she had to phone her mother at the store to remind her to pick up some medicine that was on hold. When her mother received the call at the store, she knew there was a problem, as there was no medicine waiting for her to pick up. Then Kathie told her mother that she was sending Gary to pick it up. He had returned and he had choked her. When Gary arrived, Kathie's mom laid into him and made him admit what he had been up to. She told him to get a shrink or she'd call the cops and he said he intended to.

"Within approximately two weeks," writes the reporting officer, "the defendant consulted a hypnotherapist [a Hollywood specialist on Normandie Ave.] who advised him that the problem was beyond hypnotherapy and suggested that he consult a psychiatrist."

This was all one-sided, of course. There may have been 4 points to this side—Kathie, Sherrie, Betty, Pauline— but still only one of them had turned him into the police. It was time to get Warren's side of the story.

On June 29, 1960, Gary Lee Warren was arrested. He spent 6 days in jail and was out on $525.00 bail on July 5, 1960. "The District Attorney of the County of Ventura hereby accuses Gary Warren of the crime of violation of Section 217 of the Penal code in that on or about June 17, 1960, in the County of Ventura, State of California, he did assault Pauline Kupker with force likely to produce great bodily harm with intent to murder her."

John Danch was appointed as his attorney. He pled "not guilty" and "not guilty by reason of insanity."

This naturally triggered statutory requirements. Drs. Vernon G Bugh, Philip R.A. May, and William James, of Camarillo Hospital, were appointed to examine him and give him tests to see if there was any organic reason for blackouts. This required a lot of questioning. I will not introduce separately each doctor's discoveries. I will combine them and note, when necessary, where they differ. May was by far the most investigative. Warren was intelligent, but he was being selective in his recall. He was also playing up being crazy.

Dr. May records a few choice statements. "I did something no one in his right mind would do. June 17, eight p.m., I saw Pauline on the street (Santa Barbara) and waved at her, said 'hi,' known her since last April, had seen her every night for 3-4 weeks; car hop Blue Onion—go out and have fun; no sex; kiss, nothing more." His recollection of the incident: "I was showing her around; in the back of the bedroom she said something to me; I said something to her (can't remember what it was). Everything went blank; next thing she was on bed on her side. I was behind her, holding her arms; I was shaking her; she was crying. I said let's go. According to her I pushed her on the bed, then put pillow over head, took it off, then stepped back and came at her again . . . She was crying most of the way back to Santa Barbara, said did I know what I did. I knew it had been violent. She said we had a fight and she didn't want to talk about it."

Throughout his chat with Dr. May, Warren denied any sexual intent. He wasn't aroused. But he did associate his attack with Kathie, to whom he was engaged last June. "I found out she had been taking me for a ride (6-8 months); she got plenty of presents and money spent on her. The main reason I went active in the Service, she and I broke up last January. I went active in March. Maybe back here (in head) I was trying to get even with Kathy [sic]."

He clarified he wasn't drunk. He'd had 3 to 4 cans of beer. He was not unsteady. He drove her back just fine. Let her out. She was now calm. "She says I said I was going to kill her. I don't remember saying it. If I did, I didn't mean it. I hate violence. Never threatened people." (Bugh: "He remembers being hot and flushed and frightened when he became aware of the circumstances, but otherwise, does not recall feeling strange.")

May noted that Warren admitted he was depressed at the time. He had phoned Kathie and suggested they get married. "He thinks he must have done the things he's accused of," writes May before he quotes Warren: "I probably did. It looks like it."

According to Warren, his family history was a violent one. His father, Leon Warren, had died in January 1958, of diabetes and cardiac issues. He was only 42. He was an argumentative man who used to beat his children and wife. He drank heavily and owned a car repossessing business in Burbank. When Gary came of age, he entered the business. "They didn't get along at all when Gary went into Basic Training for the Air Force, but after he returned things got better." He was beaten by his father when drunk and sober.

His mother remarried in May to Chester Partis, who had earlier partnered into the business. It wasn't working out. Gary repeatedly had arguments with Partis, accusing him of doing no work. (Bugh: "defendant describes stepfather as a person hard to get along with.") Finally he told him the business was his, and then it folded three months later. He is the oldest child, a younger sister age 17, and a half sister 13 months old "cuter than hell."

May notes there is family history of cancer and diabetes but not of mental illness or epilepsy.

As for other background, Warren graduated high school 1957, a B to C student. "Didn't like school very much," noted May. "No serious disciplinary action."

He entered the Reserves in December 1956. He had 11 weeks of basic training, then Air Force Reserve. Entered active reserve March 1960 and now changed to Regular status. He was a draftsman, Arman 3rd class. Stationed at Vandenberg A.F.B., no disciplinary problems, 4 year enlistment. "Does not plan to stay." He plans to get a B.A. in civil engineering while in the Service. During school days, he worked as a paperboy, stock boy in stores, box boy, delivery, sold used cars, May Company, gas stations. After graduation, worked in auto repo business with dad. After he let Partis have it, he worked for Pacific Finance, August-October 1959. Had girlfriend trouble then worked until February 1960 for Bank of America. He asserted he worked well and had no trouble.

As for religion, he said he was Baptist and a fairly regular attendant of church services. He has had more religion over the last 2 years. "I've been trying to live more by the Bible." After he leaves the Air Force, he said, he wants to help in church. He even thought about Seminary, but then decided against it.

I don't know how cynical May was, but I expect a shrink took much with a grain of salt, especially considering the charge against Warren. He had before him a 21 year old man who looked older than his age, who smoked 1 and a half packs of cigarettes a day, drinks a lot of coffee, and after Kathie spilt up with him spent his monthly salary on liquor. He got drunk frequently. Before the girlfriend problems, very little drinking. Now he drinks "every cent I got." No DTs, no narcotics, no shakes.

What is most curious for us at this stage is that he had no prior record at all, but he had worked with the police with car repossession issues. His hobbies are of even greater interest to us. Cars, of course, was first. He even raced stock cars on drag strips. As such, he knew the Riverside race track area. He also loved drawing— mechanical, architectural, engineering.

He claimed he only had one temper fit in his life and he knew what he was doing. "March 1960 he threw a plate on the ground and broke it in a fit of temper." (Bugh: threw it on kitchen floor.)

Psychosexual History:

Started dating at age 17. First sex relations at age 16. Has had sex relations fairly frequently since then. Denies sexual difficulty of any type or perverted activity. Engaged May, 1958. Cooled off September, 1959; he found out she was stepping out on him. They fought (argued), nothing physical; she says he slapped her once, but her father and he say it did not happen. Finally broke up January 1. He was hoping they could go back together. It was on his mind quite a lot.

Gary probably didn't realize May would check out the minutes of the first hearing and the police report and compare them to what he had told him. "After my first interview with the defendant, I read these records and noted certain matters which defendant had failed to mention—in fact, he had denied any other difficulty."

May noted he omitted his incident with Betty Jane Nunez. On June 14, he pulled the screen off Betty's window "after staying outside long enough to smoke two cigarettes (butts found outside)." Betty had awaken, screamed and ran. He got in, grabbed her by arms and waist. She broke away and ran. May also knew that Betty had warned Pauline that Gary had tried to kill her and Pauline had confronted him with this before the attack. May knew that Warren had said: "Betty wasn't kidding. I tried to kill her and I'm going to kill you tonight." After he choked Pauline, he had said: "Well, I want you to marry me."

It was time for a second interview. Gary declared he had proposed to Pauline on the way to the trailer, not after the assault. "I brought it up myself. When I think back on it I was trying to hurt Kathy [sic]—get back at her, out of spite. I don't think I would actually have gone through with it."

"Denies carrying a knife," writes May, "and then modifies it." In Gary's own words: "I never carried a knife in my life— well, I do own one (a skin diver knife) and a pocket knife." He had sold the skin diver's knife a couple of weeks ago.

When confronted by these discrepancies, Warren denied the "night episode" at Betty's. He could prove he was in bed the night of June 14, in an apartment he shares with 2 other guys. Denied attempting to kill Betty. Denied telling Pauline he said that before the assault. "Says he took Betty home from Blue Onion twice; she got into his car; first time was their first date and they went to a show. Second time— this was the time Pauline said Betty said we had a fight." In Warren's own words: "I said, do you want to go home or take a ride. Drove around a half hour; stopped. I kissed her once. I blacked out. Betty said we'd had a fight. She didn't seem upset." (May qualifies: "Parked car by trailer. Kissed her twice— then doesn't remember until Betty says let's go. She seemed tee'd off. He said what did I do now? She said we had a fight.")

Physical examination reveals a couple of intriguing points. Everything was normal, but the "left optic disc does not have the normal cup and the vessels appear to bend down to the disc. Margins somewhat indistinct. Veins prominent. Warren told May that his vision was never good in that eye. Blood pressure was 140/90.

Dr. William James was largely responsible for the physical and neurological tests. "The patient has had headaches for a period of three years that are described as a 'band around his head' usually beginning in the frontal area. They are present mostly when he has to do a considerable amount of drafting which requires close visual work. He does wear glasses and he feels he needs another pair at this time. . . No disturbance of speech except the patient states he has begun to stutter over the past two years. According to the patient, he had been under a considerable amount of pressure." Neurological tests were normal—skull x-rays, cerebral spinal fluid, electroencephalogram, pneumo-encephalograph.

Bugh: Mental Status— Defendant is an alert intelligent appearing 21 year old single white service man who showed a neat appearance, a normal stream of speech, a normal affect and no unusual mental trends. No delusions or hallucinations were noted. He concentrated well, calculated without error, made change correctly, interpreted proverbs adequately and showed no particular impairment of judgement."

Summary & Conclusions:

(Bugh) Defendant shows evidence of some emotional instability particularly since his break-up with his fiancée. He showed a certain pre-occupation with pushing his claims on girls with or without their cooperation. The marriage of his younger sister at the time of the offence may have been a part of the motivation to force someone to marry him. There are suggestions that he has considerable doubt about his masculinity. The very method by which he went about winning a wife, however, reveals a great deal of basic insecurity and ambivalence about performing as a man. He apparently tried to absolve himself of his anxieties by overindulging in alcoholic beverages and by adopting a rather brash, bellicose attitude toward girl friends. The so-called blackout episodes appear to be in the nature of a hysterical reaction, perhaps suggestive of a fugue state. However, defendant appears to have intended the threat, had an awareness that he would intimidate and otherwise threaten the victim, in order to achieve his ends and had an awareness that such threats and behavior would regularly result in legal recrimination against him.

Bugh found him sane at the present time and at the time of the commission of the offence.

(May): In my opinion, this man is legally sane at the present time in that he understands the nature of Court proceedings and of the charges against him and is capable of cooperating with an attorney in his own defense. I consider him to have been legally sane at the time of the alleged offense in that he knew the nature and quality of his acts and was capable of distinguishing between right and wrong.

Sane. At this juncture John Danch, the county appointed attorney, knew he'd have to strike a plea bargain deal. He would have to drop "not guilty by reason of insanity." He'd have to work some deal whereby the intent to murder charge is dropped. This he did. Code 217 was dropped for 245 of the Penal Code— assault with a deadly weapon— but not the intent to commit murder. Warren pled guilty.

Gary Warren was to be reexamined by the same doctors to see if he was a sexual psychopath in need of hospitalization. The court ordered it on November 22, 1960.

It is here we come across hints of the true Gary Warren. Reading Dr. May's first paragraph we get an idea Warren wanted to dissuade him from giving him a negative diagnosis.

> He states that since my previous examination he pleaded guilty and applied for probation, that he has been told, by his Probation Officer that there is no reason why he should not have probation, that it all depends on whether he is found to be a sexual psychopath, that his hearing is next Tuesday.

Gary presented a different appearance now.

> He is husky, clean, neatly but casually dressed, with his shirt open one button more than is customary, exposing his chest. He is alert, in good contact and answers questions readily but appears at times to be minimizing the extent or the seriousness of the difficulty; is almost often flippant and casual, or at least bland and offhand, talks with little emotion and involvement. He now admits that he did not tell the truth at the previous examination—says he was scared and didn't want to go to jail. Never had any blackouts— knew what he was doing all the time. First choked his fiancée Kathy [sic] Rull in September, 1959, "a couple of times in the apartment,

maybe a couple of times in the car" (!) Also admits choking Sherrie Maco, Pauline (present offense) and Betty Nunez. "I had my hand on her throat but I'm sure I didn't choke her; I kissed her; she said it hurt." Denies other events mentioned in the police reports, including threatening with a knife and breaking into a girl's bedroom.

Gary described psychiatric symptoms like tenseness, confusion, bottled-up rage. He blamed these feelings on Kathie after she gave back his ring. He stopped drinking and has started going to church. He feels better, May notes, but added in parentheses "cannot explain how." He claimed he dated a girl recently and had no trouble. "Tells a different psychosexual history, with sex relations less frequently than he said at first. Denies wish to rape." Gary also reminded May he had gone to a hypnotherapist in January— the inference being he has been trying to address his issues. "Now wishes to have probation and outpatient psychotherapy once a week."

May rendered his conclusions:

> In my opinion, this man is suffering from a mental disorder— psychoneurosis with schizoid, hysterical and anxiety symptoms. In a sexual situation with girls, he has impulses to choke them which he has carried out on several occasions, but never has such impulses toward men.
>
> I consider that these acts represent a pathological fusion of sexual and aggressive impulses and that they are sexual offenses. I consider him to be a sexual psychopath predisposed to the commission of sexual offences, and a menace to the health and safety of others. I consider him to be a sick man, sicker than he realizes, and in need of hospital treatment. I recommend that he be committed to the Atascadero State Hospital as a sexual psychopath for a 90-day period of observation and treatment trial.

Bugh offers other insights. He itemized Warren's victims. "The fourth girl is Pauline, according to the charges the present situation. He states that he had been dejected earlier in the day (on the day of the offense) because his sister was to be married that evening and he had previously planned to marry Kathy [sic]. . .The defendant denies that he has had other impulses to attack other girls. He admits that on occasion he has been angry with other men and has felt like fighting, but instead he usually walks away from the argument."

Aside from 5 sessions of hypnotherapy (in Hollywood), Gary stated he tried to see a psychiatrist at Vandenberg. "However, no appointment was actually obtained."

Further Psychosexual History
(Bugh) Contrary to information the defendant gave the examiner on previous occasions,— he now indicates that he has had infrequent sexual intercourse with girls. He states that he might average sex relations some four or five times per year. He continues to insist that he has no difficulty in accomplishing the sex act. He denies that he ever noticed an inner urge to rape or assault girls sexually. He states that he enjoys kissing girls on the mouth – pulling at their ears – and if the sex act is consummated he enjoys the relationship. He indicates that he has never been rejected by a girl with whom he chose to have intercourse.

Dr. Bugh noted the same present mental state as May had noted. "At this examination the defendant maintains a rather light-hearted attitude about his present predicament. He seems disciplined to consider himself to have serious emotional problems so far as his attitude goes. So far as his statement goes he indicates that he does have a serious problem. He doesn't have any particular notions about what sexual activity means to him. In this regard he maintains a rather vague and evasive attitude about sexual activity and aggressive activity as well."

In his summary and conclusions, Bugh applied the perfect summary of Warren's attitude. "At this examination it is apparent that the defendant has little understanding of the serious implications of recent aggressive behavior. He gives lip service to the idea that psychiatric treatment is necessary, but seems to avoid the implications of getting such treatment on an organized basis. He suggests that out-patient therapy might be helpful, but doesn't appear to be motivated in the direction of receiving such therapy."

Bugh felt that Warren was predisposed to sexual crimes "and indeed may be harmful to those around him. He appears to be relatively unaware of the nature of his sexual confusion and is not highly motivated for help."

Thus, it is the conclusion of this examiner that the defendant is a sexual psychopath within the meaning of the law. He is in need of hospital observation and care.

Two days after Dr. May had submitted his report, Bugh submitted his (November 30, 1960).

In early December, Warren must have felt he was a good option for probation. During this period he was chatty with his probation officer, Robert Ashby, and gave his take on the Kupker incident, claiming again blackouts.

> We were at my parents' trailer on the beach near the Knickerbocker Hotel. Pauline said something to me. I answered and then I went blank. The next thing I remember is Pauline saying my name. We were lying on the bed and I was holding her by her arm. I then took her back to her car in Santa Barbara. . . .As for my reason for doing what I did I can think of none. We had never quarreled before.

He proposed that extenuating factors had led to these episodes. He admitted that choking episodes were a "repeat performance" with Kathie. He believed that because of his abusive, alcoholic father he'd always been scared and afraid. "Maybe because of that I want others to be afraid of me. I know it's not right. I know that"; "I'm not normally violent. In my whole life, I've never had more than three fights." He was the victim of "this thing."

> It would happen at her house (Kathy's [sic] house) or in the car. No special place and always at night. I don't know what caused it. I know I could watch out for it, correct it, but I don't know how. I have various ideas what caused it. That what I told you about my father and quarrelling. I don't do that anymore. I keep a tight rein on myself. My nerves are shot. I'm shaking all the time. My stomach is tied up in a knot most of the time. I jump at little sounds. I feel empty since Kathy [sic] and I broke up. I can't fight fires any-

more. I was always scared but never like this. I told them how I feel so now I don't have to fight fire.

I watch myself for little things which would cause it. I analyze myself, you might say. I'm moody. Normally, I'm happy, but I get in these depressed moods. Not deep depression but I do get depressed. I'm a worrier. I always have been.

If I get probation I'm going to see a psychiatrist. At one time I did consult a psychiatrist because of this thing. I saw him four times, then he moved and I went in the Air Force. He told me he didn't know for sure. He suddenly up and left for Texas. Two days later I was supposed to have an appointment with him.

On December 13, 1960, the court convened. Deputy District Attorney Elwood Walls stood silently. John Danch stood by Gary Warren, equally silent. Judge William A. Reppy declared "the court finds that Gary Warren is a sexual psychopath within the meaning of the law, and it is therefore ordered that he be placed in Atascadero State Hospital for a period of observation and diagnosis not to exceed ninety (90) days."

Warren must have been stunned. But off he went.

He would be more stunned in March 1961 when it was time for the 90 day observation report to be sent to the Superior Court in Ventura. Superintendent Dr. William Y. Hollingsworth submitted his recommendation March 7: "In my opinion said person is a sexual psychopath and could benefit by treatment in a state hospital. I recommend the court make an order committing him to the Department of Mental Hygiene for placement at Atascadero State Hospital for an indeterminate period . . ." On March 9, Judge E. Perry Churchill agreed. Warren was incarcerated with no light at the end of the tunnel. He was also true to Dr. Bugh's summation. He had only been paying lip service to the idea of needing help. When he tried to get out in July 1963, Atascadero's Medical Director sent in a report. Gary Warren had not been a good patient.

In the hospital there has been some tendency on his part to be rather glib when talking to authorities, and somewhat restrictive and seclusive when it comes to associating with other patients or speaking in therapy groups.

This patient has been examined by the hospital staff on several occasions. Although the ward team felt on one occasion that he had his hostile and sadistic impulses under fairly good control, the final report from the ward team is that he has again resumed being quite smug and sarcastic. He expresses little remorse at all and little fear of his own hostile propensities. After careful consideration the ward team's final decision is that this patient is still a menace, and, in addition, they cannot foresee releasing him at all in the near future.

It got worse. "The patient has reached maximum hospital benefit. He has had a trial of therapy at this hospital and has continued to be hostile. He is not amendable to treatment in a hospital setting. He remains a menace to society. He should be sentenced for the criminal act if sentencing is mandatory."

There was an out— if sentencing was not mandatory, it was recommended he be sent to Chino Institute for Men.

He had to be reexamined all over again. In addition to Vernon Bugh again examining him, Dr. Donald Patterson examined him.

Bugh gives us much information, but it is best to summarize it. Gary suspected that Atascadero had sent in some report that said he was still hostile, but he insisted he was not. He attended the group meetings and joined in. He even became a projectionist and worked in the Library. He participated in "bull sessions" and believes he "got things cleaned up." He admitted he was opposed to treatment in the beginning, but came to realize that he was "a pretty sick boy and needed help." A staff conference in February 1963 regarding his disposition referred him to a study group. He didn't understand and it was then he requested to be returned to the jurisdiction of the court. He was sure he could control himself and was no longer a menace to society. However, he admitted that when the staff wouldn't answer his questions in the beginning he tended to "blow my stack." He felt this is the reason some have said he was still hostile. He told them the truth instead of "what they wanted to hear."

He states that his first attorney, he believes, did not serve his interests very well and consequently he made arrangements to change his counsel by requesting his mother to make private arrangements. He is anxious to have the opportunity to prove himself, and if allowed his release, he would be willing, he states, to continue in psychotherapy in the Santa Barbara out-patient clinic. He states he would have a job with the family business, a collection agency, with offices in Santa Barbara and Los Angeles (Associated Finance Adjusters.)

Bugh now describes Warren as 'an alert, neat appearing boyish looking 24-year-old single white male, who professes that his treatment experience at Atascadero State Hospital has been of great help to him." He does not believe the staff was fully aware of the improvements in his psychological status despite his inability to satisfy them. "He rationalizes his conflicts with the staff, and although he insists that he participated actively in all of the program, there are several references to the fact that by and large, he was rather evasive and defensive in the area of grappling with his personality problem. So far as his mental status is concerned, the examiner is not able to detect any particular difference in his overall adjustment when the present examination is compared with those done in 1960."

Bugh concluded he was still a sexual psychopath and disposed to commit sexual crimes. Since he appeared not amendable to treatment, he recommended Chino Institute for Men.

From his interview with Warren, Patterson also notes that Warren didn't believe he should have been sent to Atascadero but that he feels he did benefit from it.

He is superficially friendly, and cooperative during this interview. He appears to be at ease, as if he wishes to impress the interviewer about his lack of concern . . .Speech is very spontaneous, and somewhat overproduced in an Elaborate style. As pointed out above, the subject is obviously withholding material that he has previously revealed to prior examiners, and attempting to minimize the seriousness of things. His changeability of stories, admissions, and even development of his psychosexual processes in its variations is to be noted. This impresses the examiner that he is presently withholding material, and is untruthful for purposes of presenting a false picture. Mental context is marked chiefly by his shallowness of thought, his lack of real concern for the seriousness of his situation, and more basically his unwillingness to face his real problems indicated by his marked aggressiveness in sadistic form, as well as evidence of a psychologic block in his sexual maturity. No evidence of any psychotic content. Intelligence is estimated as average. Affect is shallow, and grossly appropriate. Emotional tone is marked chiefly by his shallowness of response, lack of real guilt or concern, about his actions. Although he would appear to "forget" (e.g., he leaves out in this present interview altogether about Betty, his third "victim"), there is no evidence of any organic impairment. Insight and judgment defective.

Patterson concluded he had a "severe personality disorder, passive-aggressive, aggressive subtype, which is marked by his hyper-aggressive, violent, sadistic types of offenses that are concerned with his sexual feelings." Thus Patterson also recommended he remain institutionalized.

The judge agreed. So much for Gary Warren's briefly published attempt to get out of Atascadero. He'd had John Danch removed as his counsel and Lawrence Chapman appointed. But it still hadn't worked. "The People of the State of California for the best interest and the protection of Gary Warren as an alleged mentally disordered sex offender . . ." and he was sentenced to Chino Institute for Men.

Much would transpire to finally get Gary Warren out on probation in March 1966, but before we go there it is best to inject here a summary of a few points. In the 1960 observations, Warren was considered nervous and claimed he had lost 12 pounds, thus usually weighing 188 or more. He was considered a "husky" guy at 175 pounds and 5 foot 9 and one half inches tall. Patterson gives us his appearance in 1963, and it is more in line with the ZODIAC. "Subject is a moderately obese adult male, who appears somewhat older than his stated age."

As we can see for ourselves, Warren was the image of the Napa sketch. This is the Gary Warren that Leigh Allen had known during the summer of 1962— hostile, seclusive, a man who had choked four girls, threatening to kill two, one with a pocket knife.

It is not surprising Allen got along with Warren. They shared car racing and mechanics, scuba diving and snorkeling, outdoorsman sports like hunting and fishing.

Still in an angry, bitter state Warren must have written that letter to Leigh sometime before 1964, complaining about his attorney,

John Danch. Joan Tucker had said the letter was full of language of a legal nature. Atascadero Staff reported that when Warren first arrived he would use "psychiatric jargon." While tending the Library he must have boned-up on some legal jargon. He may also have studied code. Warren was seclusive, to use Atascadero's own word. Such a personality would likely be drawn to code, and Omicron even used code when writing to Leigh Allen.

There should be no doubt that Gary Warren is The Omicron Suspect. Nor should we doubt that Leigh Allen knew his case well and also knew that he got released in March 1966. In October of that year, Cheri Jo Bates is brutally murdered by a pocket knife. For those who knew the circumstances of Warren's 4 victims, they should be alarmed, and Allen unquestionably knew Warren's *M.O.*

In 3 of the 4 victims, Warren took them for a drive to his mother's trailer (where he lived alone). After the event he drove them back. Bates certainly went somewhere with someone and was then brought back. It is at this time probably that she turned over her car and it wouldn't start. She then walked with somebody, ostensibly the person who brought her back, to make a call. She obviously didn't want to get back in the car with him. Then she was attacked by a man who had nothing more than a 3 inch pocket knife.

In fact, the language of the Bates confession letter is disturbingly similar to Warren's *M.O.* with Betty Nunez and Pauline Kupker.

Nunez After a few minutes, Gary said: "What would happen if I really meant that I was going to kill you?" She replied that she didn't know. "The defendant then stuck a knife next to her stomach and said: 'I'm going to kill you.'"

Kupker "He asked me if I would like to see the back of it [trailer]. Then he said 'Betty wasn't kidding. I tried to kill her and I'm going to kill you tonight.' He pushed me on the bed and put his hands around my neck."

Bates Confession Letter I told her that my car was down the street and that I would give her a lift home. When we were away from the library walking, I said it was about time. She asked me "About time for what." I said it was about time for her to die. I grabbed her around the neck with my hand over her mouth and my other hand with a small knife at her throat.

Allen would have good reasons to fear Warren was the 'Zodiac' Killer and that he had also snuffed Bates in October 1966. Since Avery had broached the Riverside connection that angle was all the rage in public chat. But why didn't Allen turn him in? It's too early to suggest an answer. It is something we must delve into later.

We must continue the narrative and uncover how Gary Warren achieved probation in 1966.

Gary remained at Chino Men's Colony until September 1964, over a year since he had sought release from Atascadero. At this point CMC recommended probation since they didn't feel he needed hospital treatment, but it obviously did not happen. He was sent back to Atascadero State Hospital. No real observational change was noted in him until May 1965. We have Atascadero's glowing report.

The Nursing Service team declared: "This patient appears friendly, pleasant and socializes with only a select few patients of his own choosing. He has not participated in any ward activities except occasionally will join in a card game with his group. He is neat in his appearance. Patient spends considerable time in O.T. shop working with rocks (Lapidary)."

The Rehab therapist had this to say: "Evaluations in Industrial Therapy Assignment of kitchen and carpenter shop rate Warren above average in attitude, adaptability, work quality and work quantity, outstanding social adjustment and dependability. Mr. Warren has participated in sports and clubs with varying degrees of interest and skill. He has continued an industrial therapy assignment in the Library as a volunteer worker for over one year with an above average record." The psychologist declared: "Testing December, 1965, compared with earlier testing indicated a change from a rigid, intellectualizing and emotionally flat individual to one who is less rigid, softened by insight and awareness of self and others."

The real kicker was by the M.D. and/or social worker: "This patient tended to intellectualize with a lack of emotion for some time after returning from the Men's Colony. There has been gradual change since about May of 1965 with significant display of feelings and concern for others. He has a good deal of insight as to why he displayed with abnormal aggression as to strangle women and has worked out more healthy channels for release of hostility. There is much more humility about this man than seen a year ago and his honesty has been noted by many."

One M.D. summarized his physical and mental status: "On admission he was cooperative, anxious to impress, but there was a lack of affect and genuineness. He over-rationalized and used a lot of psychiatric jargon." After treatment: "The overall response has been favorable with change from a cold, callous individual to one who displays feelings and concern for others."

Were they right? Or did they want to get rid of a patient? Or had the young, sadistic Gary Warren seen the light?

In the Probation Officer's report dated March 1966, the officer (David Conahey) notes Warren was returned from Atascadero to Ventura County jail in February 1966 to begin the process of a hearing for probation. He summarizes the change in Warren.

> The defendant states that he remained in custody for so long because he was "a hard headed ass." He remained as such until about May of 1965, at which time he began to gain insight into himself and his problems. He now feels that he knows himself and that he can accept his self-identification and cope with situations that in the past he would not have been able to cope with. He realizes that the most severe test of his rehabilitation begins upon his release and has indicated he will seek the guidance and counseling of the probation officer and other interested parties, to help alleviate the strain of this readjustment.

However, in substance Warren had said nothing different here than what he had said to his first probation officer Robert Ashby or the claims he asserted in July 1963 to get out of Atascadero. Apparently, it is not what he said but how he behaved which altered impressions of him.

> The defendant returns to the Court after a period of five years of confinement in treatment facilities. The probation officer was greatly impressed with the defendant's insight, attitude and over-all general appearance at this time. It is felt that a grant of probation is indicated and that the probation officer can serve as an additional buffer for the defendant, both in his initial readjustment to the community and his over-all continuing adjustment.

Conahey's recommendations were accepted by the court. Warren was returned to Ventura and sentenced to a year in county jail, which sentence was suspended. He was then given a 5-year probation. It was a fairly strict probation. Warren was to avoid establishments where liquor was the "chief item of sale." He was to maintain employment as approved by probation officer and "he shall not leave the County of Ventura nor the State of California without the prior permission of the probation officer"— a strong leash, very hard to tug at for one like Warren who liked to drive.

Finally, he was free, released in March 1966. We lose track of him thereafter, from the eyes of the law anyway, except for 1972 when he made a motion to expunge his record. This was granted. Previously, it had even been recommended by his probation officer, namely, that his probation of 5 years ends early and that he is allowed to expunge his record. A plea of "not guilty" had now been entered and the case closed. Gary had been a model of reform.

However, there are inconsistencies in his intended vocation that make it impossible to gauge just what his daily routine was like. His probation officer had said he was going to live with his mother and stepfather Eddie Cron at the trailer area on Breakers Way, but that he intended to get an apprentice carpenter's license with the Carpenter's Union in Santa Barbara. To Atascadero State Hospital, he had said he would seek employment as a gas station attendant since he had previous experience, but he lists his parents' address as a P.O. box in North Hollywood. As a part of Cron and his mother's Financial Adjusters they repossessed cars, which means he would be doing a lot of driving.

It is certain he stayed around Santa Barbara and even attained some level of education. Only a few days before Stine is murdered, a Gary Warren rates news in Goleta in reference to the Anthropology Club electing new officers. He is the new Activities Chairman. The slated field trips would be to the Channel Islands (he was an avid boater) and perhaps in December to San Francisco for a Chinese-American cultural study.

This seemed to be our Gary Lee Warren. On December 20, 1970, the anniversary of the murder of Faraday and Jensen, he would wed Phyllis Gatter in Santa Barbara. She was from Antioch in the East Bay Area. He was 10 years older than her. She was an Anthropology student at UC Santa Barbara. I suspect the connection between them had been the Anthropology Club.

The marriage didn't last long. Allowing time for things to go sour and separation, the bloom hadn't remained on the rose for a year. Already in 1972 they were divorced. It was his only marriage.

Warren obviously liked younger women. His last serious girlfriend had been Kathie, a high schooler 3 years younger. His last experience with women had been parking and choking with this general age group. He later marries one much younger, briefly.

By 1969 he had become an insurance salesman with Mutual of Omaha, based in Ventura. His time was largely his own.

So is Gary Lee Warren the 'Zodiac' Killer? He certainly becomes a prime candidate here. There is no doubt in my mind that he is The Omicron Suspect. But are they one and the same? Leigh Allen seemed to have feared so, and if he knew half of what I uncovered (so far) he had good reasons.

For instance, Warren's family business dealt in car repossession. His mother had ditched Chester Partis already and had married Eddie Cron. This is the family business to which Warren alludes in his plea to get out in July 1963. He could have easily had an old repo Studebaker and have been doing some repo and financial adjustment work in Riverside. He was superficially convivial and could ingratiate himself quickly, as noted by the carhops of the *Blue Onion*. Bates and he could have been acquainted and she felt safe with him (initially). He fits the description of the heavyset young man with the beard who didn't return for the reenactment.

In addition, it could also be Gary was preparing for the upcoming races. Of the Santa Barbarans participating in the 500 Mile Ensenada Rallye there is mention of Brock Thompson and Gary Warren driving car 100. The *Santa Barbara News* reports this on October 12, 1966. The race was to begin in West Covina. It could be another Gary Warren, but it is a fact he was an avid car enthusiast and racer. The famed Riverside Raceway lay midway between March AFB and Riverside.

An investigation of any active duty Air Force men by Riverside PD produced nothing. In 1966, Warren wasn't active duty. Indeed, after he had been sentenced to Atascadero as a sexual psychopath the Air Force had dropped him as an "undesirable" (January 20,

1961) under the heading of AFM 39-12 SDN 258— "unfitness, multiple reasons." Yet he may have kept his old low cut Air Force shoes. Bates had torn off a Timex wristwatch from her attacker, one the police discovered had been bought overseas. Warren could have bought that Timex 2nd hand during his Air Force days. A 45 dollar watch is listed as one of his recent purchases before he was committed in 1960; all very intriguing, and knowledge of which tends to create suspicion in us as it would have in Leigh Allen.

During one of their Atascadero chats Warren might have even told Allen what he did in his 11 months active service in the Air Force— draftsman at Vandenberg AFB. Specifically, he was a 22101 (classification) photo map helper. Thus it is probable he also knew what radians were.

I was fortunate that the National Military Personnel Records Center in St. Louis went the extra mile and discovered his discharge notification for me. His official military file was one of those burned in the great fire they had in 1973, which destroyed all AF records for names after Hubbard. Thus so far I could find no shred of (handwriting) evidence against him.

Warren's language, however, is that of ZODIAC's. He even refers to his problem as "the thing." Warren had draftsman skills. Z had such skills. He loved to drive long distances and could maintain any car mechanically. If he used repos as ZODIAC, the cars could not be traced to him. This would also explain why a relatively new car like the Chevy Impala at Lake Berryessa was being driven by a young man. It was a repo. It might also explain why Z didn't mind admitting he had a brown car — it couldn't be traced to him anyway.

His attitude at release may have been genuine, though it came on rather quick. They were ready to release him in December after seeing only a change starting in May. And there is nothing in the "glowing report" that says anything different than early and negative summations. It's just reworded. Instead of "seclusive" he "socializes with only a select few patients of his own choosing." His honesty is noted, but it does not qualify how weighty the context.[8]

Whether superficially reformed or not, how fast he could spiral

---

[8] In serious matters his dishonesty was constant. Almost everything he told the shrinks was a lie. In his 1963 bid to get released he claimed blackouts again.

into sadism and hostility depends on what he encountered in the real world after such a long time incarcerated. Negative experiences, discrimination, all would affect him, and he would begin to remember how excessively long he had been locked up. Bitterness might have caused him to reflect on some legally questionable influences in his incarceration. For example, the psychiatrists considered him being dishonest if he avoided mentioning all of his incidents with the 4 girls, especially if he omitted Betty. This helped get him returned to Atascadero in 1963 instead of the more customary release after 2 years. It is a fact the charges against Warren were only for assaulting Pauline Kupker. The other cases were only anecdotal, unproven by trial. By this time, his new attorney Chapman might have told him to confine himself to speaking about Kupker, the only victim who pressed a charge. Warren's diagnosis and tenure in mental institutions was, in fact, based on discussing actions not legally brought against him with charges. He had pled guilty to an assault charge, not to any sexual charges. Thus he had to be legally referred to as an "*alleged* mentally disordered sex offender." Yet he was hospitalized for this and not assault. The language of a legal nature which Joan Tucker recalls reading could have surrounded such facts.

Pauline Kupker had some reason to doubt Betty Nunez's reliability, else she would not have gotten into a car with Gary and asked him on a lonely coastal drive whether he had tried to murder Betty. She believed him when he denied it. Betty doesn't seem to tell the police about her claim Warren broke into her house on June 14. This comes out at the hearing and Warren denies it. He had witnesses that he was at his own digs. One was his roommate Marty. Rull's own father denied Warren had slapped Kathie. Warren was a sicko, but some episodes would have been challenged by a capable attorney. How bitter did he become reflecting on this . . . and how bitter about girls who go parking with guys?

If dates mean something to the psycho-babblists, then dates in Warren's life and ZODIAC's crimes should be briefly compared. His sister's wedding date was June 17, the day of his attack on Kupker. Apparently he still made it to the wedding. He was arrested June 29. He was bailed July 5. His attacks were in summer and fall/winter, and attacks came on only at night. He married on December 20, 1970, the anniversary date of the Faraday and Jensen murders.

Warren showed little interest in fighting men. Z showed little interest in his male victims. Warren left off choking women when they feigned death. When Hartnell did that, Z also stopped stabbing.

Establishing Warren as Omicron does not, however, establish him as the ZODIAC. Leigh Allen, after all, could have been wrong in his suspicions. Nevertheless, the overall scenario and profile favors Warren, and considering all they had in common it would seem likely he had contact with Leigh Allen after release in 1966.

This seems a must if he was the ZODIAC. It is hardly likely Allen was hatching his inventive Zodiac crime fantasy as early as 1962. Yet we have to confront a more logical surmise than direct contact: that ZODIAC had indirectly heard of Allen's tale through someone else in between Allen and himself otherwise he is leaving a witness who can easily identify him; and Allen would have more than the tardy suspicion he displayed in 1970. This means the link in between the two also kept silent. Why? It's not the same silence as Leigh Allen. There's the likelihood of 2 cars at Lake Berryessa. There's the Chevy Impala with a lookalike of Steve or Gary in it. And who was in the jalopy with the retread tire?

I was far from satisfied with what I had discovered. I had dug deep into the cruddy life of a 1960s' youth. What did I uncover? An obscure life turned sour shits. I had not uncovered a potential southern Cal couples' killer. On the contrary, I had uncovered a better fit for ZODIAC than Steve H.; and yet neither could be the so. Cal killer. And in Gary's case there was zero evidence against him; no handwriting sample—his military files burned. Yet *I had found* Omicron; after all this time I had *finally* found him. I was justified in my intuition there was more here. Warren had to lead somewhere. Was I chasing an autumn leaf, or was I finally on the trail to uncovering a complex crime spree engineered by someone who had boasted he was too clever to ever be outed?

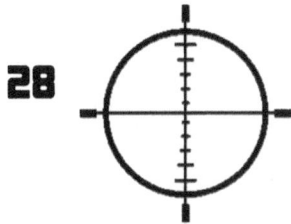

28
THE SHADOW

Everything of substance casts a shadow. When something I had found cast a shadow, I knew I had found an important clue to the solution. Leigh Allen cast the biggest shadow. It revealed Gary Warren, the spitting image of the Napa sketch. Where could his shadow lead? I wanted it to lead south, of course. The older, less documented couples' murders by .22 caliber in southern California were a shade of the ZODIAC crime series. I was seeking a link to this past, to this "Shadow Zodiac."

I did not regard finding a connection between the 2 murder sprees a vain hope. The ZODIAC had a different *M.O.* for each attack, and his first northern Cal. attack is an outcropping of the Shadow Zodiac's *M.O.* in southern Cal. Thereafter Allen's inspiration enters the picture and we have a chunky, clumsy killer who brings Leigh' fictional character to life with a ceremonial hood. I didn't think a single killer needlessly absorbed Leigh's fanciful moniker. I was seeking an accomplice, the "blonde Zodiac."

Operating under the premise Warren was ZODIAC, I had to search out those around him. Warren and Allen shared several things in common: racing cars, skin diving and sportsmanship. They shared the summer of 1962 at Atascadero State Hospital. But most importantly, the above combined, they shared Bill Henry Gosnell, for a brief time Gary Warren's brother-in-law.

In some ways, Bill Henry was the image of the SFPD sketch of the Stine killer. His brown hair had much blonde in it when young that had darkened to reddish-brown. He had green eyes and was 6 foot tall. He had perfectly chiseled lips, a thin nose, and a lifeless hound dog stare.

The clues to his character were paradoxical. He liked "smart apparel" from boutique men's stores, but he also sported a single tattoo. On his left forearm there was the death card (ace of spades) with his name "Bill."

Gosnell was born in Oklahoma on June 7, 1939, to George B. Gosnell and Irene Bohannon. George was a farmer and tractor driver for other farmers. He had already been married and divorced once before meeting Irene. About 1942, George came to California to the Brentwood area of Contra Costa County. Unemployed, they first lived at Boyds Camp, then Pease Camp, so that from a young age Bill Henry learned outdoorsman skills. After finally finding employment in farm related businesses, thanks in part to a break from fellow Oklahoman Thomas Mumford Smith, George opened up Gosnell's Grocery on Lawton Street, Antioch.

Irene and George soon divorced and she married Fred Gatter of Antioch. At 10 years of age, young Bill was given a half-sister. Bill Henry divided his time between his father, who was his legal guardian, and his mother and stepfather. His father lived in a loft on 2nd Street downtown and his mother in a middleclass home. Though he sported an Okie name his whole life (he was never William) he was thoroughly a Bay Area Californian by school days.

What his home life was like I really can't say, but something rushed him into the Air Force midway through his senior year of high school. Underage, his father and mother had to sign a Consent Form to allow him to enter in December 1956. It wasn't the Delayed Entry Program. He officially entered on January 3, 1957, and reported to Lackland AFB on January 4. He would then undergo special training at Warren AFB, Wyoming, February to April 1957.

He whisked himself into the Air Force so quickly that his senior picture still appeared in Antioch High School's yearbook. However, it wasn't until October 1958 that he would pass his Air Force GED course while stationed in Japan.

He was transferred so many times that one reviewing officer wrote that he was not going to mature into his Air Force duties unless stationed at one location long enough. This was done and Gosnell settled in to being the supply specialist, eventually promoted to

A cropped image of the above was placed in his yearbook. The humorous caption read: "Bill Gosnell: Always smiling."

Airman 2nd Class. He improved starkly, to such an extent that 3 reviewing officers praised him highly, one recommending officer training. However, Gosnell didn't seem to feel the Air Force was right for him or he was crushed by his PULHES review, in which he was given a 3 for his physical constitution. This would allow him to remain in the Air Force, but it would prevent him from being deployed. He remained the supply man at Elgin AFB, Florida, until early release for Christmas 1960 was recommended. When he officially got out in January 1961, he went into the Reserves and returned to Antioch.

So far, I had an Air Force man with a big gap in his life thereafter. The gap ended in 1976 when Bill Henry committed a strange crime. It is this crime which set me to uncover the past of Gary Warren's short-term brother-in-law and his potential influence.

From what I could deduce, he knew Warren from about 1968, when he was dating his sister and visiting her family in the East Bay Area. Warren probably already knew some of the fishing areas, but I would imagine Bill Henry introduced him to some others. After all, he was only 2 weeks younger than Warren and also an outdoorsman.

But what Bill Henry was doing in his life at this time I did not know. I did know that he liked fine men's clothes. In the Air Force he had supplied credit references. He listed James A. Davi. He was the proprietor of *James* "Men's & Boy's Shop" on Second and G Street, at the corner near where he grew up with his father.

This fit with what I already knew about his 1976 crime. The *Contra Costa Times* had reported that Bill Henry had been sentenced for attempted burglary of *Tito's* Men's Store on January 1, 1976. *Tito's* advertised itself as "Fine Apparel for Men." The Antioch location was on G Street, just around the corner from where George Gosnell lived on 2nd Street. They had more than just fine apparel. Pictures advertising *Tito's* in local high school yearbooks showed a wide array of assortments, some for the outdoorsman, including McGregor jackets (similar to what ZODIAC wore). This told me Bill Henry continued to patronize his childhood haunts around this downtown area of Antioch, near where his father sill lived.

This street and its shops obviously tell us much about young Bill Henry. In between the above was the Palace Sporting Supply emporium— a store he also patronized quite a bit.

I had to hope the Superior Court of Contra Costa County would come through and find the records of his case. The clerk had promised to look for me, then told me to call back in a few days. I did. It was most likely on microfilm, and she gave me the coveted case #. I had to write a blank check, specifying "not to exceed" a certain amount, and mail it off. This was a lot different than how Ventura operated, and it could take up to 10 weeks. . .which passed slowly.

Stewed and angry Bill Henry entered *Tito's* at 606 G Street, January 1, 1976. Combining his woodsman skills and crime, he was armed with a hatchet. His partner in crime was one Joe Sandoval. They failed and were arrested, charged with first degree burglary. Perhaps it was partying in the New Year which had Gosnell more sloshed than usual, but it was obvious he was a boozer anyway. A plea bargain reduced the charge to second degree burglary. He pled guilty on March 26, 1976. Judge Richard Calhoun sentenced him to 3 years' probation. He was to avoid "absolutely" bars and he was to abstain from alcohol. He was also to seek counseling in liquor intake management. Gosnell got off lightly for such a strange crime. He violated his Probation in 1977 and was stashed away in prison.

Probations had objected to Gosnell's original sentence, having recommended 6 months in prison followed by a 3-year probation. This told me Bill Henry wasn't a beginner.

The mystery of Bill Henry's character would be vanquished by a little more digging. I began to fill in the blank space in his life after 1961. By summer 1962 he was in bad company— Orval Lee Smith (24) and James Alex Wadkins (28). Bill Henry and Orval Lee bunked at a Pittsburg roach motel while Wadkins lived at home with his wife. Exactly 259 checks were stolen from Glass Containers Corp. in Antioch. These hot checks started to get passed for $150.00 amounts over Pittsburg and Antioch. After such a bad check was passed in early August at *Smario's* Men's Store in Pittsburg, the police began to follow their trail. Finally, the 3 were arrested. In their car were 200 of the remaining checks. They had 600 bucks in cash. They denied being involved in any burglary.

A modicum of legal wrangling ensued. But each maintained their word and didn't break. They didn't rob the company. Thus the DA had to charge conspiracy only in passing hot checks. On September 11, 1962, they pled guilty to conspiracy. As the runt, Bill Henry was treated leniently. He was sentenced to 120 days in county jail, which he would serve at the Marsh Creek Rehabilitation Center. James Alex Wadkins got 6 months. They had to pay fines of $250.00 and make restitution. Orval Lee Smith was slammed in the State Pen for an indeterminate amount of time.

Though only 24, Smith was the worst apple of the bunch. At 21 years of age, January 1959, he had robbed the Sacramento gas station where he worked as an attendant, obtaining several hundred dollars. Then in March he robbed it again. His accomplice was supposedly Travis Hunley, far older than him at 28 years. They pulled if off on March 5 and got $1,400 in cash. He supposedly gave a cut to Hunley. The Friday before his arrest (July 17, 1959) he stole $2,300 bucks from the Government Employees Enterprise service station. It was at gunpoint. He used a sawed-off .22 rifle. He gambled the ill-gotten loot away in Reno. They arrested Hunley as being an accomplice, but released him when he denied it all. Then Smith said the gun was Hunley's. They arrested him again for possessing an illegal firearm and released him since he had 7 kids to feed. Hunley pled guilty to owning the sawed off .22 (sometimes called a sawed-off pistol), and Smith cleared him of being a part of the robbery. Orval Lee requested probation. Judge Raymond Coughlin ordered him to prison.

Orval Lee had a hell of a temper. A year before his known descent into crime, the *Sacramento Bee* reports for July 21, 1958: "Loss of Temper Gets Motorist 40 Days in Jail." Orval Lee's '32 pickup stalled at the corner of 38th and Broadway, Sacramento, while pulling into a service station. The attendant Rocco Ochinero did not immediately leave off his duties and come and assist him push the truck. Orval Lee started cussing him out loudly. It escalated until Smith, in a temper tantrum, smashed several bottles of oil onto the pavement. Then he punched customer Jay Williams in the nose. Williams got in the phone booth and started calling the police. Orval Lee smashed and broke the phone booth door. The police arrived and arrested Smith. Then Ochinero and Williams filed charges against him for battery and malicious mischief. That very day he stood before Judge McDonnell and refused to pay the $200 dollar fine. McDonnell threw him in jail. "If you're in here for the next three years for losing your temper again, you'll do at least 90 days plus any other sentence I might give out."

Young Orval had egalitarian views on motor vehicle laws, ironically. A year before in the "Inquiring Reporter" section of the *Sacramento Bee*, several man-on-the-street interviews are showcased for the day, April 2, 1957. The 19 year old mechanic was asked if the President and the cars carrying his aids should be allowed to break all speed limits. "No, I do not. It endangers just as many people if he drives too fast as if somebody else does. If he is in that much of a hurry, let him take a plane. Speed laws should be obeyed by everybody—regardless of position." The accompanying photo gives us a young version of the SFPD sketch of ZODIAC.

James Alex Wadkins misused his probation. Assuming he spent a full 6 months in county jail, he bee-lined to crime after release. He robbed the Dietz-Crane construction company in Concord on June 5, 1963. He took $2,000 in office machine and equipment, which the police soon retrieved. Judge Patterson revoked his probation from the earlier conspiracy charge and ordered Wadkins to serve back-to-back sentences on October 29, 1963.

The connection between Bill Henry and his 2 co-conspirators became obvious. Orval Lee was the grandson of Thomas Mumford Smith. Orval Lee had grown up in Pittsburg where his father Orval B had worked as a foreman at Fibreboard. His grandfather Thomas still lived in Brentwood, just east of Antioch. Wadkins and Bill Henry had multiple connections through the venerated Fibreboard Company. Their big papermaking plant was in east Antioch, and Bill Henry's uncle Jody worked there too. Wadkins' father worked there and at one point so did Wadkins as a "wrapper." When Bill Henry put down names for credit and character references (in the Air Force), he listed a Mr & Mrs Bunt. Both Walter and Albert Bunt worked at Fibreboard— Albert a papermaker and Walter a foreman. Fibreboard had a lodge a few blocks from George Gosnell's 2nd Street loft. I couldn't find employment records for young Bill Henry, but I suspect he worked at Fibreboard on occasion. And, of course, the other connection between the three is the patronizing of men's fine apparel stores.

What impressed me about this trio is how they had maintained their joint alibi about not having robbed the Glass Containers Corp. and stolen the checks. Perhaps it was fear of Orval.

What also impressed me is that Bill Henry never worked alone. Joe Samuel Sandoval, some 6 years younger than he, was his accomplice in 1976. Finally, in June of that year Sandoval was declared a drug addict and sentenced to dry out at the rehab center. What may seem surprising to the younger reader is the lightweight nature of the sentences. But we must remember this was the era of reform and not punishment.

It is hard to believe that Bill Henry was clean in the interim between 1962 and 1976. I have no records for him during the late 1960s. I only know he was briefly brother-in-law to a man whom Leigh Allen seemed to suspect was The 'Zodiac' Killer. If anybody would remain mum about his bother-in-law, it's Bill Henry.

What I'm implying above is that Bill Henry could be the conduit via which Leigh's fanciful tales innocently trickled to Gary Warren. Whoever the middleman was he would have to be someone indifferent about the law. Bill Henry was not the kind to go to the law.

Nor likewise was anybody in his immediate crowd and probably extended sportsman crowd, which included Leigh Allen. I had a definite link between Bill Henry and Gary Warren; a definite link between Warren and Allen.

In any case, swatting out more potential ways via which Allen's macabre dreamwork reached ZODIAC is not the focus anymore. Uncovering the Shadow is. This being reiterated, it is hard to proceed with the hypothesis one of the above is the Shadow. I couldn't confirm prison dates for Orval Lee, but I doubt he was out of stir by June 1963. Bill Henry appears to have been free, but he's a poor fit. He comes off more as a petty stumblebum than an adroit criminal.

Potential for the Shadow to have interacted with this crowd is another matter. I had only scratched the surface, but I firmly believed that following the outdoorsman crowd was the right path to southern California. I also suspect being a mechanic is as significant. There is, in fact, a tenuous clue. There were insinuations by San Diego Police that a sawed-off .22 had been used to kill the Swindles. This would implicate experts in tool shop. All of the above were mechanics or intricately involved with mechanics. Mechanics can saw off a gun in auto/metal shop. ZODIAC's knife at Lake Berryessa appeared a homemade type bayonet.

The wandering of criminal mechanics was unavoidable theory the more I obsessed on finding a link to Shadow Z. Browsing dozens of lovers' lanes crime reports, it became obvious how service stations fit in the quilt of these crimes. Wandering mechanics are the ones who can most easily and quickly discover where the local parking areas are. It can be from customers gassing up, tow-drivers bringing in cars, often even from patrolmen visiting the station. Idle conversations would give an itinerant mechanic the info he needs.

The boldest criminals hit the parking areas. This should not be a surprise either. Each was ready and more than willing to take on a couple or multiple couples to rob them. What was surprising was the number of times two men worked together. But this should not have been surprising either. Knowing that multiple couples could be encountered, a ringleader took accomplices.

These were not professional criminals in any sense of the word. They were strange amateur highwaymen— pool hall thugs— out for easy loot but ready to take advantage of the situation for their other thrills. If the date was pretty, there could be collateral "fun." More than a few times, at gun point, often a .22, the boyfriend was taken from the car and locked in the trunk while the girlfriend was raped.

Although a series of different *M.O.*'s are apparent in the ZODIAC crimes, at Lake Herman Road he followed the *M.O.* of every so. Cal lovers' lane crime. He made them get out first at gunpoint.

The most audacious lovers' lanes crimes had been committed between Santa Monica and Newport Beach. This is the area of aircraft industry and the Hermosa oil tract. The connection to the industry of the East Bay Area is obvious. As obvious is the fact this area is equidistant between Gaviota and San Diego. Shadow Zodiac's crimes and those of the ZODIAC are rooted in the lovers' lanes crimes of Los Angeles, hug the shore or ripple out from major ports.

Suspecting the potential of a mechanic being involved, I traced the lives of those involved however ephemerally in the Lake Herman Road incident. Bingo Wesner pastured his sheep beyond the gate of the turnout, but he lived in Fairfield where his father had retired from Shell Oil and older brother had John Wesner's Chevron Station on Texas Street. John had a longstanding connection with Ben Oliver and his station on Taylor Street. They would merge in 1970 as Oliver-Wesner Automotive Service. Oliver was a volunteer fire chief, former probation officer, and Sheriff's department employee.

Any itinerant mechanic who worked at either could have learned about brother Bingo pasturing sheep by Humble Oil. Equally, any casual chat at either station could have mentioned the turnout being a petting spot. Bingo missed the ZODIAC by about an hour that tragic night December 20, 1968.[9]

The same can be said for a more provocative pathway to Lake Herman Road. Bill Henry's cousin James Gosnell ran his own Chevron Station in Antioch. After his release from the Air Force in 1961, it was to his cousin's house that Bill Henry moved. This put Bill Henry in an interesting pipeline. James was also an avid outdoorsman, eventually dying of a heart attack while out deer hunting at the age of 66. He had been within the same hunting group as the late John Atkinson, a retired boiler maker for Shell Oil in Martinez. He lived only a few miles south of Lake Herman Road. Born in England to a miner father, raised in Grass Valley, CA, since the age

---

[9] Bingo later said the oil refinery contaminated the ground and his sheep died. He quit shepherding and moved to Elko, Nevada, where he ranched and bred horses.

of 10 with his three brothers, he was a source of British English for the East Bay outdoorsmen. His brother Frank had a daughter, Jackie. She married Orval Lee Smith.

Clues infer Leigh Allen believed the old Atascadero inmate somehow got down the pipeline of his foothills fiction crime scenario. Clues indicate he believed it was Gary Warren. ZODIAC originally maintained that Lake Herman Road is where he began "collecting slaves." For simplicity sake that would be preferable to believe, but only full light can vanquish a Shadow that leads to southern California, and we are not yet there.

Gary Lee Warren remained a lifelong outdoorsman, though his life was not a particularly long one. He died in November 1989 at the age of 50. About 5 months later Bill Henry died, also at age 50. Orval Lee made it into the 21st century and died at the age of 64 in 2002. After the sins of their youth, each lived a fairly obscure life.

Everybody so far mentioned was within a detectable ripple from Leigh Allen. Thus I didn't want to contemplate that ZODIAC was entirely unconnected with any of the above, including Leigh Allen; that he was pure rogue, listening, adapting, completely unsuspected, unconnected. However, an insinuation has lasted for an awfully long time. You can throw a matzo ball in the fan for only so long.

Borsht Belt comedians have long joked that the villain in movies is never Jewish. He's always Irish. The Jewish background of David Berkowitz, the "Son of Sam" killer, was something the Jewish community tried to ignore. In 1888, no one truly wanted to believe the theory Jack the Ripper was a Jewish tailor or hairdresser. Fear *claimed* there would be riots against Jews. Today, the profile isn't exotic enough for those who wish to believe in the top-hatted gent from the West End preying on the righteous hides of the poor. Has this factor contributed to the insolubility of the ZODIAC case into the compound of crime solution?

29
JOKER IN THE DECK

Connotations of irony saturate the expression "Joker in the Deck." A Joker is someone unexpected, and he is also someone whose revelation is tinged with surprise and even mirth. A Joker can take more than one form. He can be a total innocent or a masquerade for the guilty. He is always someone unwelcome to every theory, and to every dream of anticipation he is the end nightmare.

All herein so far presented has been from following the theory that ZODIAC came from afar, from the east of the Bay Area, or from southern California through the East Bay Area, to commit his murders. It is time to swing with the pendulum and consider a very disturbing opposite extreme.

As I have already noted, for many the subject of the 'Zodiac' Killer is a real life serial franchise. Fans relish its narrative like any pulp fan of DC or Marvel. Characters within it like Leigh Allen, Dave Toschi, Bill Grant, Paul Avery, are as essential as Batman, Commissioner Gordon, or Riddler. Fans are eager for new installments in the franchise, but they don't want the franchise rewritten.

However distressing it may be to do so, it must be said that the San Francisco investigation of the Stine murder was fundamentally flawed. The original perpetrator sketch was grossly inaccurate, influenced by the false assumption a young serial cab robber was responsible. No one even ascertained why the SFPD search shifted to Presidio because Don Fouke didn't clarify matters of his sighting for a month. When he finally came forward with his "scratch," he is approached by a detective and shown the sketch of the ZODIAC based on the kids in the room with the view. He was asked if this matched the man he had seen. He said "make the subject older and heavier." This and *presumed* further input from Fouke resulted in the "amended drawing."

AMENDED DRAWING

It is possible that Don Fouke saw Robert Newton Bloch. Much later Fouke evolved his original statement and admitted that the man he had seen on Jackson did not first turn onto Maple but into a residence. He has even stated the address on camera. It is bleeped by the censors, but it's not difficult to read lips during a confessional moment.

One should be skeptical of the value of the kids' collective sketch, but the value in Fouke's amended sketch is that it reflects features of someone who would have a reason to be at the location of the sighting. The address was his childhood home, where his parents still lived. Bloch was 45 years old and about 6 foot 1 inch tall. His features remarkably coincide with the amended sketch. Patches of gray, as Fouke described the subject to have, would be far more likely on a 45 year old man.

Robert N. Bloch, as a young man. Used for U.S. Army induction.

When Fouke first mentioned it publically around 2007, he said he had never told this before (publically). How long it took for Fouke to voice his concern officially within SFPD, I do not know, but he came to believe he had put it in his "scratch" and left it to the detectives to work out. It is a fact the statement is not in the scratch. He came to speak the address publically with verve; but he was very cautious when broaching the matter, clarifying he never saw "Zodiac" get to the top of the stairs leading to the front walk and hence the front door. It is probable he had mentioned it long before in semiofficial circumstances.

I cannot say what kind of response he got, but all one needs know thereafter is the nature of the beast. A detective hears this and they will discreetly act upon it. Snippets may go through a police grapevine. Depending on the nature of the content, it could have influenced Fouke to eventually go public, and it certainly could have influenced other detectives behind the scenes.

Interestingly, by the early 1990s Roy Conway, captain of Vallejo detectives, came to the conclusion that ZODIAC had *not* murdered Paul Stine, without qualifying what was the basis for his new conviction. However, faced with the above, he could put the obvious theory together himself, namely, that Z lived in the general neighborhood and was out walking and took advantage of the situation. He tore the cabbie's shirt to use as a token to bogusly claim he had killed him. In this instance, a police investigation could never lead to ZODIAC, and this may explain why a *new* Browning automatic 9mm could not be traced to a viable suspect. A common thief may have botched a cab killing and ran off before the kids even looked out the window. The theory is, of course, highly speculative, but it is a fact the kids never heard a gunshot nor saw that WMA kill Stine. No one can account for why the suspect was initially declared a Black Male Adult and why this was broadcast over the police radios.

I am not endorsing the above. I am somewhat indulging the theory in order to flesh out the origins of Fouke's need to go public, plus give parameters to some extreme views held by select detectives. It is pretty safe to assume Fouke did not get concise feedback. It need be no more than that to prey on a man's mind, especially in an era where cronyism and cover-up were frequent accusations. For someone on the outside like Fouke, the apparent wealth of the extended family could impress upon him that political intrigue quashed an investigation, and Don Fouke was certainly on the outside, too far outside to bandy the name of a member of a wealthy and politically influential Jewish family.

Bloch's uncle Paul Bissinger was laid to rest in October 1969, during the Autumn of Angst, and due to his past political positions SFPD officers were the pallbearers. He was a holder of the Legion of Merit for his service in the US Navy, President of San Francisco's

Chamber of Commerce, member of the Police Commission, helping to reorganize the department during the first George Christopher mayoral term. He was a Director of Wells Fargo Bank and United Airlines. He was also president of the family firm. Bloch's mother's family (Bissinger) wealth was based on hides and tallow from the Pacific Northwest, and his stepfather's wealth had been from investment and brokering.

Befitting the typical affluent SF family, servants were Japanese: cook, houseboy, butler.

Minimal public reports indicate young Bloch was not a wild bachelor. Until 1960 he lists his parents' house on Jackson as his home. This year he married a woman raised in England, where he had married her. He was a chessman, and we can assume that like all chessmen he mentally labored on his moves and considered all alternatives. He merited a notice in the newspapers on November 9, 1962: "Chess sets by the great Wedgwood will be displayed by Robert N. Bloch when he tells [sic sells?] his chess collection at Sunday afternoon's meeting of the Wedgewood Society of Northern California, to be held in the San Francisco home of . . ." his parents.

At the time of Stine's murder, Bloch lived on Divisadero and could have driven up and turned on Jackson, parked up the street and was walking down to visit his parents' home, thus inspiring the amended sketch.

But this does not explain why features of the original suspect sketch share some of Bloch's features— a long, thin nose near the upper lip, a significant lower lip. Fouke amended it to give the suspect a broader chin, deeper lines, a poutier lower lip. This is essentially Robert Bloch. It is also a *fact* that the young age of the perp (25-30) contained in the original SFPD handbill was influenced by the first victim of a cab robbery on Arguello. The estimate by the kids across the street was of a man much older. I quote the report dated the very night of the murder October 11, 1969, by the first responding officers Armond Pelisetti and Frank Peda.

> Suspect WMA, in his early forties, 5'8," heavy build, reddish blonde "crewcut" hair, wearing eyeglasses, dark brown trousers, dark, (navy blue or black) "Parka" jacket, dark shoes. . . .Last seen walking north on Cherry St. from Washington St.

This original description segues neatly into Don Fouke's description of the man he saw walking down Jackson Street.

Fouke: "WMA 35-45 Yrs, about 5'10", 180-200 lbs, Medium heavy build – Barrel chested – Medium complexion – Light colored hair possibly graying in rear (May have been lighting which caused this effect.) Crew cut – Wearing glasses. Dressed in dark blue waist length zipper type jacket (Navy or royal blue). Elastic cuffs and waist band zipped part way up. Brown wool pants pleeted [sic] type baggy in rear (rust brown). May have been wearing low cut shoes."

It would seem impossible to separate these two descriptions as representing the same man. This simply cannot be left dangling. Because a police officer, a direct eyewitness, has caused this whole affair to smolder for so long, I was obliged to look into it.

The first step was to find samples of handwriting. It is interesting to note that Bloch's penmanship is suggestive of an ambidexter capable of a wide range of variation. When young he appears able to write with his left hand. In examining his 1942 Selective Service I.D. card, it is one of the rare moments in which I encountered the applicant to have actually filled out the card instead of the Registrar. The same writing is encountered in 1960 when he apparently helped fill out his 70 year old father's visa application card. The same quirky lower case two-stroke 'r' is present.

It is also interesting to note that when filling out his own immigration card in 1959, he correctly used block letters, as instructed on the card. He used his right hand.

By this time in my long investigation I had examined ZODIAC's letters enough to realize he had written both ways. The pressure points made it obvious. For example, in the Belli Letter and the Little List Letter *inter alia*, the pressure points are at the bottom of the letters whereas in other letters, such as the letter confessing to Stine's murder, the pressure points are at the top, nonexistent, or in unusual places. This is someone writing backward and forward and possibly even upside down.

The writing samples herein presented show a writer who can write in the same manner. Pressure points are sometimes at the bottom of letters, indicating left handed or backward printing. A quirky lower case 'r' is evident, as well as other letters made with two strokes that are usually made with one stroke.

Hon. Disc. (Army) 7/9/46 (Phys. Dis.)

REGISTRATION CARD—(Men born on or after January 1, 1922 and on or before June 30, 1924)

SERIAL NUMBER	ORDER NUMBER
N—	

1. NAME (Print) **Robert Newton Bloch**
   (First) (Middle) (Last)

2. PLACE OF RESIDENCE (Print) **Jackson St. San Francisco, Calif.**
   (Number and street) (Town, township, village, or city) (County) (State)

   [THE PLACE OF RESIDENCE GIVEN ON THE LINE ABOVE WILL DETERMINE LOCAL BOARD JURISDICTION; LINE 2 OF REGISTRATION CERTIFICATE WILL BE IDENTICAL]

3. MAILING ADDRESS **Same**
   (Mailing address if other than place indicated on line 2. If same insert word same)

4. TELEPHONE **BA. 3767**   5. AGE IN YEARS **18**   DATE OF BIRTH **6 2 1924**   6. PLACE OF BIRTH **San Francisco**
   (Exchange) (Number)   (Mo.) (Day) (Yr.)   (Town or county) (State or country)

7. NAME AND ADDRESS OF PERSON WHO WILL ALWAYS KNOW YOUR ADDRESS **Mr. & Mrs. Fred W. Bloch   Jackson St.**

8. EMPLOYER'S NAME AND ADDRESS **Unemployed**

9. PLACE OF EMPLOYMENT OR BUSINESS
   (Number and street or R. F. D. number) (Town) (County) (State)

   I AFFIRM THAT I HAVE VERIFIED ABOVE ANSWERS AND THAT THEY ARE TRUE.

   B (Registrant's signature)

D. S. S. Form 1 (over)
(Revised 6-1-42)

o16—21630-3

Family Name	Given Name / Initial
Bloch	Fred W
Nationality (Citizenship)	Passport Number
American	731059
United States Address	
Hotel Pierre, New York City	
* Airline & Flight No. or Vessel of Arrival / # Passenger Boarded At	
PAA - #101 / London	
Permanent Address	
Jackson St. San Francisco USA	
Birthdate	
Nov 14, 1890.	
Birthplace	
San Francisco USA	
Visa Issued At	
Passport San Francisco	
Date Visa Issued	
Feb 14, 1958	

PLEASE PRINT IN BLOCK CAPITAL LETTERS

The writing is quite similar on this 1960 US Immigration Card for his adopted father Fred Bloch as on Robert Bloch's 1942 Selective Service Card (see overleaf). Some letters like B, C, and T appear written backward, with the pressure point at the bottom. A 3-stroke lower case m and 2-stroke n.

> *Written with a right hand when he was 36 years old, it is quite evolved from his youthful penmanship on his Selective Service Card in 1942 when he was 18 years old.*

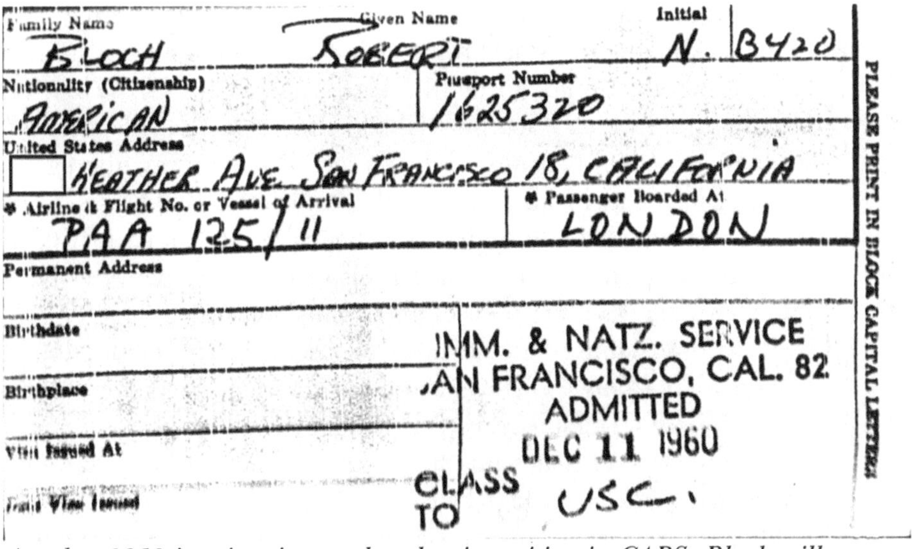

[Immigration card image with handwritten entries:]

Family Name: BLOCH
Given Name: ROBERT
Initial: N. B420
Nationality (Citizenship): AMERICAN
Passport Number: 1625320
United States Address: HEATHER AVE. SAN FRANCISCO 18, CALIFORNIA
Airline & Flight No. or Vessel of Arrival: PAA 125/11
Passenger Boarded At: LONDON

IMM. & NATZ. SERVICE
SAN FRANCISCO, CAL. 82
ADMITTED
DEC 11 1960
CLASS TO: USC.

Another 1960 immigration card— despite writing in CAPS, Bloch still wrote the "i" in lower case. The "PAA 125/11 London" is the clerk.

Bloch's penmanship shares a number of similarities with ZODIAC's. In addition, that dash of an 'r' is like an elephant coming out from the corner and sitting on the coffee table. ZODIAC had a little checkmark for an 'r' quite often. But it is interesting that on occasion it is not even a checkmark. It is merely a dash— a half of a two-stroke 'r'. In the letter bragging of Stine's murder, ZODIAC made 3 such slips.

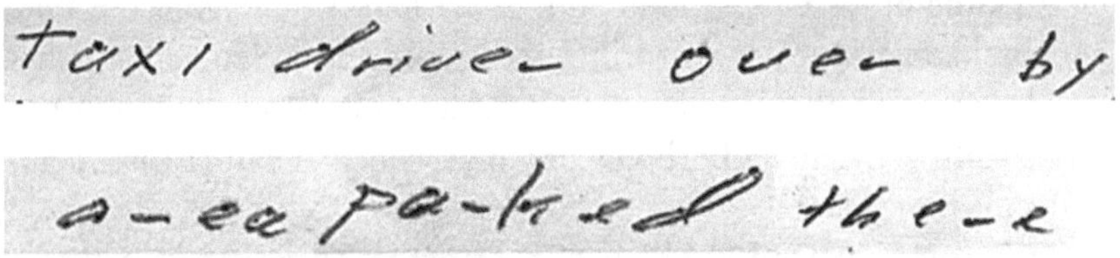

[Handwriting samples:]
taxi driver over by
area parked there

ZODIAC's checkmark 'r' (top) compared to his dash (bottom line).

His military files were largely burned in the great fire of 1973 in St. Louis, thus preventing me from getting an outright statement he was an ambidexter. (His school records might carry such a ticked box.). Both writing styles are provocative, but hardly conclusive. They are part of a fact pattern that dead ends. I, at least, could not make any connection between Bloch and Leigh Allen and the East

Bay outdoorsman crowd. The fact pattern only leads to irony. For example, Bloch was a stockbroker with offices in the Bank of America building, the building from the opening shots of *Dirty Harry*, the building from which "Scorpio" kills his first victim, a villain loosely inspired by ZODIAC. Thus while Warner Brothers was filming the movie, Bloch was in his office on the 46th floor. But Bloch didn't have a big face. I doubt he had a young voice. He connects with no evidence except the amended sketch inspired by someone seen (supposedly) walking up the steps of his parents' house.

There were immediate attempts to discredit Don Fouke. In the documentary (*This is the Zodiac Speaking*) where Fouke introduces the address on Jackson Street, Armand Pelisetti questions Fouke's reliability. He even states that he walked around the block and only saw a man walking a dog. Pelisetti's original police report is also public, and he makes no such statement therein. Nor would he have had time to walk the block before Fouke and Zelms had responded.

Pelisetti stated outright he did not believe Fouke saw ZODIAC. He noted Fouke was very detailed about the clothes and yet described no bloodstains. But there is no reason to believe ZODIAC would be drenched in blood. We don't know ZODIAC's position when he shot Stine.

From the clues in the Stine murder, it would seem ZODIAC killed Stine at a previous intersection, then seized the wheel and continued on. If the neighbors had heard a gunshot they would only see a cab passing on the road uneventfully. He pulls over and shifts into park at Washington & Cherry. The kids see a man rummaging the body and then dusting off fingerprints indicating the killer had touched the driver's side inside and out. This does not sound like a ZODIAC just strolling the neighborhood nor one who just pulled out a gun and shot him.

It is true that Don Fouke left an historical record that only contradicts his later claim. To appreciate this, I quote from his November 12, 1969, scratch. "I respectfully wish to report the following, that while responding to the area of Cherry and Washington Streets a suspect fitting the description of the Zodiac killer was observed by officer Fouke walking in an easterly direction on Jackson street [sic] and then turn north on Maple Street." Not only this but: "The subject was not stopped as the description received from communications was that of a negro male. When the right description was broadcast reporting officer informed communications that a possible suspect had been seen going north on Maple Street into the Presidio." Thus explaining why SFPD poured into the area hoping to catch the killer.

It is hard to reconcile Fouke's disparate statements separated by time except to posit that he had seen the "Zodiac" step up to the address, but when "Zodiac" noticed the police car he continued on Jackson to Maple; or in the side view mirror he saw him step down and walk toward Maple. Aside from this rationalization I cannot conceive what would cause Fouke to want to single out that address.

In any case, Bloch at least symbolizes something true— irony. He makes any investigator carefully assess the ZODIAC evidence to determine just what and who really does fit.

He's almost blonde and short to Mageau. He is blondish red and short to the kids in San Francisco. To Fouke he is a little taller but still light hair, and he strikes him as being Welsh. In between, he is a big, hulking 220 pounds or so at Lake Berryessa with dark brown hair. He wrote prolifically. Nyeah, nyeah, nyeah was his attitude. You'll never catch me. Every witness is wrong or there is (1) more here than meets the eye.

At this stage I was divided between Steve H. and Gary W. for the nomination as ZODIAC, at least the one at Lake Berryessa, essentially as the one who meets the eye. But I did not wish to give up that phantom, the blonde Zodiac.

I also needed to find a motive, a believable motive for the terror campaign. According to Chief Crumly, Cheney had said: "Allen stated how he would send notes to police or authorities to harass and lead them astray, and Allen then signing the notes 'Zodiac.'" Well, that's easy to say, but what are the logistics of someone actually doing this successfully? It requires a lot of careful forethought. The true ZODIAC did. Something more than the flippancy of impromptu foothills fantasizing must account for his inspiration and success.

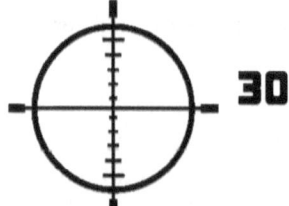

30

THE SPOOK

No police or popular suspect hitherto was ever a New Age Aquarian cycled through Haight-Ashbury. Nor was anybody a diagnosable psychotic. It is thereby obvious no professional or amateur sleuth ever believed in the hype of ZODIAC's letters and ciphers. Yet there was never any real attempt to explain why such ordinary undesirables as have been proffered should invent such an exotic alter ego on paper with those occult motives and that rambling, antagonistic madman vocabulary.

Now, when adding to the equation the cracking of the 340 Cipher in 2020, it is evident ZODIAC intended no more murders after he achieved metropolitan panic. Yet he continued to write letters for years bogusly claiming more victims, each time risking making some mistake that could lead to him. The expected question would be— why would an individual serial killer wish to go to these lengths?

For the indefatigable world of conspiracy theories, the window is herewith opened. The theory would be the ZODIAC did not act alone; he was only one cog in a greater wheel to discredit the disturbing counterculture movement.

To assert that "ZODIAC was only one cog," there can only be one other organization to make up the wheel— the often-accused-of-all-sins Central Intelligence Agency. There is indeed much documentation about whom and what kinds of movements the CIA wanted to discredit in the 1960s. One of them was, of course, the highly unnerving counterculture. It was based in San Francisco. This is where it began to bloom and reach national importance on June 14, 1967, with the coast-to-coast broadcast of the Summer of Love.

A year and a half later ZODIAC appears at the heart of Flower Power, killing in the boondocks but making San Francisco look like the base of his operations. His occult motives easily fit the counterculture, but his victims were the exact opposite— John and Jane Q. Mainstream Teenager. He soon evolves, on paper anyway, to be a kid-shooting sniper and planter of bombs. His crime spree, in fact, evolves parallel to antiestablishment until it seems to neatly fit as one section under the rubric of the New Left.

By 1969, this more than esoteric antiwar "Flower Power" was alarming society. The New Left had emerged as a student movement of extreme Marxists. They rose to true prominence in August 1968 with the Democratic National Convention riots and the trial of the Chicago 7 who instigated its violence. This inspired a main instigator of extremism, John Jacobs, to declare a course of action at the Students for a Democratic Society National Council in October: "The elections don't mean shit—vote where the power is—our power is in the street." With this the radical faction took over the SDS and set course to massive protests.

Taking courage from their 1968 news coverage, the SDS radicals advertised the "Days of Rage" over the nation in 1969. They had copied the template which had summoned the youth to the Summer of Love, but instead of joyous living being the object it was tailored to a militant agenda to overthrow the US government and end the war in Vietnam. The main instigators, the Weathermen, categorized by the FBI as the "militant faction of the SDS," expected tens of thousands of militant youth to answer. Although only a few hundred proved themselves sympathetic, there were enough to vandalized Chicago's Lincoln Park district for four days in October 1969.

The New Left was disturbingly archaic, employing the rhetoric and revolutionary methods of Red October 1917 in a society vastly different and unsympathetic. The "Days of Rage" amounted to thug warfare in which the terrorist group the Weathermen introduced themselves to the world and eventually, following Jacobs' other maxim "bring the war home," declared war on the United States in 1970.

The advent of the ZODIAC is strangely timed. He starts killing at the end of the first truly violent year of antiestablishment, with no stated motive or confession. Then his terror campaign is narrowly tailored to piggyback on an exotic element unique to San Francisco yet with a villain sounding like a radical SDS student insulting the "pigs." This sounds like someone who is cobbling together too much television. In other words, a villain is created that is an indictment of the most disturbing elements projected on evening news. Counterculture and the violent New Left are now in ZODIAC indistinguishable.

However impotent the "Days of Rage" truly were, they were real; as was the bomb igniting New Left that, seeing the failure of open combat, took to the underground afterward. By comparison, however, the ZODIAC's terror campaign is fake, fake from the very beginning when he threatened a kill rampage if his cipher wasn't published by the demand date. Fake when he claimed 2 more victims in August 1969. Fake when he threatened to shoot kids. He said so himself. "If you cops think I'm going to take on a bus the way I stated I was, you deserve to have holes in your heads." Every claim of a victim thereafter was fake. The cracking of his 340 cipher proves that. "I am not afraid of the gas chamber because it will send me to paradice all the sooner because I now have enough slaves to work for me." Fake when he imitated caller Sam in the Belli Letter. Fake when he rambled *The Mikado.*

There is no question the killer took the alter ego seriously enough to wear that ceremonial hood. But was a violent, demented man being manipulated by someone else? It is at Lake Berryessa where the clues suggest two men, coincidently or not, and it was only here where it was necessary to prove the letter-writer was at the crime scene by writing on the car door. Otherwise the terror campaign had no teeth. Thus though the clues suggest two men, the inference is only one did the writing.

While any conspiracy theory is titillating to contemplate, one logistic fact exists. If there are two men involved, one must be the "spook," the evil genius, the gloved hand. There is more than one way to interpret the "blonde Zodiac." But since he is a man with a conspicuous establishment haircut— crewcut— we'll go for the most conspiratorial first. Those of a flowery or dramatic vocabulary would label him "The Control," the handle given an intelligence agent who is working grunt assets.

From this point forward we have to deal with a fact pattern, and this fact pattern requires interpretation. Unless carefully fleshed out, the pattern will deceive more than enlighten as to what type of spook walks in shadows. There's one who can be an Intelligence operative and there is one who can be a rogue in the New Left. In some instances ZODIAC pioneers New Left methodology, which no Intelligence spook could do. For example, New Left bombings and subsequent messages to the press do not begin until August 1969. ZODIAC was already taking victims by gun and sending messages to the press in July. In others he parallels it. For instance, on the last day of the Chicago riots, October 11, ZODIAC kills a cab driver. While Chicago remains the center of news, he sends his letter threatening to snipe school buses in the Bay Area, launching the panic there. In 1970 ZODIAC begins to anemically mimic the now underground New Left. Was ZODIAC truly New Left? In his demented mind was he "ennobling" his murders to indict the establishment? Or was all this fake, a PSYOP by a member of the establishment?

To interpret the fact pattern correctly, one must understand the counterculture's origins and the Intelligence Op it *truly* inspired.

Initially the movement was projected positively by the press. Hippies were peace-loving dropouts. "Maidens" wearing coronets of spring flowers confronted riot guards by sliding a daisy stem into the barrel of a rifle pointed at them. But Intelligence knew that interwoven with these flower toting youth were radical communist students (New Left) out to overthrow the US government. The continued unraveling of the social fabric of society could only assist them. Racial tensions then rose to new heights. Then demonstrations against the war in Vietnam grew more violent. Needless to say, the potential of the counterculture was hated by the Central Intelligence Agency.

In a rather ironic twist, the CIA may have felt morally obligated to assail counterculture. Drugs, especially LSD, were at the center of its nonconformist philosophy; and in a very real way the early protagonists of LSD were in the pipeline to the public from CIA developmental experiments. Derived from ergot, an hallucinogenic fungus that grows on rye, early research had revealed that a normal person administered with a trial dose of LSD essentially mimicked schizophrenics. It was therefore declared to be a psychotomimetic drug.

This is, of course, not how it was being touted by its chief advocates in the 1960s. The leaders of young America asserted the drug opened the mind to a real universe. The counterculture took their lead from an early, arcane group of philosophic dabblers. One of the most significant was a former OSS agent (Office of Strategic Services, the precursor to the CIA) Captain Al Hubbard. After leaving the Service, he had become rich on uranium investments. Searching for greater truth he "dropped acid" in 1951 and took his first "trip." Under the drug, Hubbard saw his conception in the womb, a speck of intelligence in the primordial swamp. He was captivated by what he believed was a real journey in time and space.

Subsequently he adapted Henri Bergson's philosophy. He had proposed that the brain and central nervous system were not the center of cognition. There was a collective universal consciousness and the brain was the portal of connectivity. However, daily survival had affected its evolution. Through use and disuse the brain developed as a screening device, keeping out anything that meddled with basic survival instincts. In so doing, it had essentially shut off the mind's connection to the greater Universal Consciousness. In essence, Hubbard believed LSD opened up the brain to the connection it once had with the collective universal mind.

Through his uranium wealth, Hubbard traveled about and gave free LSD trips. After partaking, philosophers and poets agreed. This was an objective experience. The drug flung one onto the universe's conveyor belt. The mind was free and the portals were open to the channels of knowledge and reality through the infinite consciousness. Aldous Huxley endorsed it, and eventually a middle age psychiatrist and lecturer at Harvard, Timothy Leary, was "turned on" to it. Leary would become the philosophic godfather of counterculture and the brand ambassador of LSD.

Naturally, the CIA experimented with the idea LSD could enable a portal to a genuine reality, and by the time of Leary's popular conversion the secretive agency knew otherwise. From clinical trials in controlled circumstances, the LSD reaction could be classified. The reaction to the drug was very different when the subject wasn't in a relaxed environment anticipating a high. Poets and philosophers expecting a joyous experience had a Beatific encounter with the divine. In the anodyne lab, almost all reactions were "bummers"— a negative reaction imitating psychosis. Because of the inconsistency of reactions in people, the drug could not be a mind-expanding drug into a genuine universal reality. If that were the case, the circumstances should play no effect on the trip.

Long before the daisy toting counterculture took off, the CIA had seen a far more insidious use for LSD. They saw the potential for a "speech-inducement" drug— *i.e.* truth serum.

As early as 1951, one CIA report recommending LSD's study declared: "There is no question that drugs are already on hand (and new ones are being produced) that can destroy integrity and make indiscreet the most dependable individual." As a result, the CIA set its top secret course to covert mind and behavior control.

The codename was Project ARTICHOKE. Beginning as BLUEBIRD, the project had been started secretly within the CIA using unvouchered funds. By 1953 an adjunct project codenamed MK-ULTRA was developed. It was the CIA project that specialized in developing forms of drugs and their uses for covert mind and behavior control. Dr. Sidney Gottlieb, a strange little man with a club foot, was in charge of the project.

One released CIA memorandum gives a solid idea what Gottlieb and MK-ULTRA were like. It is a complaint by ARTICHOKE's personnel about MK-ULTRA's complete lack of ethics and its autonomous behavior. Under Gottlieb, MK-ULTRA was testing LSD on people completely unaware. They were using mental patients, prisoners, deviants, and prostitutes in "safe houses" in San Francisco; the latter is where agent George Hunter White sat behind a see-through mirror and watched the effects of the combination of LSD and lovemaking as a potential tool to elicit secret information.

One of the first horrors of MK-ULTRA was Army scientist and germ warfare expert Frank Olson. Gottlieb personally spiked after-dinner cocktails with LSD to see what effect it would have on those present. Olson's failure to fully recover led to his eventual suicide.

Another early case is that of Harold Blauer, who in 1953 was given a drug under Army contract by doctors working at the New York State Psychiatric Institute. The drug was MDA, similar to the rave drug "Ecstasy" of the 1980s. One of the Army researchers didn't even know what they were injecting. According to *Acid Dreams* by Martin Lee and Bruce Slain, he said: "We didn't know if it was dog piss or what it was we were giving him." Blauer died.

Gottlieb operated at this dark level. In 1977, he refused to testify at Ted Kennedy's Senate Committee hearings unless a grant of immunity was first given. Even when he testified, they adjourned to another room and the audience was only able to hear Gottlieb's voice over speakers but not allowed see the mysterious little man.

Although **ARTICHOKE** viewed themselves as morally superior, the clearing of documents under pressure at this time also revealed their ability to program an assassin involuntarily through drugs and via a "trigger mechanism" set him to his task at a later date to kill a foreign government official or American official "if necessary." The famous January 1954 memo states the problem as "hypothetical" but then presents a real subject who is a heavy drinker and works for a foreign government. Given the circumstances outlined, success at covertly dosing his cocktail at a party was considered problematic. Nevertheless, under the "appropriate authority from Headquarters the **ARTICHOKE** Team <u>would</u> undertake the problem in spite of the operational limitations," concludes the memo— a clear indication in principle it was possible.

For insight on why only a handful of CIA employees knew of the existence of **ARTICHOKE** and its ability to covertly control minds, I again turn to *Acid Dreams*. "A previously classified document explained why the program was shrouded in secrecy: 'The knowledge that the Agency is engaging in unethical and illicit activities would have serious repercussions in political and diplomatic circles and would be detrimental to the accomplishment of its mission.'"

ARTICHOKE's moral superiority lay in that they wouldn't act without direct orders, and they accepted it was unethical to involuntarily program killers. But they really didn't know what Gottlieb was doing.

The indiscriminate availability within the counterculture of a drug vital to involuntary mind and behavior control was a source of dismay. And from its history of testing, the CIA knew how dangerous it could be for mass mind programming. Through the constant cycling of radical ideas this would largely be inadvertent, but it could be intentionally manipulated by anybody who knew its inducing effects. And no paperwork needs be released for us to know the CIA always suspected the Soviets of every diabolical plot, including having spooks in the New Left driving them toward rebellion.

Thus it is time to introduce the clues that the CIA, with its massive scientific and production contacts, took matters in-hand to discredit the counterculture. Here enters the shadowy figure of Ron Stark; at the time a weird sort of schlep who in August 1969 pops up at the Brotherhood of Eternal Love near Anaheim, California. This hippie commune was run by biker gangers who converted to church-like demeanor after tripping on acid in the desert. Their commune had become a hub of LSD, cocaine, and marijuana trafficking. Stark introduces them to the largest underground stash of LSD they'd ever seen.

Orange Sunshine had hit southern California in early 1969 and had quickly become the acid of tripping preference. The barrel-like tabs were supposedly LSD-25 (basic LSD), only pigmented orange. Stark's tabs are also tinted orange, but *but* it is a fact he wasn't the original supplier and therefore they may only have been Orange Sunshine *in appearance*. Nevertheless, this meant little to the Brotherhood. They weren't too particular about suppliers.[10]

By December, Orange Sunshine tabs are flowing freely at the Altamont Free Concert. However, attendees said the Sunshine was giving off bad vibes. To quote *Acid Dreams*: "The paramedics and physicians from the Haight-Ashbury and Berkeley free clinics treated so many bummers that they ran out of Thorazine in half an hour. Thousands of others suffered cut feet, broken bones, head wounds, and worse as the Angels went on a rampage." Four attendees died, one by being beaten to death by Hell's Angels who acted as bodyguards for the significant antiestablishment concert. This shocked the stoned, peace loving crowd who realized drugs weren't the open sesame to the peaceful inner trip through the ecstatic universe. To this day, this concert is the apocalyptic benchmark in the destruction of the counterculture. Increasing "bummers" would lead to the counterculture abandoning LSD.

Was this Orange Sunshine a dangerous analogue of LSD-25? Or was this tainted LSD that produced nothing but "bummers?" Either way, the next question is whether this was intentional or accidental?

---

[10] Orange Sunshine was made by Nicholas Sands and Tim Scully in Sonoma County, Calif., beginning in November 1968. Due to its popularity various underground manufacturers also pigmented and marketed their LSD tabs as Orange Sunshine.

Either way again, how did Ron Stark get so much of the illegal tabs ready for distribution so quickly?

Uneducated and shabby, Stark would nevertheless rise to make millions in international drug trafficking. He would turn up at all the antiestablishment protests in Europe and had numerous contacts within American embassies. He finally landed in an Italian jail. Eventually he was released, and Judge Giorgio Floridia did not hide his reasons. He wrote it was because of "an impressive series of scrupulously enumerated proofs" that Stark had from 1960 "belonged to the American secret services."

Not all spy labor is an employ of the agency. They can be assets or contractors. Which one was Stark? Was he acting as a CIA contractor to supply tainted LSD designed to give "bummers"? The purpose? The counterculture would wean itself off the hallucinogenic drug. Orange Sunshine was also popular with soldiers in Vietnam. After bad experiences, they too, so one should naturally assume, would forsake the distinctive pill. LSD was eventually vilified, and even within the drug bloated 1970s it became taboo.

However, conspiracy theorists are anachronistic. They see all that spiraled into effect after the Altamont and declare all of it was carefully engineered. For conspiracy theorists, the conspirators are always omnipotent. In reality, it was logistically impossible for the CIA to foresee the scope of Altamont's aftermath. The best of intents had no doubt been to wean soldiers and kids off the dazzling drug, and that certainly had succeeded.

The torrent that had been the counterculture thinned to a trickle in the 1970s, incapable of cohesion and only doing its own thing. What remained were the meanest factions of the New Left— the bomb igniting terrorist the Weathermen and those groups that took their lead from them or from the outlaw culture, each ennobling their crimes in the name of bringing a new people's government.

The fact pattern is consistent with a subtle and brilliantly executed operation to destroy LSD. Another fact pattern is laudable to the CIA in general. This reveals how much the CIA objected to Gottlieb. His control over MK-ULTRA must have been strongarmed. Only *after* he left the Agency in 1973 did enough complaints circulate to merit the Senate investigation. At the start of the hearings, Ted Kennedy expressed his hope the hearings would "close the book on this chapter of the CIA's life."

It is impossible to conceive that the CIA at any level ever used programmed killers to discredit the counterculture, for the above gives us a healthy insight on motives and goals. Shooting teenagers at petting spots and trying to pin this on a counterculture/New Left ideological gunsel is out of the question. This does not mean, however, that CIA assets were not incidentally about.

In the 1970s, radical students knew no bounds. One cell, the Citizens' Commission to Investigate the FBI, broke into their field office in Mena, Pennsylvania, and stole boxes of documents, which included papers on the top secret Co-Intel-Pro. This was the FBI's covert Op to infiltrate and destroy groups such as the Black Panthers, antiwar movements, and even Martin Luther King. The papers also revealed that FBI agents were masquerading as militant students in various cells.

It's unlikely that CIA assets were not equally entrenched in facets of the New Left movement, rubbing shoulders with drugged militant extremists and "outlaw culture crazies." The Zodiac Crimes were also within Gottlieb's dark and autonomous era, and things can go wrong. Gottlieb used mental patients, which are by nature unstable. Outside of stealing documents, however, there is no way to prove what influence, incidental or not, an individual asset had.

Intelligence networks exist within the world of Induction. Success at Inductive Logic is the supreme reflection of the investigator's talent. But Induction also requires the final reveal, the moment where the curtain is pulled back to prove all clues, evidence, and circumstances were interpreted correctly by the investigator and he had followed them to the right culprit. This is not possible with Intelligence agencies. They need never pull back the curtain. They always hide their culpability. The reveal can never happen. Intelligence ops leave fact patterns, discernable only over decades. This leaves the investigator with dots, very far apart, to try and connect. And each dot's value needs to be weighed.

So far, as it pertains to ZODIAC the biggest dot has been Leigh Allen. How can one draw a line from Allen to a spook theory? Sadly, one can. It only convolutes things, but we must get it out of the way, at least.

One, as a convicted felon he was not legally allowed to own guns and certainly not bombs. Yet when an arsenal was uncovered in his basement in 1981 he was not indicted. District Attorneys are not unaware of poetic justice. If they truly believed Allen was ZODIAC, but also knew they couldn't convict him, they still had an airtight case to put him away for a long time for multiple felonies. Yet he walks, Scott free. As in the Stark case, this suggests a man whose basement belongings had some Intelligence coverage.

Allen is always somehow at the center of constant ambiguity, balancing on a teeter-totter that can send him to the bottom of New Left conspiracies or opposite to being an intelligence asset. Like Ron Stark he was an oddball, but he was a fairly well-connected oddball. He was a professional student with a (proffered) antiestablishment focus which placed him within the University system, the medium of the New Left's extreme bomb igniting factions. He certainly knew how to store bombs. Piloting and car races brought him into a more affluent crowd, and so did his background. He was once well-covered in the newspapers when young, winning awards for swimming and diving. Often pictured, he was the 1950s' example of the blonde American boy-next-door. The veneer hid a very dark truth. He had friends and sportsman companions all over the state, which included affluent people. For whatever reason, he also had lots of friends who were the antithesis of the affluent and fanatic— ex-cons.

The entire Leigh Allen factor is a hard thing to weigh. The problem, of course, is LARPing— Live Action Role Playing. Assuming the paper character in real life takes a lot of devotion. Does a copycat who steals the inspiration from another have such devotion? Copycats don't have inner inspiration and originality else they wouldn't be copycats. It always comes back to that ghastly hood at Lake Berryessa. The victims were to have died. ZODIAC was sure in the phone confession that he had murdered both. No one was to have known he had worn that dramatic hood. It was all for himself that he wore it. For me that represents a hell of a lot of originality and devotion.

I cannot explain how a "serial killer" can ape someone else's fiction plot directly and not fear exposure. After all, he's leaving a witness who can identify him. If he's down the pipeline from Allen and hears secondhand then someone else in between is also keeping quiet. It would seem this is someone Allen can't turn in as well.

If Allen was a CIA asset, I have no idea what it was about. But among the dots we have, there is that particularly curious one: his suspicion as to how deep his Zodiac story had run and his refusal to name anybody even to get the heat off him.

From this dot we can draw a line back to a group better at subterfuge than the CIA and just as fractured. The New Left was full of hatred in the late 1960s and heavily interwoven with the counterculture. The most vitriolic went on to become the most dangerous terrorist of the 1970s, and their method of communication and ZODIAC's are a mirror image. They also maintained a cult level of silence.

Up to 30 practicing hardcore members, for example, and yet no Weatherman ever turned on another. A more shadowy group was the New World Liberation Front, a particularly audacious and violent Bay Area cell of bombers active 1972-1978 headed by drug addict Ron Huffman. Only after he ax-killed his girlfriend in 1979, apparently believing she was possessed by demons, was he identified by fingerprints as one of those responsible for some 22 bombings. Most of the other members of the cell were never identified.

The New Left rose to national prominence in Chicago, but it incubated in Berkeley where some of the most vicious members of the Yippies (Youth International Party) were fomenting hate since 1967 and proving themselves an influence on the SDS Weathermen.

A founder of the Weathermen, Mark Rudd, later admitted what their attitude was like after My Lai (March 1968). "At that point in our thinking there were no innocent Americans, at least not among the white ones. They all played some part in the atrocities of Vietnam, if only the passive roles of ignorance, acquiescence and acceptance of privilege. All guilty. All Americans were legitimate targets for attack."

There is more than enough room for a different kind of spook, not a government one, but a crazy radical who early-on drew his inspiration from the far left. Rogue, however, would be a big word here. The ZODIAC and/or any possible accomplice were not independently fulfilling some New Left agenda. This was a personal application to politicize murder by an individual(s) sympathetic to the New Left but fundamentally rooted in crime already.

"Outlaw culture" dominated the youth scene. Older "crazies" with a past in crime were all around the New Left. "Prince Crazy," 30-something George Demmerle, earned his nickname because he wore a golden Roman centurion helmet and purple cape at the protests. He manned a militant booth at Woodstock, where he met Sam Melville and later became one of his New York terrorist group. Demmerle was also the FBI nark who engineered Melville's downfall. One of the Chicago 7 was a World War II draft dodger. California had more than its share of establishment age cranks who were drawn to the militant movement because of their predisposition to crime. A neat middleclass crewcut is curious on such as this, but not impossible. The aforesaid 30-something Melville shed his hippie appearance for mainstream togs to fit in while planting his exploding press releases. He was even dressed in Air Force gear when captured near an army depot in 1969.

Doubtless the ZODIAC's style did not inspire the many political statements to the press by 1970s' left wing bombers, but rather both emerged from the same fomenting heap of discord in the 1960s. For example, "This is Unit Three of the New World Liberation Front," a typical preamble by Huffman's Bonny Doon bombers. Weather Underground's political statements were worded as retaliation for some establishment act or corporate policy. Communiques sometimes began by declaring their number per the example when they took credit for the bombings in San Francisco and Sacramento on August 28, 1971, in response to the death of inmate George Jackson during his attempted escape from Soledad prison: "This is the twelfth communication from the Weather Underground. . ."

ZODIAC is strangely ahead of the game in his preamble, declaring himself first and making his demands and threats. There is another similarity. Like many radicals, the ZODIAC went underground after publically establishing himself. "At the end of the sixties or the beginning of the seventies," said Joanne Chesimard (Assata Shakur), "it seemed like people were going underground left and right. Every other week I was hearing about somebody disappearing."

Specifically, they were going underground because of the failure of the Days of Rage in October. They had broadcast their hate for years in sarcastic street demonstrations. Cheers emboldened them to believe there would be enough for open combat. Each was so well known to law enforcement that they had no choice but to go underground when they publically failed.

A famous militant example is the Weathermen. After three of

their members accidentally blew themselves up on March 6, 1970, while making a bomb, which resulted in a massive conflagration which destroyed a New York City townhouse on East 11th, the FBI knew these radical high profiled SDS students were preparing mass murders. Key members earned top 10 status on the FBI most wanted list. The entire militant faction went underground, with a cell in Sausalito in the Bay Area. It was only now that they referred to themselves as the Weather Underground but vowed to continue their revolutionary agenda.

Prior to their vow in 1970 not to kill anyone (at least according to some members), they held violent extremist views per Mark Rudd and could only have attracted likewise. When the New York cell, led by member Terry Robbins, blew itself up, the bomb was intended to be deployed at the noncommissioned officers ball at Fort Dix— its purpose to blow the arms and legs off the families and friends enjoying the gala.

Obviously, the ZODIAC murders were before the Weathermen's anemic repentance in 1970. Some ephemeral militant may have aligned with a former inmate at Atascadero, introduced perhaps somewhat incidentally by the bomb hoarding Leigh Allen. Thus if there are two, they conceive a way to make utilitarian murder a pathway to societal terror, using Leigh Allen's fanciful tale. Necking white teens, which were ZODIAC's victims, certainly fit the criterion of guilty white Americans of acquiescence and acceptance.

This does not make it any easier to identify the "Blonde Zodiac." All the radical far left groups, though considered autonomous, were known to interact, such as Weathermen with The New World Liberation Front, Black Liberation Army, and even counterculture crime communes. A notable example is when the Weathermen were involved in assisting in breaking Timothy Leary out of prison in September 1970. It later emerged that the Brotherhood of Eternal Love, dear old Ron Stark's suckers, had paid the Weathermen $25,000 to get him to Algeria. Money can buy you talent, but it can't endow you with it. These radical students had crime contacts that ran very deep, and they were floating on money from bank robbery, armored car robbery, and "donations" from undetermined sources.

Outlaw culture was so pervasive within the New Left it is impossible to separate their terror style from that of a killer like ZODIAC.

For example, despite Bernadine Dorhn and Bill Ayers, two key members of the Weathermen, later accentuating the care they took to never hurt anybody in their bombings, it is true that Dorhn issued the following recorded statement sent to news outlets after they assisted Leary and his wife's escape to Algeria. "This is the fifth communication from the Weathermen Underground. Rosemary and Tim are free and high. We are building a culture and a society that can resist genocide. It is a culture of total resistance to mind controlling maniacs. A culture of high energy sisters getting it on, of hippie acid smiles and communes and freedom to be the farthest out people we can be. Now we are everywhere, and next week families and tribes will attack the enemy around the country. We're not just attacking targets. We're bringing a pitiful, helpless giant to its knees. Guard your planes. Guard your colleges. Guard your banks. Guard your children. Guard your doors."— Yet when added to their vow not to hurt people, such blowhard language is purely for terror, terror which can bring about no utopian goal. It is little different in character than ZODIAC's empty threats or the Bates confession letter.

Intent to terrorize will naturally employ a certain lingo, but the fact pattern indicates ZODIAC was on the fringe of the outlaw culture of the youth movement.

The righteous antiwar attitude of the New Left created a permissive attitude condoning any expression of violence. After being asked by a reporter to verify the voice above was her sister's, Jennifer Dorhn was then asked:

"How do you feel about what your sister is advocating?"

"I think it's right on. I think she's far out, and all Weathermen are far out."

"Can you explain that?"

"They are our brothers and sisters in the underground. They're forced to be outlaws by the way society is run, and we think they're great."

The Yippies traveled over the country for demonstrations. Prior to the 1968 DNC riots in Chicago, the Yippies were regarded as engaging in only street theater and pranks to draw attention to the antiwar movement. So it is not surprising under their tutelage the extreme Marxists of the New Left turned the DNC demonstrations into riots; nor that the Chicago 7 contained more than one Yippie. Nor that the bloodless bombings of the Weathermen, influenced by Yippie *M.O.*, amounted to only destructive urban theatre.

As the bombings of the Weather Underground grew more audacious in the 1970s, so did the Yippie endorsement. After the Capitol bombing in March 1971, notorious Yippie Judy Gumbo was quick to get her face in the camera before the ravaged Capitol. "The Weather Underground bombed the Capitol to bring joy, to bring joy to America, to bring a smile and a wink to all the kids who hate the American government. We didn't do it, but we dug it."

After the end of America's active participation in the Vietnam War in 1973, the antiwar movement dissipated and with this the motive for the "ennobling" ideology of the radical left bombers. Interestingly, ZODIAC also decided to quit, sending his last letter in January 1974 under that grand criminal moniker. Anti-government anti-corporate bombings continued for a few years, but it was in the hands of the outlaw culture and not ideologists. In a few years Weathermen started surrendering. Most of the others got nailed for armored car heists, murder, and bank robbery in the 1980s. But not the New Left imitating ZODIAC.

This chapter is a way of trying to get into a sealed mind and explain the aggravating contradictions between the killer's actual murder cases and the goal of his alter ego's paper persona.

As such I cannot avoid returning to the significance of LSD in this period. Researchers into the Manson murders have long suspected that Manson would not have had the mesmeric control over his "Family" without the free flowing use of LSD, the main drug the CIA discovered was best for covert mind and behavior control. Although conspiracy theorists speculate whether there was any indirect CIA involvement in the Manson murders, the fact pattern and collective evidence suggests something more fearful— that the mind programming was incidental.

Due to the philosophy that LSD opened one up to objective truth, the constant reiteration of militant ideology while "tripping" became a powerful conditioner reconfirming the communal beliefs, inspiring moral superiority, the urgency of action, and personal empowerment.

More than one Weatherman later admitted the inability to explain why they did what they had done, linking it to insanity. In particular Cathy Wilkerson, one of the survivors of the accidental townhouse explosion, told author Bryan Burrough: "It's all so fantastic to me now. It's just so absurd I participated in all this." He told her (*Days of Rage*, 2015) that his difficulty would be explaining to his readers why this era didn't seem as "insane then as it does now."

Within the annals of crime, the Zodiac Murders and his strange New Left militant terror style have stood out as uniquely insane. With the dissolution of the militant youth culture in the 1970s universities, plus the taboo upon LSD, did the ZODIAC also lose inspiration and come to view his crime spree as having been pointlessly bizarre? His Badlands Letter of 1974 is taken as sarcastic. But is it? "In light of recent events, this kind of murder-glorification can only be deplorable at best (not that glorification of violence was ever justifiable) why don't you show some concern for public sensibilities + cut the ad?"

One thing I know for certain. It is impossible to divorce the paper persona's terror campaign from the *M.O.* of a New Left radical group. Equally, it is impossible to explain it as the acts of a serial killer. The logical conclusion is that it is a combination of both. But is it an individual who decided to combine both, or are two men (?) involved?

Another thing I know. The Zodiac Murders are street theater. The first two attacks are drive-by shootings— undeniable street theater. Lake Berryessa is most certainly street theater. POSH Presidio is a very specific kind of street theater. The ZODIAC could have murdered a couple in their house. But that is not public theater. There need be no spook for us to know the murders were a form of PSYOP. All of this comes from a demented mind saturated by the tactics of the youth movement and New Left.

It is finally time to sort out the hard facts and evidence.

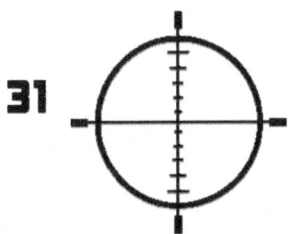

31

THE ZODIAC CLUB

I HAVE FOLLOWED SEVERAL PATHWAYS IN MY JOURNEY TO THIS END. The first was to search out those who may have fallen through the cracks. This led to Steve Haeberle, a close approximation of the Napa sketch of the young, heavyset "suspicious" man.

More impressive than similar style, Steve's printing displays the same wide variation ZODIAC made. From his background it should be certain he knew what radians were. He matches the stats of the killer at Lake Berryessa. He also would have "Wing Walkers" from the correct period of manufacture. He had a "big face" per Mike Mageau's one certain description. He was ensconced by the Air Force for essentially 90 days, the usual observation period to determine if a subject should undergo long term psychiatric treatment.

Second, I followed the shadow of Leigh Allen. He has been the most popularized suspect because of the accusation by occasional hunting companion Don Cheney. This accusation was, namely, that Leigh had doped out the basics of the ZODIAC crime spree— striking lovers' lanes, using "Zodiac" as the killer's handle— at least a year before the publicized lovers' lanes murders under that moniker took place. Despite Allen denying knowledge of such a conversation, it seems likely he did babble on about such an inventive fiction crime scenario. It is possible therefore that at some point in time the actual killer must have heard of Allen's tall tales.

More than once Allen displayed particular interest in a letter a mysterious inmate at Atascadero State Hospital had sent him, which according to witnesses contained lettering suggestive of ZODIAC's writing and code making. Allen had been a teacher/technician at the hospital during the summer of 1962. Probing into inmates housed there at that time led me to Gary Lee Warren, the dead ringer of the Napa sketch. The summer of 1962 at Atascadero State Hospital was one of the darkest periods in Warren's stay at the hospital. Furthermore, he shared all of Leigh Allen's hobbies. Warren was intelligent and crafty. He had been a draftsman in the Air Force at Vandenberg AFB. He likely also knew something as arcane as radians. His psychiatric background is almost a prerequisite for ZODIAC's actions.

From his behavior during police questioning in 1971, Allen was preemptive in a way that suggests he was being guarded about what could be construed as his complicity in unintentionally (presumably) inspiring the real killer.

As a snorkeler, Haeberle was likely downwind of the convivial Allen's stories during a critical time in his recovery from psychiatric issues which had forced him from the Air Force. It is far more likely, however, that Gary Warren is the one Allen had suspected. In 1970, his suspicions seemed to crystalize. He became bold enough to share that letter from a past Atascadero inmate. Coincidently, in 1970 Warren became affianced to the half-sister of Bill Henry Gosnell, a hatchet wielding petty East Bay criminal whose immediate clique was hardly comprised of John Q. Upstanding Citizen.

Through Bill Henry we come upon Orval Lee Smith. Like Leigh Allen, Orval did not like his first name and preferred to be called Lee. Like both Gary Lee and Leigh, Lee Smith was a journeyman mechanic and obviously very much into cars. How far he routinely traveled for business and car races, I do not know. He did head hours away to Reno just to gamble away the money he stole a few days before he was arrested. That was enough for his young wife. She divorced him for cruelty. It is interesting to note that her father Frank was an English national. He had not become a naturalized citizen. He was one of 4 brothers born in Lancashire who came with their miner father to Grass Valley, California, in 1913 to what was essentially a colony of English and Welsh miners. One of the brothers, Oval Lee's wife's uncle John Atkinson, eventually moved to Martinez, a few miles south of Lake Herman Road. ZODIAC was thought to use British English on occasions. Orval Lee had frequent contact with the East Bay and Contra Costa County. He had much family there and school days friends like Gosnell and others.

The above, in a strange way, constitute The Zodiac Club. Through their collective backgrounds they could have easily and unknowingly inspired the actual 'Zodiac' Killer's paper persona. We must remember that Leigh Allen used the expressions "trigger mech" and the English "Happy Christmas" too. He may have seen more than just the purloining of his crime scenario in ZODIAC's letters. He was seeing the use of expressions within a certain crowd of East Bay outdoorsmen comprised, in some cases, of ex-cons. He would not have been out-of-line to think one became ZODIAC.

Third, I acted upon officer Don Fouke's far from subtle insinuation about the address on Jackson Street. Robert Bloch is a very unlikely addition to this club. Ironically, he is an afterthought even though he is the only person who can be identified as having a reason to be at the location where the sighting took place and he matches the amended features of a "Zodiac" composite based on Fouke's observations. He was spared contemporary triaging because of the inexplicable kibitzing of Don Fouke.

It would be convenient to dismiss Fouke's amended memories, but then we would have to explain why his "Zodiac" was dressed the same as the original description given by the kids.

What someone like Bloch represents is also unwelcome— a rogue. Not just in the sense of someone who is seemingly unconnected with the others, but someone who is so unconnected to the pillars of evidence in the 'Zodiac' case he makes it look as wooly as the legend— the young man in the Impala becomes a coincidence, maybe even the jalopy a coincidence, even Leigh Allen and all his game playing, a young man's voice confessing, the long lock of brown hair in the eyelet.

In some ways, the reader may feel I have unnecessarily convoluted what should be a streamlined thesis. Instead of limiting myself to the process of elimination I have on occasion engaged in the process of inclusion. I have not only sought to add the Shadow Zodiac crimes to the case, but I have also opened the loop about an accomplice in the northern California ZODIAC crimes without offering a viable second man in order to close said loop. It is not for want of effort, I assure you, that I have not uncovered the "blonde Zodiac."

I lashed out in many ways from the "club" and found another 37-year old version of the Napa sketch, but I did not find any viable young or middle-aged blonde.

I do not excessively rely on police sketches, but I am impressed by consistency. The blonde or light-haired ZODIAC is first described by Mike Mageau. Secondly, he is described by the kids and Don Fouke. In between there is Lake Berryessa where the heavyset man is the antithesis: he has full styled dark brown hair. ZODIAC is not going to disguise himself to look blonde for night attacks and then remain undisguised for a daytime attack. Logically, he would disguise himself during the daytime attack, not at night. This can call into question the value of the Napa sketch. Or it means there are 2 men and neither particularly disguised himself.

This I take to be the case. Mageau's "almost blonde" attacker has somewhat curly hair. Cut into a crew, the light blonde curls would be gone, leaving the light-brown/reddish-blonde hair of the SFPD villain. This does not sound like disguise. It is but a haircut. He didn't wear a full wig at Lake Berryessa. Anybody could recognize that on a young man. Why wear a wig and then put a hood over the wig?

If not accepting this, we can convince ourselves as SFPD did, namely, that ZODIAC had reddish-brown hair in San Francisco and Mageau's assessment is worthless. It is a puzzlement I fully kept in mind during the whole of my pursuit. It grew smaller with my discovery of 2 viable candidates who looked like the Napa sketch, one of whom definitely had contact with Allen and the other quite possibly downwind of him through their mutual hobby. I found it hard to fully embrace SFPD's rationalization. Naturally, what I was left with was to suspect the existence of a second man, the blonde ZODIAC.

Police charge. The District Attorney accuses. The accusation is often just a single sentence. They like to keep things simple to assist in winning. They don't mess with a case they don't think they can win. The learned wisdom of the profession should be adopted here.

The simplest approach to the solution is to accept the Lake Berryessa sketch by the coeds as representing *a* definite ZODIAC. They estimated the young man to be 6' to 6'2", heavy (200-225 lbs.), with dark hair. Bryan Hartnell estimated the killer was about 5 foot 11 inches and heavy, 200-250 lbs. "Victim stated he could also see hair through the mask's eyelets and observed the hair to be dark brown."

Although the coeds' sighting was not in perpetration, Hartnell's was. Therefore it should be taken as established that the killer had brown hair at Lake Berryessa. Hanging down far enough to be seen in the eyelets would indicate hair too long to be in a crew at this time.

From the collective evidence we must catalogue who fits best.

Subject	Hair	Height	Eyes	Weight	Complexion
Haeberle	brown	5'11"	blue	220+	light
Warren	brown	5'9.5"	brown	200+	med.
Bloch	brown	6'1"	blue	200+	ruddy
Gosnell	brown	6'	green	180+	fair
Smith	brown	6'	brown	180+	med.

The lot falls to Steve H. or Gary W. Of the above we know they were moderately obese. Either fits the description of the young man in the Impala and the heavy perp who left "Wing Walker" footprints, and indeed Steve was turned in because of the broadcast of the Napa sketch. Both would have a young voice to match the one who confessed in the phone calls. Based in Ventura/Santa Barbara, Warren would have been completely unsuspected. Steve did not have a known violent background. Warren did— a particularly stubborn, strange, and sadistic one.

So it would be easiest to say that Warren is our man, at least at Lake Berryessa. Based on his criminal and psycho record, it would seem safe to consider Warren the prime candidate, but the vicissitudes of fate have destroyed records via which to access historic samples of his printing. As Omicron he is the writer of the letter that so suggested ZODIAC's felt tip style.

Steve H. is the second option. He fits the height, weight, everything. He got his blue eyes from his grandfather, who also had red hair. His brown hair likely had red in it. He is the only known deadeye in the group, established so as an Expert in his Air Force records. His handwriting is suggestive. Though impressive, it remains unchallenged by samples from Warren. Hartnell said ZODIAC spoke with a cadence to his voice he could not identify. Raised in Kansas, Haeberle may have had a cadence. Fouke described the man walking on Jackson as "at no time appeared to be in a hurry, walked with a shuffling lope slightly bent forward head down." One walks downhill at this point on Jackson, and this may account for the limp-like stride. However, Haeberle had a 6 inch vertical scar on his right calf.

No one can get into a mind this long after death unless there are clues. Haeberle doesn't seem flamboyant. With Warren his North Hollywood background is a clue that does suggest a dramatic alter ego like ZODIAC would appeal to him. After all, he went to a Hollywood hypnotherapist to gain insight into his murderous urges with parking dates. Someone who goes to such lengths to design and sew that ceremonial hood is likely to be a bit theatric in real life in addition to being crazy.

Warren's known circumstances also fit the militant language of ZODIAC's letters. Though much older he was immersed with a younger crowd in education in an area like Santa Barbara/Isla Vista where the antiestablishment youth movement was very strong. Although it broke out a bit later than at other universities, it was far more aggressive. In February 1970 the UCSB student body War and Peace Committee learned Bank of America had investments in the Vietnam war. A protest mob burned down the local branch building. In May 1972 in response to the US bombing of Hanoi, a sit-in of some 2,500 students shut down the airport.

Warren looked older than his age, according to some reports, and from pictures I have it is noticeable even when a teenager. If he is the same killer in San Francisco, he might have looked even older with a crew. But this is hopeful rationalizing that doesn't fit the fact pattern. The killer may have disguised himself at Lake Berryessa, but he didn't switch cars. Who drove the jalopy with the retread? A coincidence? I would prefer to think so. But . . . we are back to the spook, the blonde ZODIAC.

I had wanted this "potential other" to be an accomplice and in turn to be a link to the Shadow Z, but no one somehow linked to Allen or Warren looked viable. It is still possible I am correct, and this faceless form is the ultimate joker in the deck. I only entered Leigh Allen's shadow through Atascadero. His crowd extended far and wide over California and Nevada.

However, for the rest of his life Leigh believed his connection to ZODIAC was through Atascadero. Graysmith writes that Allen also told a man named "Craig" that the codes ZODIAC used were developed by a criminally insane murderer at Atascadero, who then taught them to ZODIAC while he was also there— an evolution to what he had told Phil and Joan Tucker.

No one has ever bothered to offer a reason why Allen continued to make such claims, but a reason does suggest itself when Warren is inserted into the context.

By late summer 1969 Allen had reasons to believe ZODIAC was downwind of him, but in November ZODIAC tipped his hand when he tried to set him up for a patsy. "To prove I am the Zodiac, Ask the Vallejo cop about my electric gun sight which I used to start my collecting of slaves." This is an accusation, pure and simple, against Leigh Allen. He often shot his mouth off about how his flashlight/gunsight design was real innovative. There are too many witnesses to support that. Allen also wasn't quiet about being a suspect. The real Z's comment came only a month after Allen had been visited by John Lynch. If SFPD and VPD had followed through with ZODIAC's suggestion, Allen would have soon materialized as a good suspect, as indeed he did 2 years later.

We know from the cracking of the 340 Cipher that ZODIAC was done killing now in November 1969 when he incongruously included that misplaced statement in his long-winded letter to the San Francisco *Chronicle*. What better way to get the heat off him than to setup someone as easy as Allen.

The inference is unavoidable. ZODIAC had been downwind of Allen's tale and didn't believe Allen knew who he was.

Clues indicate it didn't take Allen long to figure it out. Only a couple of months later he starts sharing that letter from an Atascadero inmate. He seems suspicious and eventually he begins to get the word around that ZODIAC had been at Atascadero. It's an interesting move. He's basically warning ZODIAC that he knows who he is and he'll go down with him if he tries that again. He's also implicitly admitting he knows there are ears about and the message will get back. Only one person in Allen's extended outdoorsman crowd fits, and this is Gary Warren. He was safe in Santa Barbara with lots of ears in the East Bay Area. Only one pathway between the two presents itself: the East Bay sportsman crowd of ex-cons and/or bombing left, the ones who never betrayed an accomplice.

Of Allen's contacts, who was mental enough and dramatic enough to have worn that hood? This could be quite a few. But which one do we know was at Atascadero when Leigh was? It is Gary Warren who was single, had a nasty background and 5 years in State bumper rooms.

In 1969, Warren turned 30 years old. Prime years of his youth had been wasted in Atascadero State Hospital before came sudden recovery. He reenters a California on the cusp of counterculture. Antiestablishment grew more violent. Counterculture grew more bizarre. The preaching was to confront the pigs. Down with the fascists! The ruling classes were exploitive imperialists suffocating society. The civil rights movement had underscored that even racism in America was the product of white imperialism of another people. Violence was advocated. It was revolution, and pacifism and nonviolence were only excuses for not struggling to fulfill the revolutionary goal to overthrow the imperialist system, to paraphrase Jeff Jones, one of the founding Weathermen.[11] How would a dramatic but psychopathic mind like Warren's hybrid this, especially if inspired by some bitter idealist? They were all over Santa Barbara, and Warren had gone back to school at the precise time students were forming their militant groups. Inspiration was all around.

Older militants were also about, decaying freaks, lechers, ex-cons like Charles Manson, child molesters like the Santa Barbara loving Leigh Allen. Perhaps even a blonde killer of couples. Warren didn't go hippie. He remained established looking and became an insurance salesman. But whether blonde- or brown-haired, ZODIAC also remained establishment looking, even obsolete. Warren is the perfect compromise to be ZODIAC— established but saturated with the youth counterculture and the militant style of the New Left.

According to Dr. May, Gary Warren was a natural killer. I can see the bitter Warren using something as dramatic as Leigh Allen's fanciful tale. He indulges his own yen for murder and also mocks the establishment that sent him away for 5 prime years of his life.

The theatric ZODIAC crimes are fundamentally southern California in origin and manifestation. Chicago, New York, and San Francisco were the centers of militant leftists and somewhat potted Marxists, but Los Angeles was the center, as always, of theatric indulgence. Of all the counterculture communes how many camped out

---

[11] Emile de Antonio's 1976 documentary *Underground*.

at an old movie backlot and part-timed as actors? Only the Manson Family. They were also the only ones to use white imperialism and black power as a sham to cover their true motives for their murders. Though I hardly think ZODIAC mixed with the Mansons, his murder spree excuse was as false as Hollywood.

Inspiration for ZODIAC came from more than one source. Perhaps more than one acted it out. Perhaps there was more than one motive.

Thus I have not streamlined upon Gary W. and excluded any other. I got within a web that connects with Leigh Allen, and I am certain the complete answer lies within it; meaning if there is an accomplice he also interacted with it. Meaning also if there was a conspiracy of silence it extended beyond Leigh Allen.

The reader must weigh and consider why Allen never turned in Warren. The reader must also account reasonably why Allen would continue to wear that Zodiac Sea Wolf watch and babble on about his electric gunsight, to the point even Ted Kidder suspected him in 1971.

Regardless of a conspiracy of silence, who pulled the trigger? Who plunged the knife?

Purely on induction therefore I would have to state that the lot falls to Gary Warren. The blonde ZODIAC is a dreadful thing to consider. I fear there is a joker in the deck. Whether there was more than a conspiracy of silence in the Zodiac Murders will remain an open verdict.

About the Author

A native of California, Gian J. Quasar has his roots in the Bay Area and family in Vallejo. He first achieved public acclaim in Y2K for being the subject of several History and Discovery Channel documentaries for his investigation of world mysteries. While still in MS form, his book *They Flew into Oblivion* inspired a Resolution in Congress in 2005 sponsored by Congressman E. Clay Shaw. He was also a central figure in the public reintroduction of the investigation of The East Area Rapist (2014). At the same time he was immersed in this present work. His writings have appeared in *Boy Scouts* and the *Journal of the Oxford Philosophic Society*; his works have been cited in Thomas Nelson and Cambridge University Press, *inter alia*. He has been the subject of dozens of TV documentaries and is a frequent guest on radio. Because of the diversity of the subjects he has investigated— from the Occult to True Crime topics— he has been dubbed "the real life Kolchak."

Index

Allen, Leigh 181, 197-205, 216-218, 235-248, 256-266, 286-88, 291-295, 301-305, 315, 334, 327-329, 339
    Letter to Lompoc friend 244-245
    Salt Point Ranch alibi 239
Armstrong, Bill 108-115, 123, 176, 181, 183, 189, 191, 197, 203, 236-242, 257-258, 314
Ashby, Robert 282, 289
Atascadero State Hospital 241, 243-244, 248, 256, 263-68, 280, 283-85, 287-293, 295, 303, 333, 339
Avery, Paul 133, 135, 140, 157-159, 165-170, 175, 205, 226, 228, 230, 257, 259, 288, 305
Axe, Helen 33

Baker, Bill 175-176, 179, 181
Bates, Cheri Jo 160-171, 203, 226-231, 240, 287-288, 291-192
    Confession Letter 162
    1968 Berkeley incident 230
Bates, Joseph 169, 228
Belli, Melvin 118-122, 138-142
Belli Letter 147, 152, 250, 261, 309
Bird, Wade 124
Bissinger, Paul 307-308
Bloch, Robert N. 306-309, 311, 313, 335, 337
Blue Meannie 146, 156, 171

Blue Onion 267, 269-271, 274, 277, 291
Blue Rock Springs Park 33, 35-39, 45, 48, 54, 57, 59, 64, 204, 216, 232
Bonine, Dave 168
Bugh, Dr. Vernon 274-276, 278, 280-285
Burd, David 28
Butterbach, Russell 25, 27-29, 265
Burton, Ricky 29, 32

Caen, Herb 158, 192
Cahill, Thomas 113, 115
Caller "Sam" 119-122, 133, 152, 260, 262
Carpenter, Sheriff John 179-181
Chapman, Lawrence 268, 286, 293
Chino Institute for Men 267-268, 284-86, 288
"Christmass" 60, 66, 156, 181, 317
Clark AFB 68
Collins, David (Ranger) 83-84
Columbus Pkwy 33, 36-37, 39, 41-43, 45, 47, 92-93, 204, 211, 212, 218
Conahey, David 289-290
Confession calls:
    One, 47;
    Two, 80
    Comparison 103
Connelly, Robert 30, 265

Conway, Roy 45-46, 124, 152, 250, 261, 309
Cron, Eddie 290-291
Cronkite, Waler 117, 122
Cross, Irv 165-170
Crow, William 33
Crumly, Charles 236-237

Danch, John 273, 279, 283, 286-287
Davis, Ray 178-179, 303
Days of Rage 317-318
Deer Lodge Prison 75, 76
Del Buono, Linda 199-200
Domingos, Bob 174-175, 178-181, 231
Drinkwater, Terry 117-118
Dunbar, Jim 118-122, 140-141

Edwards, Linda 174-175, 178-181, 231

Ferrin, Darlene (Dee) 37, 40, 46, 48-54, 57-59, 62, 70, 197, 198-200, 202, 205, 207, 213, 237
Fibreboard Company 301
Fisher, Carol 112-113
Furlong/Snoozy murders 69, 133

Garlington, William 237
Gasser, Frank 30, 265
Gaviota 172, 176, 179, 183, 303
George Washington High 217, 223
Gnesa, Lee 174
Gomez, Ricardo 142, 230-31
Gosnell, Bill Henry 295-299, 301, 303, 334-337
Gottlieb, Sidney 321-322, 325
Grant, Bill 198-2005, 269-90, 305
Graysmith, Robert 197-205, 218, 239, 245, 246, 257-59, 321

Haeberle, John 221-222
Haeberle, Steve 217-220, 221-222, 235, 256, 294, 315-316, 337-338
    Printing comparison 251-253
Haight-Ashbury 18-20, 25, 68, 70, 146, 149
Haight, Wayne, 86-87, 98, 290
Harden, Don/Bettye 67, 102, 117
Hartnell, Bryan 71, 77-79, 82-84, 87-88, 96, 100-101, 123-124, 136, 208, 216, 231-233, 294, 336, 338
    description of Zodiac's hood 101
Hoffman, Richard (VPD) 45-46
Hollingsworth, Wm. Y 283
Humble Oil Refinery 24. 29-30, 211, 224, 303
Husted, Jim 198, 201-202

James, DR. William 274, 277
James' Men's & Boy's Store 298
J.C. Higgins Model 80 (.22 pistol) 28-29, 174
Jensen, Betty Lou 24, 26-29, 33-34, 48, 53, 59, 62, 172, 175, 210, 290, 194
Joannides, George 319
Joe's Union Gas Station 48
John Burroughs HS 267, 272
Johns, Kathleen 151-152

Kat Pad 55
Kidder, Ted 240-41, 341
Kinkead, Thomas 165
Knickerbocker Motel 270-271, 282
Kupker, Pauline 267, 269, 273, 282

La Grange, Charles H. 222
Lake Berryessa 71-72, 80, 82, 86, 97,

100, 102, 104, 115, 122, 124-125, 127, 136, 165, 170, 174-175, 204, 209-210, 213, 217, 225, 231-233, 239, 264, 292-294, 302, 315, 318, 320
Lake Herman Road 23, 28-29, 31, 33, 43, 60, 90, 151, 172, 179, 210-212, 224, 231, 264, 303, 304
Land, Dennis (Ranger) 78, 83-85
Lee, Martin 114-116, 119, 124, 133, 135-137, 211, 293
Lonergan, Richard 81-88
LSD, CIA and 321-327
Lundblad, Leslie 24, 27-29, 32-33, 265
Lynch, John 46, 56-57, 70, 216-18, 236, 239, 259

Macko, Sherrie 272
Mageau, Michael 38-39, 43, 45-46, 49, 52-57, 66, 70, 88, 100, 104, 182, 201, 207-08, 213, 232, 315, 336
Manson Family 16, 145, 248, 340
March AFB 161, 170, 226
Marshall Ranch 30
Marshall, Rick, 198
Maupin, Armistead 191, 193-194, 196-197, 203, 259
May, Dr. Philip 269274, 279, 282, 340
McDonnell, Brian V 147, 247
McNamara, Michael Sebastian 239
Medeiros, Stella 24, 30, 31-32
Melville, Sam 328
Mr. Ed's Drive-In 36, 38
Meyring/Lindemann, VPD Officers 45
Modesto Bee 152, 207
Modglin, Dr. Rene 164
morbid poem 166-168, 170, 227-228, 231, 259
Morrill, Sherwood 167-170, 193, 215-218, 228-229249, 256-59, 322
Mount Diablo 150-151, 156
    Diablo Code 151, 156
Mulanax, Jack 88, 237-242, 246
Narlow, Ken 81-88, 99, 168, 208, 233
New Left 13, 15, 247, 317-318
Nicolai, Mel 168, 176, 228
Noeller, Agnes 224
Noeller (Wilcox, Haeberle, "La Grange," Osborne, Rogachefsky), Helen 221-224
Nunez, Betty 270-71, 276, 280, 287, 293

Oceanside 178, 303
Omicron Suspect 236, 242, 246, 248, 256, 262-265
Ordione, Ken 46-47
Osborne, Charles H. 224
Owen, James 30-32, 213

Panzarella, Santos 236-237
Patterson, Dr Donald 284-286
Partis, Chester 267, 275, 291
Peda, Frank 106, 108, 111, 308
Pelisetti, Armand 106, 108, 314
Presidio Heights 105-07, 110-111, 135, 211, 217, 223, 305, 314
Press Enterprise 161, 166196, 227
Project Artichoke 322-324, 326
Project MK-ULTRA 322-324, 326
Prouty, Robert 193

Radetich, Richard 149, 195
Rayfield, Dr. Clifford 85, 99, 208
Rayfield, David 85, 98-99, 208, 233, 338
Riverside City College 160, 168, 170

Roed, O.J. 177
Roger, Jerry, Debbie 42-43, 45, 47
Rull, Kathie 272-276, 280, 282, 291, 293
Rust, Ed 46, 52-53, 56, 70, 207

Sanders, Prentice Earl 190
Sandoval, Joe 298, 301
S.F. Chronicle 60-64 (cipher 63), 102-103, 110-114, 129, 133-135, 140, 147, 149, 156-159, 166, 168, 184, 186, 191-194, 197, 229-230, 259
S.F. Examiner 60-66 (cipher 63), 70, 102-103, 113, 157, 207, 213, 249, 255
"Shadow Zodiac" 231, 234, 292, 302-303, 335, 339
Shephard, Cecelia 72, 78-79, 87, 97, 127, 233
Shimoda. John 192-193, 229
Shirai, Dr. Satoshi 50-51
Slaight, David 80, 98, 123
Slover, Nancy 47-48, 123
Smario's 299
Smith, Arlo 117
Smith, Orval Lee 299-302, 304, 334-335
Snook, Harold 81-82, 84-85, 88, 231
   Karmann Ghia report 84
Stiltz, Jack 58, 62 64-66, 102, 128, 135, 210
Stine, Paul 105, 109-111, 113, 122, 128, 135, 138-141, 191, 217, 233, 250-251, 256-257, 260, 262, 295, 305, 307-309, 313-314
Studebaker (car) 165, 226, 291
Summer of Love 7, 11, 17-18, 21, 34, 39, 69-70, 221
Suennen, Leo Sr. 49

Suennen, Leo Jr 205
Suennen, Pam 199
Swindle, Johnny (Joyce) 177-178, 231, 302
SLA 14, 16, 183, 185, 187.

Taft, Rolland Lynn 231
Tate/La Bianca Murders 16, 69, 70, 146
The Doodler 195-196
The Mikado 154, 182, 184
The Most Dangerous Game 123, 203, 240, 242-243
Tito's Men's Store 298
Toschi, David R 108-115, 123, 168, 183, 189-197, 202-203, 216, 238-242, 246, 257-259, 305, 314
Townsend, Don, 85, 97
Tucker, Joan 246, 263, 287, 293, 321
Tucker, Phil 240-241, 246, 263
Union Oil & Gas 238-239

Vallejo Times Herald 34, 59, 61-62 (cipher 63), 103, 157, 207
Vandenberg AFB 176, 275, 281, 292, 316

Wadkins, James Alex 299-301
Walls, Elwood 283
Warren, Gary Lee 266-298, 301-304, 316, 319-322
Warren, Leon 267, 275
Warren, Barbara Hope 267
Waters, George 55-57, 216
Weil, Eric 141
Weather Underground 147, 247-248, 317, 327--331
Wesner, Bingo George 23, 254, 303

Wesner, John (Chevron Station), 303
White, Archie/Elizabeth 78
White, William (Ranger) 78-79
Wogan, Harry 238

Your, Homer/Peggy 29-32, 265
Yippies 327, 330-331

Zebra Killings 14, 16, 183, 185, 187, 190
Zodiac
  first usage 65
  coeds' description of
    86, 98, 100, 208, 232 (318)
  S.F. Handbill description 110
  first sketch 98
  outfit 74, 101
  Fouke description 136
  first cipher 63
  translation 67
  name cipher 146

  car door 83
  bus threat 113
  uncovering symbol meaning 116
  a serious problem 118
  amended sketch 123
  opinions about 124
  pop psych 126-172
  begins false victim clams 129
  340 cipher 130
  perhaps Welsh 137
  Belli Letter 139
  writes LA Times 171
  Exorcist Letter 184
  Badlands 195
  Red Phantom 186
  Evidence for two 209, 231-33
  Cars 214
  340 cipher cracked 260-261

www.ingramcontent.com/pod-product-compliance
Lightning Source LLC
Chambersburg PA
CBHW020349170426
43200CB00005B/101